P-829

Travel and
Older Adults

Choices and Challenges:
An Older Adult Reference Series
Elizabeth Vierck, Series Editor

Housing Options and Services for Older Adults,
Ann E. Gillespie and Katrinka Smith Sloan

Mental Health Problems and Older Adults,
Gregory A. Hinrichsen

Older Workers, Sara E. Rix

Paying for Health Care after Age 65,
Elizabeth Vierck

Travel and Older Adults, Allison St. Claire

Volunteerism and Older Adults, Mary K. Kouri

Forthcoming

Legal Issues and Older Adults,
Linda Josephson Millman and Sallie Birket Chafer

Travel and Older Adults

Allison St. Claire

Choices and Challenges: An Older Adult Reference Series
Elizabeth Vierck, Series Editor

ABC-CLIO
Santa Barbara, California
Oxford, England

Cover Design/Graphein

Library of Congress Cataloging-in-Publication Data
St. Claire, Allison, 1942-
    Travel and older adults / Allison St. Claire.
       p. cm.—(Choices and challeneges)
    Includes biliographical references and index.
    1. Aged—Travel. I. Title. II. Series.
  G151.S7 1991   910′.84′6—dc20   90-24411

ISBN 0-87436-573-2 (alk. paper)

98 97 96 95 94 93 92 91   10 9 8 7 6 5 4 3 2 1

ABC-CLIO, Inc.
130 Cremona Drive, P.O. Box 1911
Santa Barbara, California 93116-1911

This book is Smyth-sewn and printed on acid-free paper ∞.
Manufactured in the United States of America

This book is dedicated to the thousands of seniors who have touched my life and made it better. I hope the information contained here will serve to suggest innovative experiences and define new paths that will expand their worlds as they have expanded mine.

Contents

Preface

One day, at the beginning of my research for this book, I stood in my local library in front of the shelves housing the travel books. My mind boggled. I couldn't even begin to calculate the number of linear feet those books occupied, but it was enormous. Where to start?

I'm fortunate enough to have one of the world's largest bookstores nearby. I visited it. The shelves of travel books there extended even further than the library's. My eyes glazed.

Then I sat down at the computerized catalog system of the Library of Congress, called up the "Travel" category and was overwhelmed even further. The computer sensed the predicament as it cautioned me: "Don't you want to narrow your search? This category contains thousands of entries." How could I ignore such an admonition from a supposedly unfeeling machine?

On the other hand, only a meager handful of resources came up when I requested the categories of "Travel" and "Older Adults." How dare my editor suggest I research such a subject when there wasn't anything out there to examine? Suddenly I had a worse problem—trying to deal with too little rather than too much.

Overwhelmingly, older adults, not the young folks, are the ones standing in front of those shelves or hunched before a computer screen trying to sort through the mess. Survey after survey has shown that the number-one priority for retirement is travel. Even in preretirement years, older adults are the ones with the most time, money, and desire to enrich their lives with travel.

But at least I now knew exactly what they must feel—frustrated, confused, unhappy, ready to take anyone else's advice about what to do and where to go and how to get there—anything but try and tackle that vast array of general travel information with only a minuscule amount of specific information aimed at their own particular needs and circumstances and interests.

Their questions abound: Where do I want to go, how do I get there, once I am there will I be surrounded by rock-and-rollers on spring break? Would I be happier on a guided group tour or exploring on my own? How do I recognize true value as opposed to a cheap price? Yes, I've enjoyed camping in the past, but isn't my husband out of his mind to want to sell the house and all our possessions and travel full-time in a recreational vehicle? And what do you mean, take a walking safari at my age? Next thing, you'll suggest I study the habits of Siberian dwarf hamsters and the effect of the local environment on them. No! There's already a group of senior volunteers doing that? Where does this all end? Where do I begin?

They begin, I hope, with this book. Whether a novice or veteran sojourner, there's much yet to discover in this wide world—and it's all listed here for their convenience.

For answers I went straight to the source—hundreds of them—all older travelers.

As editor of *Senior Edition USA,* a general-interest senior newspaper with national circulation, I am in nearly constant terminal envy of all my traveling readers.

They send letters. "Just got back from our 12th Elderhostel trip. Why don't you hurry up and grow up so you can join us?" "You would have loved the reaction of a group of Japanese children who'd never seen anyone with completely white hair before. They dared to touch mine—gingerly—giggling incessantly." From an 85-year-old adventurer: "Just got back from attempting the Machame Trail up Mt. Kilimanjaro. That's the difficult one, not the 'Coca Cola' tourist route."

They send photos. "This is me several years ago at age 80. That's my backpack, the only luggage I carried on my 176-day trip starting at the Himalayas. Slept at hostels and did the whole trip with several stops around the world for only $24 a day, including an Aegean cruise and airfare." "Our cruise up the Amazon was outstanding, only no one told us about the nightly attacks of killer insects. . . ."

And most of all they send stories. Hundreds of manuscripts have helped me be one of the world's most blessed armchair travelers. "My heart patient husband never thought he could cruise again having to face all that glorious food, until we discovered a cruise line that serves an American Heart Association—approved entrée at every meal." Before the era of Glasnost in Russia: "I didn't mean to elude my Intourist guide, but I'm a speedwalker and I did get to see a lot of things on my own." Or "Just piled the grandkids into the camper and took off for Disneyland." "Just got back from the nicest tour of New England's fall foliage," " . . . the Grand Canyon," " . . . my ethnic roots in Yugoslavia," " . . . the World War II battlefield I thought I'd never escape from alive," " . . . the most exciting river rafting trip down the Colorado, just for grandmothers."

The list goes on, as do mature travelers. Since older adults constitute the bulk of pleasure-travel business, especially that related to recreational vehicles and camping, followed by group tours, cruises, train trips, and then literally everything else, almost every travel business finds itself catering to the senior market. Some organizations are very age-specific. One must be 60 to attend Elderhostel. Vacations for Women over 40 is self-explanatory, as is the 70+ Ski Club. The Grandparents Travel Club implies a certain age bias.

Other organizations, although they set no age limits for membership, naturally attract a preponderance of older travelers. Over 75 percent of recreational vehicle (RV) travelers are retirees, and the large number of service and social organizations that serve them reflects the same percentage of older members. Singles groups that help locate travel companions report a large percentage of older members, once again reflecting the demographics of that population.

In other words, there's no lack of travel resources and services poised to serve older travelers, but which may be hard to find because they do not emphasize age in their marketing materials, or because one just doesn't know where to go to find them. Almost any travel book contains information pertinent to any age traveler but again, why spend the time searching through many when one or two have just what's needed.

To help sift through those resources and avoid the need for puzzled frowns when contemplating vast shelves of travel books, I've narrowed down those resources and organized them in an easy-to-find, easy-to-read format in this book. Part One explores the abundance of current senior travel styles and answers a myriad of travel questions: How to get a passport, what are the age limits on car rentals, what's involved in selecting a group tour, are cruise ships handicap-accessible, what is Elderhostel, what types of adventure travel are suitable for seniors, how does one find a travel companion? The chapters in Part One look at specific travel issues for older adults: travel basics, travel health and safety, disabled travel, cars and RVs, cruising, trains and planes and even camelback, plus a plethora of specialty and adventure travel possibilities. Sources for the information contained in Part One include a broad array of travel literature and professional travel materials. All of them are listed and annotated in Part Two.

Part Two supplies a comprehensive list of companies, organizations, clubs, books, periodicals, pamphlets, and other resources to assist mature ravelers in finding exactly what they need for the travel time of their life. All the resources in Part Two have been specifically recommended by my hundreds of traveling sources and by other senior-service providers.

Thanks, sources. You've given me hours of pleasurable reading and conversation, in addition to invaluable information.

And to all you readers, Bon Voyage! Or, if you haven't got a serious case of wanderlust yet, keep reading. You will.

Acknowledgments

My thanks to Elizabeth Vierck, who attracted my attention with her outstanding book, and who had enough confidence in me to allow me to try one too.

I also thank Lynn Bradley of Mile Hi Travel for a starting boost of inspiration and information, and Wendy Robinson of Robinson Travel for a final confirmation that I'd gotten it all right.

And I extend an extra measure of gratitude to one son, two dogs, three cats, four fish, and a multitude of friends and relatives who cheerfully put normal life on hold while this book took shape.

Finally, to Jason—that very special son who has been my life's largest blessing—I can't thank you enough for your love and encouragement and the chores you've done so willingly, nor can I promise that dinner will ever yet be on time, but our travel time together will surely be better than ever!

How To Use This Book

Each book in the Choices and Challenges series provides a convenient, easy-access reference tool on a specific topic of interest to older adults and those involved with them, including caregivers, spouses, adult children, and gerontology professionals. The books are designed for ease of use, with a generous typeface, ample use of headings and subheadings, and a detailed index.

Each book consists of two parts, which may be used together or independently:

A narrative section providing an informative and comprehensive overview of the topic, written for a lay audience. The narrative can be read straight through or consulted on an as-needed basis by using the headings and subheadings and/or the index.

An annotated resource section that includes a directory of relevant organizations; recommended books, pamphlets, and articles; and software and videos. Where appropriate, the resource section may include additional information relevant to the topic. This section can be used in conjunction with or separately from the narrative to locate sources of additional information, assistance, or support.

A glossary defines important terms and concepts, and the index provides additional access to the material. For easy reference, entries in the resource section are indexed by both topic and title or name.

Travel Basics

Chapter 1

Planning Ahead

FACTS OF INTEREST

- The mature population is responsible for more than 80 percent of all leisure travel, according to the American Association of Retired Persons (AARP) and the National Tour Association, Inc. (NTA).

- In 1988 and 1989, adults age 55 and over took over 225 million trips each year, according to the U.S. Travel Data Center. The most popular destinations in the United States for those age 55–64 were the South Atlantic, Northwest, Central, and Mid-Atlantic regions. Those over age 65 preferred the South Atlantic, Mountain, and Pacific regions.

- The most popular transportation modes for older adult travelers in the United States are (in order of rank) automobile and/or recreational vehicle (75–80 percent), airplane, bus, and train (the latter used mostly by the 65+ crowd; there's very little use of trains by the 55–64 age category), says the U.S. Travel Data Center.

- Seventy percent of those 50 and over take at least one vacation of a week or more per year; half take more than one. Seventy-four percent take at least one long weekend trip per year and two-thirds take more than one, according to the U.S. Travel Data Center.

- Older Americans account for over 35 percent of all package tours, according to AARP and the U.S. Travel Data Center.

• The NTA, in a national random-sample study conducted in 1989, found that mature Americans who are active and travel, specifically those who travel on group tours, are also more likely to feel happy, healthy, optimistic, friendly, and energetic than those who don't.

Common wisdom and everyday observation—as well as the conclusions of a number of scientific studies—confirm that older Americans' number-one desire for retirement is to travel. A majority of preretirees are on the go as well, according to travel industry statistics. With children generally grown, mortgages often paid, and jobs and careers well established or now behind them, older adults are on their way to broadening their horizons anywhere and everywhere—especially away from home.

Part of the excitement and adventure of travel for some people is the thrill of the unknown, the challenges of new places and new cultures, or the vagaries of unfamiliar transportation, service, and accommodations. For others, even the thought of less-than-customary standards in food or bathroom conditions, of being bumped from a flight, or the fear of missing a major attraction in the city they're visiting because they didn't know about it is enough to make a trip a miserable memory.

Good planning lays the groundwork for a successful trip regardless of one's travel style. Witness some examples.

A 60-year-old couple from Michigan found themselves with time and resources to travel when the husband accepted an early-retirement program from his company. Their only prior travel involved fishing trips around the state or visits to nearby relatives. Being such novices, they decided they wanted a risk-free, no-hassle vacation with everything planned and done for them. Their group tour to Europe was full of friendly people, hosted by a congenial expert guide, and visited popular sites they'd always wanted to see. They were miserable. He wanted to be outdoors more; she wanted to rest more than the pace of the trip allowed. They felt herded around, the hotel accommodations weren't what they expected from the tour brochure, and some attractions they wanted to visit at a leisurely pace were simply viewed from the tour's motorcoach. Their problem: neglecting to decide their own personal travel style and not questioning their travel agent or tour operator closely enough to be sure they understood all the tour conditions.

Another very similar couple, however, knew they loved to leave the driving to anyone else, wanted to know in advance exactly what their expenses would be, and wanted to spend every minute of their trip soaking up sights and sounds—from the bustling crowds at the airport to quiet contemplation of the passing scenery—and never worry once where their luggage was or how to carry it or what to tip at the restaurant. But they started by poring over tour brochures, asking questions, and querying their travel agent and all their traveling friends. They've taken seven tours now, both domestic and foreign. Their next one will combine a flight to Orlando with a tour of southern Florida, followed by a four-day cruise out of Miami.

Yet another older couple are true travel gypsies. They read travel books by the armload, belong to a discount travel club, and take off on nearly a moment's notice when an inexpensive fare or travel package comes along. On their way they peruse travel guides for the area, bone up on the historical and cultural background of the area, and listen to language-learning cassettes. When they arrive they're poised for adventure and surprise and the chance to "go native" as much or as little as they like.

The variations on travel themes are as endless as there are individuals taking off to pursue their travel dreams. Whether single or coupled, whether staying close to home or visiting the other side of the world, whether going it alone or joining a group, be it on land, in the air, or on the sea, solid planning is the key ingredient to a memorable travel experience.

Where To Go

There seem to be only two limitations to senior travel today: one's own imagination, and locations and activities on this planet—at least as of this writing.

There are nearly endless sources for discovering intriguing travel destinations. Inspiration might come from wanting to experience the locale where a favorite fictional heroine fell in love, to wanting to visit the archaeological site that was the source of a pottery masterpiece on display in the local museum.

Most older Americans want to visit national parks, natural wonders, historic sites, warm-weather locations, areas of fall foliage, and special events and festivals on their vacations, according to a National Tour Association survey. Others travel to trace family roots, to expand a hobby, pursue a favorite sport, volunteer a needed skill, learn a new language, or pursue a lifelong dream such as learning to sail or studying an active volcano or researching the communication patterns of dolphins.

One's purpose for travel also affects choice of destination. Is the goal to relax, to learn, to soak up sights? Other choices may be for adventure, volunteer opportunities, educational experiences, a lively urban scene, or a chance to commune with nature. The better that travelers can define their travel goals, the clearer their choices become for appropriate destinations.

Finances, too, obviously play a big role in choice of destination. However, if one's dream is to see Paris, the number of ways to get there are abundant. A little well-spent research time will locate discount fares, inexpensive tours, bargain accommodations, or whatever is needed to make that dream come true.

How To Go

Package Travel

Older Americans account for over 35 percent of all package tours, according to AARP and the U.S. Travel Data Center.

Package travel arrangements combine a number of travel services into an all-inclusive price. These may include any of the following elements: lodging/accommodations, ground and/or air transportation, cruises, meals and beverages, sightseeing, entertainment, airport transfers, car rentals, and taxes. These services are planned, marketed, and implemented by wholesale tour operators and are sold primarily by retail travel agents. Tour operators contract for these services in bulk and pass the volume purchasing savings on to consumers. Often they are able to secure accommodations, airline space, and other arrangements that are nearly impossible for individuals to obtain.

For example, a Colorado public relations executive in her mid-50s and a friend wanted to visit Hawaii. They bought a ten-day travel package consisting of air transportation, food and hotel vouchers, car rental, and a four-day cruise to several islands. While the cruise portion was a planned tour of several ports, their remaining time on one island was spent as they pleased—exploring, shopping, or relaxing on the beach.

Package tours can encompass independent tours and vacation packages such as the one above to all-inclusive, fully escorted tours of specific itineraries.

Group Tours

The National Tour Association, in a national random sample study conducted in 1989, found that mature Americans who are active and travel, specifically those who travel on group tours, are also more likely to feel happy, healthy, optimistic, friendly, and energetic than those who don't. An overwhelming 92.1 percent of mature Americans surveyed who have taken a group tour consider themselves "friendly" and 81.4 percent consider themselves "happy."

Mature Americans have a strong aversion to risk and are seeking security and worry-free experiences, says Richard Balkite of The Mature Market Network. "Consequently, escorted tours are growing in popularity among people 50 years of age and older because the group travel experience offers security, value and convenience as well as education and companionship," he notes.

There are over 300 independent tour operators in the United States, which can be located through a travel agent. A listing of those that cater specifically to mature travelers or whose trips older adults have found especially attractive can be found in the General Travel Organizations, Specialty Travel Organizations, and Disabled Travel listings in Chapter 7.

It is important to check out a tour company thoroughly before committing any money for a trip. Every year a few companies fail financially, leaving travelers stranded, occasionally in a strange location far from home. Travel agents can recommend reputable companies they have dealt with before. Tour operators that are members of professional trade organizations such as the NTA and the United States Tour Operators Association(USTOA) must meet certain professional and financial qualifications. The associations can offer some recourse for consumers if a member company defaults.

Travelers should also check to see that a tour departure is guaranteed. Most companies will cancel approximately 30 days before departure and will return full refunds if a trip is canceled for lack of bookings. However, 30 days might be too short a time for some travelers to plan an alternate vacation.

The tour brochure should contain all the information travelers need to know to ensure they will get the travel experience they want. They should read tour brochures carefully and thoroughly for cost comparison and trip details. They also need to ask the travel agent or tour operator as many questions as needed for complete understanding of all terms and conditions.

Some questions to ask in choosing a tour:

Is the price all-inclusive or does it cover only land arrangements?

Is there "add on" airfare from one's home city?

Will there be optional excursions, service charges, or taxes?

Are there supplemental charges for single rooms, or seasonal surcharges?

What level of accommodation is supplied? Even in a supposedly elegant hotel, rooms reserved for the group might mean a lesser quality room than one might normally expect. What does a term like "deluxe hotel" really mean in that area?

Is the trip fully escorted or are hosts available at each destination?

What sightseeing is included?

Are the events especially arranged for members of this tour, or are they open to the public?

Are the various sites and cities on the itinerary to be visited or simply driven through?

Are meals run-of-the-menu or set dishes? Are there explanations for various meal terms such as "continental breakfast" or "full board"? Exactly which meals are covered?

How much walking is required to enjoy the various stops? Are there any barriers or limits to accessibility?

How much free time is available for individual activities or rest? How many actual days are spent in a particular area, not counting travel time?

Is shopping available on one's own or only at stores selected by the guide?

What are the penalties if one needs to cancel or interrupt a tour? Is there insurance against these possibilities?

Is there a limit to the size of the group?

What tips will participants be responsible for, excepting tips to the driver and guide?

What additional services does the company offer, such as reading lists, background material, packing tips, travel accessories, etc.?

Traveling Alone

Travelers seem to be gregarious types, and single travelers, whether they join a group tour or sail off on a cruise on their own, seem to get swept up quickly in the general vacation camaraderie.

The downside to solo traveling is the single supplement, an extra charge levied by most cruise lines and hotels, which may mean paying up to 200 percent of the regular rate. For example, if the normal double-occupancy rate for a room is $80, each person is being charged $40. The rate for a single to occupy that same room might be $65 or even the full $80.

Some cruise ships offer a limited number of single rooms at premium prices, but will charge the single supplement for most cabins. If traveling alone, one option is to request a "guaranteed share" rate. This means the cruise company will either find a roommate to share the cabin or will guarantee half the regular double-occupancy rate if no one can be found. Another option, the "guaranteed single" rate, guarantees space and a standard rate ($900, for example) but does not specify a cabin. At sailing time the single traveler is placed in any cabin still available, which cannot be valued at less than the amount paid, and, in fact, is often a much higher priced room.

Some tour groups also help pair up travelers to share rooms for cost savings. In addition, a number of clubs and groups help locate travel partners. Some are fairly elaborate matching services with personality questionnaires, a specified number of guaranteed matches, and nationwide newsletters with hundreds of travel partner "personals" ads. Some are specifically designed for singles driving recreational vehicles, while others feature ads for companions for cruises, safaris, or any other type of travel plan.

Choosing a Travel Agent

A good travel agent can be an invaluable resource in planning any trip, whether the vacationer be a novice or veteran traveler. Almost all the services travel agents provide are free because the agent receives a commission from the vendors. Special services such as long-distance calls or telexes are usually billed to the customer, as is the time needed to create a custom-tailored tour for independent travel. Reputable agents will explain consultation fees, or the costs for any other extra services, in advance.

Among the services provided by travel agents are: arranging transportation, accommodations, sightseeing, car rentals, escorted tours, and admission to theaters and sporting events; selling insurance to cover the traveler, baggage, and cancellation penalties; helping obtain passports and visas; advising on clothes, gadgets, weather, health, where to shop, and who and what to tip.

Just as in choosing a doctor, lawyer, or other professional, the best sources for information are personal references from friends and acquaintances who have received good service from a particular agent.

Travel agencies that belong to the American Society of Travel Agents (ASTA) must have been in business at least three years under present ownership or control, and are subject to strict business practices and ethical standards. ASTA is a valuable resource in resolving complaints concerning services sold by its member agencies.

An agent with a CTC (Certified Travel Counselor) designation means the agent has at least five years experience and has completed a two-year graduate-level program developed and supervised by the nonprofit Institute of Certified Travel Agents (ICTA).

Whether or not to use a small, local travel agency or one affiliated with a large national chain is purely a matter of individual preference. What matters most is that a travel agent spend adequate time with customers to ascertain their likes and dislikes, budget parameters, and any special needs in order to guide each client to the most fulfilling travel experience.

Bargain Travel

A number of travel agents sell discounted travel services. Some buy blocks of seats or cabins in volume on certain flights and cruises and then sell them at deeply discounted rates. Since these agencies generally do not do research or provide customized service, vacationers need to know exactly which cruise ship, sailing date, or flight arrangements they would like and then see if they are available through the discounter.

Last-minute travel clubs, or travel clearinghouses, sell last-minute seats or cabins at deep discounts to travelers such as retirees who are flexible enough to take advantage of such offers with very little lead time. Most of these companies charge a membership fee and provide regular newsletters and/or telephone hotlines offering information about available deals. Travel agents will not refer customers to these groups since they do not pay commission to the agent, but it would be wise to check them out with a friendly travel agent who would know if they are reputable or a fly-by-night operation. Some have operated for years with no complaints; others have found posing as such an operation a convenient way to separate people from their hard-saved vacation money. Travelers can find such companies through newspaper or magazine travel articles and advertising.

Travel Insurance

Although most older travelers enjoy uninterrupted, peaceful vacations, additional insurance should be considered for a number of different potential problems. The following list details items that can be insured against.

Accident or illness while traveling

The need to cancel a prepaid cruise, tour, or other item due to illness or accident

Added expenses if a trip must be canceled or interrupted

Evacuation assistance if emergency assistance is not available where a traveler is stricken

Transporting a dead body

Being stranded or losing a prepayment if a carrier or company defaults

Damage, loss, or theft of personal effects

Emergency expenses due to lost or delayed luggage

Personal liability for claims lodged against the traveler

Some of these incidents or losses may be covered by one's current homeowner's, medical, or umbrella insurance policies. Most "comprehensive" travel insurance policies don't cover everything, so careful comparison and choice of the most necessary individual coverage are strongly advised.

Cancellation insurance is almost a must in today's world where so many fares and expenses must be paid in advance. It usually covers travel by air and sea, and often bus and rail, as well as ground arrangements such as hotels, meals, car rentals, escorted tours, or any other prepaid travel service. The reason for collecting is usually restricted to illness or death of the covered traveler, or death or alarming illness of an immediate family member or close relative, whether on the trip or prior to leaving.

A useful formula for calculating the amount of cancellation or trip-interruption service is to ask: How much money would not be refunded if the trip had to be canceled immediately before departure, and how much money would be forfeited if forced to return home once the trip begins? The latter should include additional airfare to return home before the originally scheduled date.

Finding Information

Tourist Offices

Every American state and nearly all foreign countries maintain tourist offices. These are outstanding resources for area maps and guides, and information on camping, accommodations, climate, attractions, special events, and more. Foreign tourist offices also provide information on cultural expectations, language, currency regulations and equivalencies, vaccination and visa requirements, and so forth. Complete listings appear in Chapter 7 under Foreign Government Tourist Offices and State Tourist Offices.

Books and Periodicals

Many mature travelers enjoy beginning their trips at home with a book. Some start with novels set in the region they plan to visit, or they read up on the history, culture, art, or lore of that area.

Next they seek out travel guides. *Going Places—The Guide to Travel Guides,* by Greg Hayes and Joan Wright, provides a comprehensive review of travel books. A local bookstore, library, or travel-specialty book outlet also is a good place to compare a number of guidebooks. Some guidebooks are oriented toward sightseeing and special events and attractions. Others offer specifics on hotels, restaurants, and entertainment, complete with prices. Some guidebooks employ a rating system to compare value; others are oriented specifically toward budget travel. Yet others delve deeply into historical and cultural backgrounds; a few are aimed at exotic locales. Seasoned travelers generally carry only one guidebook on a trip to keep baggage weight to a minimum.

Some of the more popular guidebooks among mature travelers are: AAA Tour Books, Baedeker's Guides, Berlitz Travel Guides, Birnbaum Guides, Fielding Travel Books, Fodor Guides, Frommer Guides, Let's Go Series, Lonely Planet Guides, Michelin Guides, and Mobil Travel Guides. An annotated listing of travel guides appears under Books in Chapter 8.

In addition to the materials provided by automobile clubs, a number of outstanding atlases and road guides provide valuable and interesting information to the traveler on wheels. Highway travelers should check public libraries, and both general and travel-specialty bookstores, for the ones most suited to their individual needs.

For additional information, a number of travel-related directories list backcountry expeditions, llama treks, canoe trips for older women, senior hosteling excursions, outstanding train trips, nudist resorts, or golf vacations, among many other travel possibilities. Some of the most comprehensive are listed in Chapter 8 under Books.

Travel magazines and newsletters are flourishing these days, and offer every conceivable type of up-to-date travel information. Some focus on particular destinations, describing accommodations, restaurants, and attractions at those sites. Others compare values among cruises, tours, or independent travel packages. Yet others present enticing travelogues of a particular region, replete with dazzling photographs. Many target varied travel styles, such as camping in recreational vehicles, cruising, or sports vacations. Although any travel periodical will have much to offer the older traveler, two publications, *The Mature Traveler* and *Travel 50 & Beyond,* are targeted solely to the mature market. A listing of travel magazines is supplied in Chapter 8.

Video Travel Guides

The electronic era has spawned travel videos, which are gaining in popularity and availability almost daily. Until recently, there were only a few marketing videos for use at travel shows or by travel agents to promote a particular cruise line or various resort attractions. Now, complete lines of travel videos—from explanations of how to pack efficiently, to what to do in Rio, to how to tour the wine country of France—are available at libraries, video stores, travel bookstores, and other retail outlets.

From the National Geographic series of documentaries on various regions of the world to cruise lines' and resort areas' promotional videos, there is little that the questing tourist can't see on a TV screen before leaving home. Series like the National Geographic are available in most public libraries and retail video-rental stores. Travel agents carry a full supply of promotional videos for travel products they handle. Sporting goods outlets often have promotional tapes on golfing vacations and outstanding fishing spots. Recreational vehicle outlets often carry RV and camping-related videos or information on where to get them.

Audio Travel Cassette Tapes

Audio tapes have also become a valuable traveler's aid and, like video tapes, are too numerous to specify. Tapes available range from language lessons to audio tour guides for a museum, a city walking tour, a national park driving tour, or even complete travel books on tape. Public libraries and private companies lend or rent various books on tape, and both general-interest and travel bookstores carry a wide array of travel tapes. Guided tours on tape are available at visitor centers at a number of tourist attractions, museums, city hospitality centers, and other tourist locations.

Audio tours of various cities, national parks, and historic sites have become especially popular with highway travelers. The tapes offer a chance to learn about an area while touring it in their vehicle. The guided tour for Glacier National Park, for example, notes what to look for at various mile markers or scenic turnoffs, offers a running commentary on the history and development of the park, and comments on contemporary usage of the area. The narrative is backed up with appropriate music and wildlife sound effects. Such tapes are rented or sold at visitor centers; often, portable tape recorders may also be rented.

Transportation

The most popular form of vacation transportation for seniors is by car or RV, accounting for 75–80 percent of older adult travel, according to the U.S. Travel Data Center. Due to its overwhelming popularity, car and RV travel is covered separately in Chapter 4.

Train trips are becoming increasingly popular as a focus for senior vacation travel, however. And, of course, air travel has become almost a necessity as mature travelers choose to spend more of their time at their vacation destinations.

Trains

From the nearly decrepit, if not practically nonexistent, passenger rail systems of only a few years ago, Amtrak has rolled forward to provide not only routine destination-to-destination travel in America, but also full vacation travel services. Currently offered in addition to rail travel, for example, are hotel packages, escorted tours, national park tours, and "circle tours," which visit a number of cities in a particular region. There are also time-saving rail/air packages and rail/sail combination packages, combining rail travel to major passenger cruise ship ports, followed by an ocean cruise.

Amtrak's All Aboard America fare allows a round-trip within one or all of three north-south geographic regions in the country. One fare allows unlimited travel through that region; accommodations are extra. It also allows visits at three places and provides sightseeing packages and hotels at each destination, if desired.

The Amtrak Auto Train operates between Lorton, Virginia (located near Washington, D.C.), and Sanford, Florida (near Orlando), carrying vacationers' cars on special flatbed railcars. Many seniors in the Northeast use this method for transporting their vehicles for use during their winter stay in the South.

One-way discounts on Amtrak are available to seniors 65 and over and to handicapped travelers. Discounts cannot be applied to premium Metroliner Service or Auto Train travel. Interested travelers should consult with a travel agent or with Amtrak for fares and schedules.

An additional resource is *The Official Railway Guide* from National Railway Publishing, with comprehensive rail timetables for Canada, Mexico, and the United States, plus fares, services, and rules. It is published eight times a year.

FOREIGN TRAINS

Great train trips exist all over the world, from those simply moving passengers from one destination to another to scenic vacation trips. A good rail guidebook like Turpin and Saltzman's *Eurail Guide—How To Travel Europe and All the World* describes fascinating rail trips all over the world, along with pertinent advice and information.

According to Gene and Adele Malott in their book *Get Up & Go: A Guide for the Mature Traveler,* varying senior citizen discounts or rail passes are available in the following countries: Austria, Canada, Denmark, Finland, France, Great Britain, Greece, Italy, Norway, Portugal, Sweden, and West Germany.

The Eurailpass began in 1959 and remains one of the best bargains for travel in western Europe. The pass is a single ticket that allows virtually unlimited first-class rail travel in 16 countries, within a stipulated time period. Sponsoring countries are: Austria, Belgium, Denmark, Finland, France, West Germany, Greece, Ireland, Italy, Luxembourg, the Netherlands, Norway, Portugal, Spain, Sweden, and Switzerland. (Not valid in Britain where a BritRail pass is needed. See below.) It is also good on many boat and intercity bus services. It is designed for foreigners to use, so Americans must buy the pass in the United States. Eurailpass applications require a passport number. Passes are available from travel agents, travel information sources such as the Forsyth Travel Library, and many of the national railroad or tourist offices for the countries involved.

A BritRail pass allows unlimited travel on any train in the United Kingdom for a set fee. Special senior citizen passes are available at a discount. BritRail passes must be purchased in the United States from a travel agent or any of a number of other groups authorized to sell them.

Planes

Almost all airlines in the United States, and many foreign lines as well, offer at least a 10 percent discount on any published fare to travelers age 62 and older. Many also extend the same discount to a companion or spouse of any age, if traveling the same itinerary. However, these and other discounts seem to vary almost with the weather, so it is important to check specific details for any trip.

Additionally, some airlines offer trip coupon books for a set rate of, say, $350 for four coupons. Each coupon is used either as a one-way ticket or for travel up to 1,000 miles, for example. Some airlines will allow use of a coupon for round-trip flying within a certain mileage limit. Restrictions vary as to days the coupons can be used and available destinations.

Yet other airlines also offer a comprehensive senior discount program allowing almost unlimited flights, during a year's time for, say, $1,500 for coach-class domestic flights, and $3,000 for first-class international flights. Restrictions may apply as to black-out days, number of trips to certain destinations, and so forth.

BEREAVEMENT FARES

Some airlines will waive restrictions such as advance purchase requirements or length-of-stay stipulations in case of death or serious illness of a family member, in order to allow the most economical air travel possible. These programs depend completely on the whim of each airline. If available, minimally they require a copy of the death certificate or other documentation from the hospital or medical provider.

CHARTER FLIGHTS

A charter flight is one in which a tour operator charters the use of an entire aircraft and then sells seats on that plane to the general public. Charter flights depart only on dates selected by tour operators to a specific destination.

COMPLAINTS

Travelers who experience problems with loss of luggage, being bumped from a reserved airline seat due to overbooking, flight cancellations, or other, unfortunately common, airline problems should complain to the U.S. Department of Transportation's air travel complaint hotline at (202) 366-2220.

Buses

Although intercity bus service has dwindled greatly in the past few years in the United States, older travelers may still find some bargain fares for getting to their vacation destinations, especially in foreign countries where bus travel is more common. In the United States, Greyhound-Trailways has a regular senior discount on fares, and periodically offers a deal similar to Amtrak, where passengers can travel unlimited miles for a set fee during a set time period. Most intercity coaches are modern and comfortable, and include on-board bathrooms.

BUS TOURS

Bus tours are ubiquitous—from a simple Gray Line tour around a city to weeks-long tours of an entire region or foreign country. Bus tours appeal to vacationers who like to have everything arranged for them—transportation, itinerary, meals, accommodations, baggage handling, admissions, and escorts who offer interesting, informative commentary on the locale.

Bus tours originate from almost anywhere. A travel agent can often find discounted flights to the takeoff point, or the tour may provide a flight as part of its package price. Bus tours may also combine with other types of transportation, say a helicopter ride over a scenic area inaccessible by ground transportation.

Some important questions to ask when comparing bus tours:

Is smoking allowed on the bus?

Are seat assignments rotated so everyone has an opportunity for the preferred seats?

Is there a lavatory on board?

How frequent are stops?

What is the tipping policy?

Is there a baggage limit?

Is there a choice in pickup spots within the city?

Accommodations

The array of accommodations available to travelers is enormous. From inexpensive to superdeluxe, mature travelers can find the right place for the right price with just a little planning ahead.

Youth hostels aren't just for the kids these days. The American Youth Hostel Association plans worldwide adventure trips specifically for those over 50. Inexpensive rooms can also be found on college campuses, in private homes, and in apartment and condo rentals. A number of seniors exchange a stay in their home for a stay in a private home or RV at their destination spot, or visit friends made through penfriend clubs or service groups.

Home exchanging has become particularly appealing to retirees who want to visit a new area before retiring there, as well as to those who desire inexpensive "homey" lodgings. By trading homes with someone from that area, visitors get the chance to truly experience what living in that neighborhood, town, or region is like, without expensive rental accommodations for several weeks. Refer to Chapter 7 under Accommodations for home-exchange services.

Some large campgrounds, especially those in the Sun Belt states of the United States, cater almost exclusively to senior campers, and offer a full spectrum of social activities aimed at the mature traveler. There's even an RV exchange club, patterned on home-exchange programs, for those who wish to sightsee by RV in a foreign land.

Nearly every major hotel and motel chain, recognizing the growing number of mature travelers, offers a senior discount of some sort. Some require proof of membership in an organization such as AARP, while others offer discounts based solely on proof of age. It's always smart to ask what might be available. Some chains also offer expanded "senior clubs," which extend discounts to car rentals, admissions to local attractions, and more. Hotel and motel chains offering senior discounts are listed in Chapter 7 in the Accommodations section.

Finally, B&Bs—bed and breakfast accommodations—are an increasingly popular option for older adults. Travel industry statistics show that over 50 percent of European travelers already use B&Bs at least part of the time.

A decade ago, a B&B was primarily considered an inexpensive mode of accommodation in a spare bedroom in a private home. They were peaceful, charming, and offered a chance to visit with the hosts. Today, larger and generally more upscale B&B inns and hotels are available as an alternative to standard hotel or motel lodging. B&Bs are usually located in historic or otherwise unique dwellings that reflect the character of the region.

Planning Foreign Travel

Passports

Passports allow U.S. citizens to depart from and reenter the United States and to enter most foreign countries. Passports are not needed for most Caribbean islands, Canada, Mexico, and some parts of Latin America. First-time applications must be made in person at any state or federal court, or at any U.S. post office that accepts passport applications. Applicants must present a birth certificate, proof of birth in the United States, or proof of naturalization; two identical photographs; and other identification. Cost for a passport is $35, plus a $7 service charge. A passport is good for ten years from the date issued.

A passport is generally the best form of identification in a foreign land for cashing traveler's checks or otherwise establishing credit. A passport is also required for a Eurailpass, which allows virtually unlimited rail travel in western Europe.

It usually takes about three weeks in off-peak travel times to receive a passport, but may require three to six months in busy vacation seasons.

Visas

A visa is the host country's permission for travel in that country. It is the endorsement or stamp placed in a passport by a foreign government permitting the bearer to visit the country for a specified purpose and a limited time. In some instances photographs and fees are required. Information about which countries currently require a visa for entry can be had from the U.S. Department of State or from travel agents. Visas must be secured before leaving the United States. They can be obtained from travel agents, or from the embassy or consulate of a particular country.

Tourist Cards

Some countries, such as Mexico, allow American citizens to enter with a tourist card and proof of U.S. citizenship. Tourist cards can be obtained from travel agents, that country's embassy or consulate, and airlines serving that country, or at ports of entry.

Other Identification

Some countries that do not require a passport still demand proof of U.S. citizenship, such as a voter registration card. It is also wise to have a driver's license and a major charge card as additional forms of identification.

Vaccinations

No vaccinations are required for Americans returning to the United States, but some countries may require immunizations to enter. Specific information can be obtained from local or state health departments, private physicians, and private or public agencies that advise international travelers. Foreign tourist offices should be able to offer information on needed vaccines, but travel experts have found their data is often out of date or inappropriate. The most highly recommended source is a recently installed international travelers information line at the federal Centers for Disease Control in Atlanta, Georgia, (404) 332-4559.

Customs

U.S. citizens are permitted to bring back duty-free up to $400 worth of goods purchased abroad, including up to one liter of liquor or wine. Goods purchased in the U.S. Virgin Islands, Guam, or American Samoa can have a value up to $800 per person; a maximum of five liters of alcohol is permitted from these areas. Meats, fruits, vegetables, plants, and plant products will be impounded by U.S. Customs unless they are accompanied by an import license from a U.S. government agency. Americans abroad can mail home gifts of not more than $50 in value ($100 from the U.S. possessions in the Caribbean and Pacific), except liquor and tobacco products.

In addition, duty preferences are granted to certain developing countries and territories under what is known as the Generalized System of Preferences (GSP). Some products from these countries have been exempted from duty that would otherwise be collected if imported from other countries. The U.S. Customs Office leaflet *GSP & the Traveler* offers full details.

More specific customs information can be obtained from travel agencies, through several helpful U.S. government pamphlets available from the U.S. Department of State, or at Government Printing Office outlets. Especially helpful is the U.S. Customs booklet *Know Before You Go*, available from any Customs Office or the U.S. Department of Treasury.

Medical Assistance

It is especially important for older travelers to know that Medicare does not provide coverage outside the United States. Private Medicare supplemental ("medigap") insurance plans may offer coverage in foreign countries, but it is not required and often not offered except as an additional-charge rider to standard coverage. Travelers covered by other private medical insurance or with membership in a health maintenance organization (HMO) should check on out-of-country coverage and/or restrictions.

The International Association for Medical Assistance to Travelers (IAMAT), a long-established, nonprofit organization, supplies information on English-speaking doctors around the world and refers travelers to IAMAT clinics where available.

In addition, several private insurance companies offer medical-assistance plans for travelers to foreign destinations. Depending on the level of coverage and assistance services purchased, travelers can receive medical and hospital referrals and assistance, help in locating and contacting relatives, follow-up on medical services, assistance in obtaining cash, translation services, and transportation arrangements. If a death occurs abroad, these programs help obtain necessary documents, explain procedures, and transport remains. Some companies include varying degrees of financial coverage for medical emergencies and may include cancellation insurance for terminated trips. Companies offering such medical services are described in Chapter 2 under Travel Precautions.

Exchanging Money

Social Security checks can be mailed anywhere in the world, but the best advice for mature travelers is to have Social Security checks deposited directly into their bank account at home.

Currency requirements vary from country to country, including the amounts one may carry into or out of the country. Information about these regulations can be obtained from travel agents, government sources, and that country's tourist bureau, consulate, or embassy.

Exchange rates for foreign currencies are generally less favorable if money is exchanged in the United States. Once in the destination country, rates still vary from one exchange source to another, such as airports, hotels, banks, or even the black market, but there seems to be no overall rule of thumb as to which is best from country to country. Vacationers generally get a better deal exchanging traveler's checks rather than hard cash for foreign currency.

Most travel experts advise carrying at least one day's incidental expenses in cash in the country's currency to handle taxi fares, tips, food, and other items until a larger amount can be exchanged. Traveler's checks in that currency are also recommended if weekends or holidays will intervene. Excess cash in a foreign currency, especially change, is generally of little value except as a trip memento when brought back to the United States.

Deak International, a private company with offices in several major cities, specializes in foreign currency exchange. Travelers may also be able to exchange American currency for foreign currency through some larger U.S. banks, as well as through travel agents. Travel agents work through Deak International and generally require 48 hours to complete a transaction. Currencies fluctuate against the U.S. dollar on an almost daily basis in international financial markets, so vacationers are advised to check with appropriate sources close to the time of a planned trip to see how much money will be needed to cover travel plans.

Helpful pocket-sized calculators to figure prices in a foreign currency are available through a number of travel retail outlets.

Travel Advisories

The U.S. Department of State maintains a travel advisory hotline with up-to-date information on areas abroad that may offer dangerous conditions for foreign travelers. The 24-hour hotline number is (202) 647-5225. Travel agents and some travel clubs also maintain current travel advisory information.

The Wise Travel Consumer

Despite the most meticulously prepared vacation plans, things still do go wrong. Sometimes nature intervenes—floods, hurricanes, tornadoes, mudslides, and volcanoes have a tendency to be very unpredictable and completely unfeeling about disrupting one's vacation of a lifetime.

Sometimes standard business practices—such as hotels and airlines overbooking reservations in anticipation of a normal quota of cancellations—leave travelers' plans less than fulfilled. And finally, outright greed, dishonesty, and deceit have ruined many vacationers' plans and dreams.

"The truth is that laws and regulations in the travel field, such as they are, are stacked much more in favor of the suppliers of travel facilities than the travelers," says Paul Grimes in his book, *The New York Times Practical Traveler*. "Much of the field is simply unregulated, notably in the United States. Nonetheless, a large number of travel agencies, tour operators, hotels, and airlines have made a point of responding positively to substantiated complaints and paying refunds promptly. Sometimes, in questionable cases, they even give the consumer the benefit of the doubt. But more often than not, complaints are ignored or the restitution offered is insultingly nominal."

An important step for any traveler is to attempt to avoid obvious pitfalls. Weather patterns are reasonably predictable in certain areas. If, for example, an outstanding price is available for a

Caribbean cruise because the ship sails during hurricane season, travelers need to consider their own desires for the trip. With today's outstanding weather-tracking and prediction capabilities, no ship is likely to be in the path of a hurricane. However, in case of severe weather, the trip might switch to alternate ports, or be interrupted or canceled altogether.

Checking Out the Suppliers

Almost certainly no one will ever really win a travel bargain through computer-generated mail or a random phone call into one's home, although equally certainly older adults will be bombarded with such offers. These "free offers" always contain hidden costs, restrictions, and loopholes, and should be ignored. True travel bargains come through dealing with legitimate travel service companies.

A good place to start is with travel agents and tour operators that have been in business successfully for a number of years. Membership in one or more professional trade organizations generally ensures some degree of financial stability and appropriate business dealings. Some of the better-known trade organizations are the American Society of Travel Agents (ASTA), the United States Tour Operators Association (USTOA), Cruise Lines International Association (CLIA), and the National Tour Association, Inc. (NTA).

Older travelers should also check various friends' experiences with travel companies and heed their recommendations about who has treated them courteously and fairly.

Hotel Reservations

Travelers should always request a confirmation of reservation. Many hotels will require a deposit to do so, but it is worth the effort, especially in peak-season travel at popular destinations. The hotel may still overbook and create a problem, but one must have documentation to pursue a refund or damages from the establishment when bumped without adequate alternative resources. Confirmation slips for hotel and motel reservations also detail each company's policy on check-in time, cancellation, what rates include, and what form of payment is required.

Tickets

Transportation tickets delineate what the carrier's responsibility and liabilities actually are, and what the customer's rights are. The fine print on tickets also informs travelers how close to departure time a refund may be requested, and how much, if anything, would be refunded.

Ticket stubs or carbons should always be saved. If there is a need to complain later, one must have a stub or coupon as proof of travel at a particular time and date. Ticket copies also help in obtaining refunds in case a flight, bus, or train trip is canceled. They are important aids to locate lost baggage and identify employees. Originals should never be sent with letters of complaint; always send photocopies and retain the originals.

Complaints

Travelers who encounter problems with accommodations or other travel services should always try first to resolve the complaint on the spot. They should complain to the manager or other appropriate parties involved and demand correction. If the proper remedies are not made, they should write down any relevant information, including names of involved parties, get corroborating evidence from other members of the group, if any, and save all receipts and other pertinent evidence. These, plus a written summary of the problem, can be given to the travel agent who made the arrangements for further action or recommendations.

For suspect business practices of any travel-service provider, travelers should first contact the American Society of Travel Agents, Consumer Affairs Department, (703) 739-2782. Additionally, they may want to inform the local Better Business Bureau, Chamber of Commerce, state attorney general's office, and/or state consumer protection office in the area of the problem.

For airline complaints, travelers should call the U.S. Department of Transportation at (202) 366-2220. For a list of government and trade organizations that help resolve travel complaints and problems, see Consumer Information and Complaints, Chapter 7.

Legal Problems

Every year, 10,000 American travelers are arrested and jailed in foreign countries. Some incidents are drug-related; others concern smuggling or currency violations. For the large majority of American travelers, however, trips abroad are trouble-free.

Some innocent travelers, however, have been caught unwittingly in legal snarls. Two examples offered by the International Legal Defense Counsel, a private law firm specializing in defending Americans arrested in foreign countries, are these: A middle-aged cruise vacationer bought some old masks in Istanbul. A customs check as she reboarded the ship found the masks to be 800 years old and covered by Turkish antiquities laws. She was imprisoned for a month. In another case, a traveler made a purchase in Greece that put his credit-card bill $40 over his credit limit. This is a criminal offense in Greece, and this traveler faced up to 12 years imprisonment. He served five days in jail without food until the credit-card company extended his credit limit so that the charges were dropped.

Laws vary widely from country to country. Alcohol restrictions and penalties are severe in Scandinavian countries; alcohol is completely forbidden in many Islamic countries. Travelers involved in accidents may find the foreign legal system arbitrary or confusing. Foreign travelers are strongly advised to check with the U.S. Department of State's Bureau of Consular Affairs for complete information on the destination country's laws and cultural mores.

Travelers who are arrested abroad have the right to meet with a U.S. embassy official. The consular officer can visit the detainee in jail, provide a list of local attorneys, notify family or friends, relay requests for money or other aid, and otherwise be sure the person's full rights are protected under local law. The embassy cannot demand the person's release, give legal counsel, or provide government funds for personal or legal use.

Chapter 2

Health and Safety

- One traveler in four will experience at least one illness while abroad.

- Cruise ship doctors report that the two most common medical problems among cruise vacationers are sunburn and forgetting to bring prescription medications.

- Tooth and gum problems tend to be among the more common health-related complaints experienced by international travelers, according to the U.S. Public Health Service and travel medicine practitioners.

- Approximately 6,000 Americans die outside the United States each year.

The majority of vacationers, both in the United States and abroad, enjoy healthy, positive, memorable travel experiences. However, many areas of the world still harbor strange diseases and bacteria, food is not always prepared in the most sanitary manner, and pollution fouls water and seafood supplies. Hotel fires happen anywhere. Crime against tourists is an unfortunate way of life in many places. Driving habits don't always conform to familiar highway and traffic patterns. And, although an unlikely occurrence, terrorists and hijackers are still at large in the modern world.

While these problems face any traveler regardless of age, older travelers need to assess thoroughly what impact their own medical, physical, or other special needs or limitations may have on their travel plans.

A diabetic couple from Alabama had dismissed the possibility of traveling far from home. He was insulin-dependent, and neither wanted to face the possibility of erratic mealtimes and no control over menus. They've since become ardent cruise vacationers, carefully planning ahead with both airlines and cruise lines to be sure their special needs are handled.

A widower from South Dakota looked forward to retirement as an opportunity to do the traveling that his life's work as a church camp director had never allowed. There were parts of the United States he longed to see, as well as friends and relatives still living in eastern Europe he wished to visit. He was in excellent health, but his hearing was very poor. Announcements in airports and train and bus depots were unintelligible, no matter what language they were in. Tour bus intercoms garbled every word the tour guide said. He was never sure when he had to reboard the bus for the next leg of the trip, or what amount the taxi driver had settled on before the ride. Signing up with a tour company that specialized in trips for the deaf and hard-of-hearing opened up all sorts of pleasurable travel experiences he had thought were no longer possible.

Medical Precautions

The most important health precaution any older traveler should take is to have both a thorough medical and dental examination prior to leaving. Dental problems are among the most common health difficulties faced by travelers, and a checkup could help forestall such problems.

Returning travelers, especially those who have been abroad in high-risk areas or for extended periods of time, need to be suspicious of symptoms such as high fevers, persistent diarrhea, itchy skin or rash, or an asthmalike cough for as much as six months after return from their trip. Specialized tropical and travel medicine clinics have been developed specifically to deal with diseases these symptoms may indicate. The American Society of

Tropical Medicine in Newton, Massachusetts, provides lists of more than 70 doctors across the country who are familiar with the prevention and treatment of exotic diseases encountered by travelers.

Medical Information

Travelers with any type of special medical problems should carry a medical report from their doctor listing name and address; Social Security number; insurance company and address; name, address, and telephone number of person to identify in case of emergency; and medical history, including blood type, current medications and dosages (in generic name), allergies, etc.

Older travelers should also consider wearing a medical identification tag or bracelet or carrying a medical alert card if unusual or serious medical conditions, allergies, or unique medical problems require special treatment. Medical assistance programs that sell short-term medical insurance and/or medical advice and assistance will make such information available to doctors and hospitals, but it might not be available in time for emergency treatment that could be required before the assistance service is contacted.

Medications and Health Supplies

Vacationers should pack an ample supply of prescription medications in original containers, especially if going abroad. Because of varying (and generally strict) narcotics laws around the world, travelers should also bring along copies of prescriptions and a letter from the prescribing physician if it is an unusual medication. It is also wise to carry the generic names of any medications since brand names will vary overseas.

Travelers should carry medications in hand luggage on planes, trains, and buses, since checked luggage will be unavailable until reaching a destination, and there is always the possibility of lost or stolen luggage. Buses and trains have ample space for small coolers to store medications as needed.

Older vacationers should consider carrying an extra pair of eyeglasses or contact lenses, as well as ample batteries for hearing aids, all of which may be unavailable or very expensive away from home. Carrying a prescription for replacement glasses may be sufficient when traveling in the United States, but even domestic tour schedules or vacation locations could make getting a new set of glasses difficult, if not impossible. A backup supply of medication in a separate bag is a good precaution as well.

A complete first-aid kit is a must for car and recreational vehicle travel. Cruise ships offer medical supplies and pharmacy services, but vacationers are still advised to carry a personal medical kit with individual preferences in pain relievers, vitamins, antacids, diarrhea medications, sunscreen, and any other personal health items, in addition to prescription medications. Cruise-ship doctors report the two most prevalent medical problems among cruise passengers are sunburn and forgetting to bring prescription medications.

The same type of personal medical kit should be carried by travelers on group tours; independent travelers need to augment these basics with first-aid essentials, plus insect repellent, antibiotics, spray anesthetic, or other items dictated by their itinerary and planned activities. Dr. Robert Lange's *The International Health Guide for Senior Citizen Travelers* offers a good checklist for a travel medical kit, along with other important advice for senior travelers. (See Health and Safety listings in Books, Chapter 8.)

Immunizations

Information about areas where immunizations are required and health precautions are advised for travelers can be obtained from local health departments, the U.S. Public Health Service, private doctors, travel clinics, and travel agencies. Foreign tourist offices supply information on needed vaccines, but the most highly recommended source is the international travelers information line at the federal Centers for Disease Control in Atlanta, Georgia. Older travelers, especially, should heed their doctor's advice on local conditions such as high altitude or evidence of flu strains that might be particularly troublesome or even dangerous to older adults.

Travel Precautions

A number of outstanding books offer comprehensive information on health precautions and practices while traveling. A listing of the most valuable books for seniors appears in Chapter 8 under Health and Safety. Mature travelers should consider consulting at least one or more such books, as well as their personal health advisers, as part of their travel planning. Travel agents and tour operators also have access to important travel health materials and advice. The following are some of the health topics older travelers may need to consider:

Immunizations

Air travel problems such as jet lag, constricted circulation and lack of exercise on long flights, and the effects of air travel on various medical conditions

Motion sickness

Sunburn or overheating

Care of the skin

High-altitude problems

Food and water precautions

Traveler's diarrhea

Malaria or other disease risks

Use of insect repellents

Swimming in strange waters

Traveling with various conditions such as arthritis, diabetes, heart disease, high blood pressure, mobility restrictions, or circulatory or pulmonary problems

Insurance

Mature travelers need to be sure they understand thoroughly the limitations to their medical coverage before leaving for a trip either in the United States or abroad.

Medicare does not cover travelers outside the United States. Medicare supplemental insurance ("medigap") plans often do not cover persons outside the United States except through special riders attached at extra cost to the basic plan. Health maintenance organizations (HMOs) may not cover travelers outside a particular service area except for emergency treatment. Some medical insurance plans only cover charges from selected health-care providers.

There are several options to consider for medical coverage while traveling. Short-term health insurance is available for both domestic and foreign travel. Travel agents can recommend companies that provide special travel health insurance. (See Chapter 7; a listing of such companies appears under Health and Safety.) Tour operators often provide some health and accident insurance coverage in the cost of the tour package, or will make it available at additional charge.

Medical Assistance

The International Association for Medical Assistance to Travelers (IAMAT), a long-established, nonprofit organization, supplies information on English-speaking doctors around the world and refers travelers to IAMAT clinics, where available, that are staffed by physicians trained in North America or Europe. There is no charge for the service, but donations are accepted.

Additionally, several private companies sell medical assistance plans for travelers to foreign destinations. Depending on the level of coverage and assistance services purchased, travelers can receive medical and hospital referrals and assistance, help in locating and contacting relatives, follow-up on medical services, and assistance in obtaining cash, translation services, and emergency transportation arrangements. If a death occurs abroad, these organizations help obtain necessary documents, explain procedures, and transport remains. Some companies include varying degrees of financial coverage for medical emergencies and may include cancellation insurance for terminated trips.

Travelers should check on the following important benefits in evaluating and comparing medical assistance plans:

Assistance in locating English-speaking medical care, and/or provision of translation services

Guarantee of any deposits hospitals may require before admission

Payment of the hospital and/or medical bills when due

Payment for evacuation of the patient if adequate treatment is not locally available

Payment for emergency transportation for the patient or family members

Assistance in the event of death, including evacuation of the remains

When a Death Occurs

Approximately 6,000 Americans die outside the United States each year. In case of death, the nearest U.S. embassy or consulate, or the U.S. Department of State's Citizens Emergency Center, should be contacted. The State Department can help by notifying the American's family and will inform them about options and costs for disposition of remains either for local burial or return of remains to the United States. The disposition of remains is affected by local laws, customs, and facilities often vastly different from those in the United States. Costs for preparing and returning a body to the United States are high and are the responsibility of the family. Often local laws and procedures make returning a body to the United States for burial a lengthy process.

Travel Safety

While a substantial number of mature travelers find health problems affect their travel plans, fortunately only a small number experience physical danger or life-threatening situations. However, theft and fraud are prevalent in a number of areas, both foreign and domestic, and the possibilities of fire, earthquakes, tornadoes, accidents, or terrorist activities cannot be ignored.

Details for ensuring personal security range from common-sense advice such as not traveling with large amounts of cash or expensive jewelry to precise psychological reasons to react in a certain manner if involved in a hostage situation. A number of devices, from portable smoke alarms to personal money belts, are available for added security.

Travelers are strongly advised to read one or more of the excellent books available on travel safety. A listing of the better books on this subject is included in Health and Safety, Chapter 8. Topics that should be considered include: protecting one's home while away; handling money and credit cards; protecting luggage; personal safety in accommodations, in public areas, while driving, or on public transportation; how to deal with terrorism or hostage situations; and travel safety devices and accessories.

Travel Advisories

The Citizens Emergency Center administers the State Department's travel advisory program. Advisories are issued to inform traveling Americans of conditions of risk abroad such as physical dangers, serious health hazards, or arbitrary detentions. Travelers can call a 24-hour hotline or can access various online computer services by modem on personal computers.

The Citizens Emergency Center also assists with information and advice if an American is arrested abroad, and helps track Americans whose families have not heard from the traveler or who need to get notification to a traveler about a family crisis at home. The center also works with U.S. consuls abroad to assist Americans who become physically or mentally ill while traveling. It locates family members, assists in transmitting private funds, and, when necessary, assists in the return of sick or injured Americans to the United States by commercial carrier. The Emergency Center can be reached by telephone Monday through Saturday at (202) 647-5225, or through the Department of State on Sundays and holidays at (202) 647-4000.

Chapter 3

Disabled Travel

- Some airlines have begun adding "skychairs" to certain aircraft, allowing mobility up and down the aisles for disabled passengers.

- Almost every Amtrak train includes accommodations for the handicapped in one or more coaches and, when available, sleeping cars.

- The Greyhound-Trailways bus line has begun to encourage travel of the handicapped by allowing a companion to travel free, and by transporting wheelchairs, walkers, or other equipment outside normal baggage limits.

- In 1985, only two cruise lines with four ships had cabins that could accommodate passengers completely confined to a wheelchair. According to Tom Gilbert, president of OPT (Organization for the Promotion of Access and Travel for the Handicapped), there are now 13 lines with 22 ships.

The experiences of thousands of handicapped and older travelers, who in prior years might have felt limited to a spot no farther from home than the edge of the front porch, have shown that today almost no limitation exists beyond their own attitude or budget as to where they can go and what they can do.

An eager traveler in her early eighties found a deteriorating nerve condition limited her walking. Since art was one of her most ardent interests, museums played a big part in her travel plans. But walking the distances required in most museums or galleries became impossible. She simply let tour guides know that although she required no special assistance into or out of tour buses, part of her luggage would be a folding wheelchair for use in viewing attractions that required a lot of walking.

A 67-year-old woman, living with the consequences of polio since age 45, had been housebound except for required trips for shopping, to medical appointments, or to the beauty shop. Recently, trips to a newly constructed senior center were her only recreation outside her home. When her schoolteacher daughters encouraged her to travel with them on summer vacations, they found that new accessibility guides for everything from individual cities to national parks enabled her to see many barrier-free vacation attractions she'd previously thought were unavailable to her.

A World War II veteran's children gave him a specially adapted van complete with wheelchair lift for a retirement present so that he and his wife could realize their dream to travel. A rapidly deteriorating health condition had made walking and several personal tasks impossible without the help of a companion. When his wife's poor health restricted her from helping him, he located a companion to assist him, through a travel group that supplies such assistants. His next foray will be abroad with a tour group designed especially for veterans, to visit the areas he'd known on his tour of duty 50 years ago.

Finally, a heart patient who didn't consider himself disabled, but who required a slower pace than most and frequent rest periods, didn't want to exclude himself from the vacation tours he loved. He simply worked with a tour group for the handicapped that also designed tours especially for older travelers like him.

A number of tour companies have specialized for many years in travel for the disabled and have access to buses and vans with lifts and other accoutrements especially for their disabled passengers. Given an additional challenge, these companies' travel planners have gotten disabled passengers aboard an elephant or chuck wagon or ocean cruise or camel or river raft or ride at Disneyland. The possibilities are almost unlimited. Refer to Disabled Travel in Chapter 7 for a listing of tour companies for travelers with disabilities. A listing of books with further information for older disabled travelers can be found in Chapter 8.

Transportation for the Disabled

Cars and RVs

A number of large car-rental agencies in the United States and a very limited number abroad have specially equipped cars and vans for handicapped drivers. Prices vary, and availability outside of major metropolitan areas is problematic. Most companies need up to two weeks advance notice, so thorough advance planning is a must. Handicapped travelers should also be sure to request written confirmation of the order, and to verify the confirmation and availability of the vehicle a few days prior to departure.

A growing number of handicapped travelers in the United States are taking to the road in specially modified RVs, and have even formed social clubs to cater specifically to the disabled RVer. RV travelers should check with individual RV dealers or an RV travel group such as the Good Sam Club or Escapees for specific information and resources in local areas.

Airlines

Both domestic and major international airlines have begun adopting new procedures and new equipment to assist handicapped passengers. Several airlines fly Boeing 767s, which are outfitted with a few aisle seats with folding arms to allow easier access from a wheelchair to the seat. Some also have new "skychairs," which allow mobility down the aisle during a flight. However, every airline has different policies regarding quotas on the number of wheelchair passengers per flight, restrictions on oxygen use, the need for a companion, pricing for guide dogs, and so forth.

The first important step for any disabled traveler is to check and compare various airlines' requirements, and to plan as far ahead as possible to have individual needs met. Explaining exactly one's limitations or needs is extremely important. One older woman who required a portable oxygen tank had become so accustomed to pulling it with her everywhere—on buses, in cars, in stores—that it had become as commonplace to her as her glasses. She showed up for her first flight since requiring the oxygen without having notified the airline first. She nearly wasn't allowed on the flight.

Carriage of oxygen on aircraft is subject to FAA regulations concerning hazardous materials. Passengers may bring their own oxygen into the plane only if it has been packed by an approved company. Otherwise, airlines can supply oxygen to those who require it, but they must have advance notification.

FAA regulations also govern transporting a battery-powered wheelchair aboard a plane. The regulations differ for spillable and nonspillable batteries, so again travelers need to make adequate advance preparations.

Most domestic airports and an increasing number of foreign airports are now handicap-accessible, with ramps, specially designed bathrooms, and motorized carts for use between airline gates or out to airplanes parked away from the terminal. Some have added "climbing chairs," which allow two attendants to get a wheelchair passenger up the steps to an airplane without the need to lift or carry the passenger.

Airlines provide their own wheelchairs for use on the jetways connecting the airplane to the terminal, allowing the passenger's chair to be loaded into the baggage compartment for the flight.

It is important that older travelers with disabilities arrive at least one hour prior to departure at domestic airports and at least two hours early at foreign airports to allow time for the extra services required. Airlines always allow passengers with special needs, such as those using canes or walkers, or needing a wheelchair, to board before other passengers.

Some of the innovations airlines have adopted in recent years include:

On-board "aisle chairs" or "sky chairs" allowing movement around the cabin

In some 767 aircraft, a handicap-accessible bathroom with specially adapted fixtures and additional space allowance for a companion or in which to maneuver the on-board wheelchair

Closed-captioned in-flight video safety demonstrations

In-flight safety briefing books in Braille

Training for personnel to sensitize them to the special needs of elderly and handicapped travelers

Trains

Amtrak has made substantial progress in making rail travel accessible to handicapped travelers. Almost every Amtrak train includes accommodations for the handicapped in one or more coaches and, when available, sleeping cars. Priority is given to handicapped and senior passengers who wish to reserve special roomettes (on eastern routes) and special bedrooms (in the West).

Battery-powered wheelchairs can be transported in at least one passenger car on all trains. Disabled travelers should inquire about size and other limitations. Wheelchair lifts, or manual assistance when needed, can be provided with advance notice.

Oxygen may be carried on board Amtrak trains, with some limitations. Call ahead for information and advance arrangements.

Special diets such as kosher, vegetarian, or low-sodium can be accommodated on Amtrak with advance notice. Car attendants can provide meal and beverage service from the dining and lounge cars for passengers unable to move about freely. Seventy-two-hour advance notice is required for special food requests.

Medication should be carried in hand luggage, as checked baggage is not available during a train trip. Amtrak will supply ice for medications carried in coolers.

Passengers requiring special assistance need to arrive at the station at least one hour in advance.

Unfortunately, train travel in other parts of the world has yet to catch up with American efforts to make trains and train depots handicap-accessible. Organizations for the handicapped or travel agents specializing in travel for the disabled should have the most up-to-date information required by travelers to accommodate their own special needs.

Buses

The Greyhound-Trailways bus line has begun to encourage travel by the handicapped by allowing a companion to travel free, and by transporting wheelchairs, walkers, and other equipment outside normal baggage limits. Its two-for-one-fare program, "Helping Hand for the Handicapped," requires a doctor's written statement that the passenger requires a companion for physical assistance. Bus employees will assist in carrying the passenger on board since there are no boarding chairs similar to those on airlines.

Handicapped travelers may still find their way completely barred if, for example, they arrive at a local city tour bus depot to take the next circle tour of the city and the only bus available is for able-bodied travelers only. However, with careful advance planning, almost no attraction or event should be written off as unavailable. A number of tour companies have specialized for many years in handicapped travel. They have access to buses and vans with lifts, and will either offer or be able to arrange a similar tour of the area.

Bus depots vary in degree of accessibility. Disabled travelers should check with a travel agent or Greyhound-Trailways for barriers that may still remain at individual depots on the itinerary.

Cruises

All cruise ships are accessible to any person in a wheelchair who has limited mobility and can walk behind the chair for support, or walk with a walker, cane, or crutches, according to Tom Gilbert, president of OPT. In 1985, only two cruise lines with four ships had cabins that could accommodate passengers who were completely confined to a wheelchair. Now, according to Gilbert, there are 13 lines with 22 ships.

Working with knowledgeable travel agents is a must for disabled travelers. The agents should be able to understand the special needs of the traveler and realize what barriers each ship might present, such as raised doorsills, little maneuvering room, or other architectural blocks. Many of the books on cruising listed in Chapter 8 that rate various ships also indicate accessibility on those ships. Louise Weiss's *Access to the World* (see Chapter 8) includes a valuable outline of services for the disabled aboard a number of ships.

However, many older travelers with disabilities are not necessarily limited in their mobility; instead, they may require the use of oxygen or dialysis, or need assistance with activities of daily living such as bathing or eating. Again, working with a knowledgeable travel agent is strongly suggested to be sure a ship's staff and facilities can accommodate the services needed.

The International Cruise Passengers Association (see Cruising in Chapter 7) provides information and support for the handicapped cruise passenger, and works to establish guidelines for the provision of shipboard support facilities for disabled travelers. It does not book cruises.

Chapter 4

On the Road: Cars and Recreational Vehicles

FACTS OF INTEREST

- Of the trips taken by adults 55+ in the last half of the 1980s (generally over 250 million trips each year), 75−80 percent were by car or RV.

- RV trips account for 18 percent of trips taken by seniors, with 72 percent of all RV trips made by travelers age 50 and over.

- Seniors age 55 and over constitute 44 percent of America's RVers.

- Camping is third only to swimming and fishing in popularity among American adults, of whom 39 percent prefer RV camping.

- Senior RVers take trips two to three times as long in duration as their under-50 counterparts.

- There are 20,000 campgrounds throughout the United States on both public and private lands that accommodate RVs.

Americans love the open highway, and older Americans express their continued adoration by taking over 80 percent of their trips on wheels—in cars or RVs, and by bus.

Of the 226 million trips taken by adults 55+ in 1988, 75–80 percent were by car or RV. According to a recent University of Michigan survey, 44 percent of America's RVers are seniors age 55 and over. The American Automobile Association (AAA) reports that the average age of its club membership in Colorado, for example, is 55—in a state with only about 11 percent of its population over that age. A random survey of automobile clubs in other states reveals the same trend.

Car and RV travel particularly appeals to independent travelers who want to choose their own itinerary and enjoy it at their own pace. Two retired couples from Nebraska, for example, have been friends since school days. Free now from daily farm chores, they take off together in a comfortable station wagon to visit craft fairs and regional festivals they'd always wanted to see. Depending on the appeal of a festival's offerings or attractions nearby, they stay as long as they choose at their destinations.

Driving One's Own Car

Driving Classes

Because the aging process alters various reflexes necessary for safe driving, it is wise for older drivers to take periodic defensive-driving classes to update their driving skills. Driving schools across the country welcome drivers of any age for refresher courses, but the 55/Alive Defensive Driving class, offered by the American Association of Retired Persons (AARP), is designed specifically for the older driver. Fees are nominal and the classes are open both to AARP members and nonmembers. The national AARP office in Washington, D.C., can supply the name and phone number of a local contact for the 55/Alive program across the United States. Many insurance companies offer discounted rates for older drivers who have successfully completed the 55/Alive or other authorized driving course.

Mature drivers should also check with their state department of motor vehicles for licensing requirements. Some states have adopted a more frequent driver's license renewal program for older people, or require a road test as well as a written test above a certain age.

Automobile Clubs

The American Automobile Association is the pioneering and probably still most widely known and used automobile club in America. AAA, as well as several other similar clubs, offers emergency road service, trip planning, travel guides, some insurance, and various discounts. Some clubs also issue credit cards; plot itineraries; offer discounts at selected hotels, motels, and restaurants; and assist in obtaining emergency cash.

Clubs other than AAA include the United States Auto Club; the National Automobile Club; those sponsored by oil companies such as Amoco, Chevron, Exxon, and Shell; and those by national retailers such as Sears (Allstate) and Montgomery Ward. Senior travelers should check to be sure the club chosen offers the services needed—especially universal road service—and whether it also covers emergency road service for RVs.

QUESTIONS TO ASK

Is membership open to anyone or are there requirements to purchase insurance or a credit card first?

What is the annual fee?

Are there any discounts for age?

What services are provided for that fee?

What additional services are provided? At what fee?

How available and accessible is road service?

Is equal road service provided for an RV?

Is service provided in Canada, Mexico, or overseas?

Getting a Car to a Destination without Driving

Several alternative methods allow seniors to get their own cars to a destination without having to drive them there themselves. One New Jersey widow, for example, drives each fall to the

Washington, D.C. area. There, she and her car board the Amtrak Auto Train, which takes them to Sanford, Florida, just a few miles from Orlando. From there it's an easy drive to her winter condo in Tampa, where she enjoys the use of her own car all winter. Recent prices for the Auto Train were $207 for the car one-way, plus $140 one-way rail coach fare, meals included. Rates vary by season.

A car-delivery service will transport a car by trailer truck to a vacation or temporary residence location. The cost from New York to Florida was about $500 in 1990. While this cost initially seemed high to one Connecticut couple, it actually became a bargain for them. The husband was the only driver, and a medical condition made it impossible for him to drive long distances. They shipped their car to their Gulf Coast winter home and flew there themselves. They enjoyed full mobility for shopping, visiting, and errands during the winter, especially since public transportation was not easily available to them in their small town.

Yet another method for getting a car to a destination is to use car driveaway services. Driveaway companies supply certified drivers to deliver cars to vacation areas. Some older people have also found college students, wanting to go to the same destination, to drive their cars. Others request a friend or family member to drive them to a destination and then provide airfare back home for the driver.

Renting a Car

Many seniors do not own a car, or choose not to take their own car to a vacation site. A retired couple who live in a suburban New York City retirement complex, for example, have exemplary public transportation anywhere in their town and in New York City as well. They have chosen to forgo the expense and upkeep of a vehicle. A San Francisco widower owns a small "city car" for nearby errands, but he wants something more comfortable and roadworthy for long-distance trips. A Des Moines couple want to be able to explore an area such as New England or the Cascade Mountains by car, but they do not want to spend long hours on the road to get to an area halfway across the continent from their home. A Texas widow and her companion want to explore the back roads of Europe. For any of these older adults, a car-rental agency is the first stop for an automobile vacation.

Every car-rental agency both in the United States and abroad offers a discount for *something*. It may be because a customer is a senior citizen, is a member of an organization such as AARP or a professional group, is picking up the car in midweek or at a downtown rather than airport location, or any number of current marketing gambits.

The most important step in finding the best car-rental deal is to call around. Every car-rental agency has a free 800 telephone number. Older travelers can avoid confusion in terms by specifying the make and model of the car wanted, i.e., a Cadillac Seville or "the smallest car available." A generic term like "subcompact" could mean anything from a Chevy Sprint to a Ford Taurus—all at the same subcompact price, depending on the rental company.

Car renters should also check for group discounts as well as any weekly, seasonal, or geographic special prices various companies may be offering. Group discounts are usually deducted from the full-rate schedule, while other types of specials may offer substantially larger discounts.

Travelers should also check on all other charges, which generally are not quoted in the base rate. These include taxes, fuel charges if the car is not returned with a full tank, and mileage limitations. Insurance fees and drop charges can also add a significant amount to the final bill.

Car-rental agencies have been the focus of consumer protest in recent years over excessive and often redundant insurance fees for rental cars. In many cases insurance coverage for one's personal car will extend to damage done to rental cars as well. Checking first with one's insurance agent about personal coverage can help the traveler avoid unnecessary or redundant insurance charges.

Drop charges can also be an expensive item. One couple, for example, wanted to fly into Baltimore, Maryland, to begin an automobile exploration trip from the nation's capital to New England. They had hoped to leave the car in Boston and fly home from there. However, with careful checking, they found that both the airfare and car-rental prices were much higher when not purchased on a round-trip basis. The additional day's travel time and expenses and mileage charges to return from Boston to Baltimore were more economical than a one-way trip.

Major car-rental companies in the United States do not set maximum-age restrictions, but some smaller companies may.

QUESTIONS TO ASK

Is a security deposit required?

What is the fuel service fee? Should the car be returned with a full tank?

Is there a drop charge?

Is there unlimited free mileage? If not, what is the daily/weekly limit?

What insurance is needed beyond that provided on one's own vehicle policy?

Can more than one person drive the car?

What is the procedure if repairs are needed? Who authorizes such repairs, to what limit, and who pays?

What are the charges if the car is returned one or more days later or earlier than originally contracted for?

Are there discounts for age? Are such discounts better than any other special offers?

Are there any age limitations to rent a car?

Driving Abroad

Renting a Car

The same questions to ask about requirements when renting a car at home apply when renting abroad. However, older travelers who want to rent a car abroad may discover that companies will not rent vehicles to drivers above a particular age due to the prohibitive cost of insuring older drivers in certain countries.

Maximum-age limits vary from country to country and from company to company. It's important to ask around. Avis, for example, may impose a restriction on anyone over the age of 60 in Sri Lanka but not in Western Samoa. Hertz's and National's age limits may differ in the same locations.

AGE LIMITS (60 AND UP) FOR CAR RENTERS

Avis, Budget, Dollar, Hertz, and National have age restrictions in the following places:

Europe
Britain: Budget, 75
Channel Islands: Avis, 69 (unless driver purchases collision damage waiver)
Denmark: Budget, 75
Finland: Budget, 70
Gibraltar: Budget, 65; Hertz, 70
Isle of Man: Avis, 70
Hungary: Budget, 70
Ireland. Budget, 75, Dollar, 69, National 75
Italy: Budget, 70; Dollar, 70
Madeira: Hertz, 75
Malta: Hertz, 70; National, 70
The Netherlands: Budget, 65

Middle East
Israel: Budget, 75; Hertz, 70
Jordan: Avis, 70; Budget, 68
Kuwait: Budget, 65
Lebanon: Budget, 70

Africa
Egypt: Budget, 65
Ivory Coast: Budget, 65
Kenya: Avis, 75; Budget, 70; Hertz, 70; National, 70
Malawi: Avis, 65; Hertz, 65
Morocco: Budget, 60
South Africa: Budget, 70
Southwest Africa: Budget, 70
Togo: Budget, 65
Uganda: Hertz, 60
Zimbabwe: National, 65

Asia and South Pacific
Brunei: Avis, 60
Fiji: Budget, 65

Indonesia: Avis, 60
Malaysia: Budget, 65; Hertz, 60
New Caledonia: Avis, 70; Hertz, 65
New Guinea: Hertz, 70
Niue Island: Budget, 65
Philippines: Avis, 65; Budget, 65; Hertz, 65
Solomon Islands: Budget, 65
South Korea: Avis, 65
Sri Lanka: Avis, 60; Hertz, 65; National, 65
Tahiti: Hertz, 75
Western Samoa: Avis, 75

Latin America and the Caribbean
Aruba: Avis, 70; Budget, 65
Bahamas: Budget, 70
Bonaire: Avis, 70
Brazil: Avis, 70
Costa Rica: Avis, 70
Curaçao: Budget, 65
Dominican Republic: Avis, 60; Budget, 70
Ecuador: Avis, 60
Grand Cayman Islands: Budget, 75
Guadeloupe: Budget, 75
Grenada: Avis, 65
Jamaica: Budget, 70; Hertz, 65
Mexico: Avis, 70
Panama: Avis, 70
St. Martin: Budget, 70
St. Croix: Budget, 70; Hertz, 70
Venezuela: Avis, 65.

From "Travel Advisory" (Older Drivers, Varying Rules), *New York Times,* February 19, 1989. Copyright © 1989 by The New York Times Company. Reprinted by permission.

Insurance

Insurance regulations and driving requirements vary widely from country to country. Closest to home, Americans driving in Canada don't need extra insurance, but do need a Non-Resident Inter-Province Motor Vehicle Insurance Card, which provides evidence of financial responsibility. These cards are free from one's car insurance company.

Domestic insurance does not provide coverage in Mexico, however. The Mexican government does not recognize foreign coverage, although some U.S. companies have coverage that extends within limited areas of Mexico. Appropriate insurance can be purchased from automobile clubs or from agents of Mexican insurance companies found in almost all American cities on or near the border.

In Europe, foreign motorists must have an International Motor Insurance Certificate or "green card" to prove the car is insured. Without it, the car can be impounded. AAA offers European Automobile Tourist insurance for 1 to 12 months, which includes the green card.

Driver's License

Although not required in all locales, 60 countries require an International Driving Permit (IDP). IDPs are available for $5 from AAA to anyone, member or nonmember, age 18 or older, with a valid U.S. driver's license. Two passport photos are required for an IDP.

Recreational Vehicles

Probably nowhere is the allure of the open road more enticing than when one's own home can be brought along. So great is this fascination that 30 million Americans owned or rented an RV in 1989, 9 million of them age 50 plus, according to the Recreation Vehicle Industry Association (RVIA). An estimated 100,000 permanent nomads comprise the ranks of "full-time" RVers, whose only home is their RV. Over 90 percent of these full-timers are retirees.

In the 1980s, the growth in RV ownership was greatest among households age 55 or older says the RVIA, while AARP found that RV trips account for 18 percent of trips taken by seniors, with 72 percent of all RV trips made by travelers age 50 and over. According to a recent University of Michigan survey, 44 percent of America's RVers are seniors age 55 and over.

In 1985, an A. C. Neilsen poll found that camping is third only to swimming and fishing in popularity among American adults. The study also showed that, among campers, 39.1 percent preferred RV camping.

A recent cost comparison by the international accounting firm Pannell Kerr Forster found that RV vacations are overwhelmingly more economical than traditional trips by car, bus, train, or airplane, regardless of trip destination or duration. Most RV trips cost one-quarter to one-half as much as a comparable vacation by other means. Senior RVers take trips two to three times as long in duration as their under-50 counterparts.

RVs have special appeal to mature travelers, who can have nearly all the comforts of home while on the road. One couple in their seventies both require special diets. They prepare all their meals in their camper and forgo the hassle of finding appropriate—and often expensive—restaurants along the way.

Another retired couple enjoy a nap in the middle of the day—a luxury never afforded them on group tours. Any roadside rest area, or even the outer edge of a shopping mall parking lot, provides that opportunity. Or, with miles to cover before nightfall, one sleeps on a comfortable bed while the other continues driving.

A retired nurse from Cleveland loves the freedom her camper offers. She moves with the sun to enjoy summer in her home state and winter in the South. On the way, she visits grandchildren scattered across the Midwest. Two of her children live in small homes, so she sleeps in her RV parked in their driveway. Some of the grandkids think it's a special adventure to sleep overnight in Grandma's camper.

A 67-year-old widow had lived full-time on the road with her husband in their RV for two and a half years before he died. Although now living on a fairly modest income, she wouldn't dream of giving up her RV home. She belongs to an RV singles group with chapters in nearly every state. She joins them for potlucks, dances, and campouts, or finds nearly nonstop activities at RV campgrounds that attract large numbers of senior campers. At least once a year she joins a caravan of RVers who tour Mexico, Alaska, and other areas in the United States or Canada. The chance to meet new people and enjoy an ever-expanding "family" of friends are, as she says, "worth my RV's weight in gold."

What Is a Recreational Vehicle?

Recreational vehicles are defined as any pleasure vehicle that contains living accommodations, ranging from simple pickup-truck camper shells and folding camping trailers to van conversions and pull-along travel trailers, to elaborate fifth-wheelers and luxurious motorhomes. RV is a generic designation for any recreational vehicle.

Standard designations for RVs are as follows:

Motorhome: A camping and travel vehicle from 24–34 feet in length, built on a self-propelled truck or bus chassis. Contains kitchen, sleeping, bathroom, and dining facilities, accessible to driver's area. Living systems include electrical, heating, air conditioning (optional), water, propane gas, and waste collection. Sleeps two to ten people. Living systems are self-contained, but when staying at campgrounds most users hook up to electricity, water, sewer drain, etc.

Mini-motorhome: A scaled-down version of larger motorhomes, from 20–28 feet in length, built on a truck chassis, usually with sleeping bunks atop the cab. The living area is accessible to the driver's area. Sleeps two adults, or up to six people including children. Has fewer features and less space and privacy than larger units, but is more economical to operate and is easier to drive and park.

Van conversion: A regular van with a raised roof, from 16–21 feet in length, customized to include side windows, carpeting, custom seats, and accessories. Can sleep from two to four people, but has minimal kitchen and toilet facilities, and little space to move about inside.

Travel trailer: Requires a heavy duty-vehicle to pull. Towable units, 13–33 feet in length, have full living facilities, which are illegal to use while under way. Best when parked at campground for extended period while using the towing vehicle for local transportation and sightseeing.

Fifth-wheel trailer: Differs from conventional trailers in the way it is coupled to the tow vehicle (a pickup truck). The hitch is centered over the truck's rear axle, providing excellent stability while traveling. The trailer's front overhang section usually is used as a bedroom. Fifth-wheel trailers range from 17–40 feet.

Truck camper: Camping unit mounted on the bed of a pickup truck, 18–21 feet in length, including the truck. May have kitchen and bathroom facilities. The cabover section contains a bunk; other seats may fold down to sleep two to four more people. Some of the larger self-contained campers may require a dual-rear-wheel truck.

Folding camping trailer (sometimes referred to as tent trailer or pop-up trailer): A lightweight, towable unit 10–15 feet in length, often light enough to be towed by any car larger than a subcompact. They have collapsible sides that fold down for towing. When set up, they provide kitchen, dining, and sleeping facilities for up to eight people.

Driving an RV

There are no special licensing requirements for driving an RV, except for a few states that may require special training for driving a fifth-wheel-type rig. Older vacationers should check with the Highway Patrol or state highway department safety division in their home state to see if this or other special RV requirements exist. Drivers are bound only by the regulations in the state from which they obtained their driver's license.

However, since both towing a vehicle and driving lengthy recreational vehicles offer considerable challenges beyond those of normal driving conditions, mature travelers are strongly advised to check with local RV dealers and service agents for RV driving classes and instructors. Many full-timers also tow a car behind them for use once their motorhome is parked at a camping location, creating additional length and driving problems in transit. Richard Dunlop's *On the Road in an RV,* Bill and Jan Moeller's *Full-Time RVing: A Complete Guide to Life on the Open Road, Trailer Life's Guide to Full-Time RVing* (see Chapter 8 for book listings), and especially the AARP booklet *Safety in RV's, A Moving Experience* (see the pamphlets section in Chapter 8 under RVs and Camping) offer good advice on handling various road and weather conditions in an RV.

Additional insurance coverage is required for recreational vehicles. Any insurance agent who regularly sells car insurance can offer information and pricing for RV coverage.

Renting an RV

Seniors who are eager to try the open road in an RV are encouraged to rent one or more for several weeks or months, not only to experience the lifestyle, but also to experiment with various types of vehicles.

For those who like RVing enough to want to consider living in one full-time—the consensus of best advice from current RV "full-timers" is clear—try it out first! Even if one has camped in a recreational vehicle frequently—or especially if one has never experienced life in an RV, at least two months on the road without returning home is recommended for making the decision to go full-time. Innumerable details of day-to-day living will be different—from having a stable home base to living in cramped quarters. RVing means much different expenses—lower than a home mortgage and home maintenance but higher for health care, shopping, and other items that one knows where to find at lower prices in familiar territory. Full-timing can mean never seeing the same dentist or doctor twice, and having nowhere to escape when a traveling partner is sick in bed all day—and that bed is in the middle of the living quarters. It can also mean the heady freedom to go precisely when and where one wants to go, following the seasons, meeting a cornucopia of new friends, enjoying a multiplicity of new experiences.

The Recreational Vehicle Rental Association offers a complete U.S. and Canadian province listing of RV dealers who rent RVs. Also, some truck rental agencies such as Hertz, U-Haul, and Avis rent RVs.

Life on the Road

Since most RVs are self-contained with independent water, gas, and electricity, as veteran RVer and author Kay Peterson says, "Home is where you park it." The choices of where to park are almost unlimited—from the spartan trailer lot or open field to the plushest resort. There are free or inexpensive state and local parks, wilderness Bureau of Land Management areas, commercial campgrounds, and elaborate and luxurious "membership" campground resorts.

Campgrounds

There are 20,000 campgrounds throughout the United States on both public and private lands that accommodate RVs. Most numerous are commercial campgrounds such as KOA (Kampgrounds of America), Jellystone Parks, Good Sam parks, etc. These operate on a first-come, first-served basis, but reservations are accepted and are often necessary for busy weekends. They generally offer a full range of facilities from tent camping spaces (no hookups) to drive-through spaces with full hookups for large rigs. Almost all have full bathroom and shower facilities. Additional services such as laundry facilities, game rooms, and sports areas or swimming pools vary from location to location.

Membership campgrounds operate somewhat like "camping condominiums." That is, members purchase the right to a guaranteed full-service hookup for unlimited usage at a local resort and then may stay at affiliated clubs for a small fee. These campgrounds—or camping resorts—generally are highly developed, with extensive recreational facilities such as golf courses, tennis courts, or health spas.

There are 440 developed campgrounds offering 29,000 campsites at the nation's 354 national parks. Campgrounds in popular national parks and forests generally do not require advance reservations, but reservations, if accepted, are recommended during peak tourist seasons. State and local parks may have spaces available, but California, for example, requires advance reservations for all state parks. Occasionally "drop-ins" may find space during quiet weekdays; some other states set aside a portion of their campground sites for first-come, first-served visitors.

Discount Passes

Golden Age passes are available free to travelers 62 and older. These passes provide free admission to national parks and wildlife refuges, plus 50 percent discounts on park user fees, including RV camping. They are also accepted as proof of age for discounts or free camping at most state park campgrounds as well. Golden Age passes must be obtained in person from any

National Park Service or Forest Service headquarters, or regional offices of other federally managed areas.

RV Support Systems

Membership in an automobile club generally offers both car and recreational vehicle support services; various RV clubs such as the Good Sam Club, the National RV Owners Club, Escapees, and the Family Motor Coach Association (FMCA), among others, offer a wide variety of specific RV support services. These include mail forwarding and message services (several other groups provide this service alone), discounts at campgrounds, insurance, lost-and-found services, and publications with travel tips and important "how-to" articles. A listing of RV support-system groups, both technical and social, is included in Chapter 7.

Social Life on the Road

The RV lifestyle fosters a sense of community and offers seniors a valuable network of friends who share a common interest. Camping and RV clubs hold annual conventions, regional rallies, campouts, and other events to bring RVers together and provide an active social network on the road. Clubs such as Loners on Wheels and Loners of America cater to single RVers, most of whom are 50+. They offer social events, group caravans, and newsletters to help members stay in touch. Yet other groups cater to RVers with handicaps or to those who wish to travel together in foreign countries.

Working on the Road

Retirees with their own RV rig can camp free for a month or more at a national park, state park, or Forest Service campground by volunteering to be a campground host. Hosts greet campers, assign sites, police the campground, and do other campground managerial duties. Information on volunteer duties and openings can be obtained from the National Park Service or through the booklet *Helping Out in the Outdoors,* published by the American Hiking Society. Other enterprising seniors have managed private or commercial campgrounds during one or more seasons in return for an RV space and hookups, while others travel to regional craft fairs and flea markets to peddle homemade crafts. Yet others write and do photography for travel publications, take temporary jobs, or provide services to fellow RVers.

Chapter 5

Cruising

- Over 95 percent of those who have taken an ocean cruise return to do it again.

- Seventy percent of cruise vacationers are over age 50, according to the U.S. Travel Data Center.

- Cruise vacations these days not only encompass ocean liners, but also freighters, ferries, barges, and even sailboat charters.

- Some major cruise lines have begun catering to mature passengers with special menus, activities, and programs.

- Solo travelers are welcomed aboard cruise ships, with events and activities planned especially for singles. Older male hosts are on board some ships to socialize with the many mature single women on cruises.

- Many cruise lines now feature specially designed programs for grandparents and grandchildren.

For the older adults who comprise the majority of today's cruise travelers, the traditional enticements of cruising such as outstanding (and plentiful) food, romantic settings, camaraderie, activities, and entertainment are just the beginning. There are also fascinating innovative ships and alluring new ports of call added yearly to various cruise lines' itineraries, specialty cruises

61

focusing on jazz or gourmet cooking or art history, and ships and programs geared especially for grandparents and grandchildren.

But what if, like one former professor from Georgia and her husband, a mature traveler fancies a bit more peace and quiet and serene communion with the ocean than is sometimes available on activity-filled cruise ships? Freighter cruising—the old days' "slow boat to China"—is attracting ever-increasing numbers of aficionados, especially retirees who have the luxury of less rigid schedules and more time to spend at sea.

In yet another cruising alternative, an older Massachusetts housewife and her sister have joined the ranks of those who have grown to love smaller specialty cruises. These set sail to whale watch or glacier gaze or simply slip into quieter, more secluded anchorage than big ships can manage, to observe local flora and fauna and enjoy unique shore excursions.

Then there are the travelers who enjoy the placid backwaters of Europe or Britain, whose time aboard a working or hotel barge allows a long, slow, up-close and personal look at a region. They may want to explore an area known for its wine . . . or cheese . . . or simply savor a tranquil pastoral vista, untrampled by tourist hordes. On the home front, thousands of vacationers each year enjoy leisurely, nostalgic paddlewheel steamer explorations of the Mississippi River, or a casual motorboat jaunt along the Inland Waterway.

There are those, like the 56-year-old Texas rancher and his companion, who want to combine the lure of the open highway in a car or RV with ferry-liner cruising. These travelers stop where they want for as long as they choose to visit or sightsee, then hop aboard the next ferry along for the subsequent leg of their trip.

Finally, boat and yacht charters serve many vacationers, like one 75-year-old retired Florida doctor and his wife, who no longer are eager to pay dockage or maintenance fees to own a boat. These intrepid explorers choose the waterway of their dreams, rent a boat, and take off to explore the world.

Ocean Cruising

Ocean cruising aboard luxury vacation liners has attracted only 5 percent of the traveling public, according to industry statistics, but of those, 95 percent book another cruise. And the majority of those passengers are older adults.

"One of the myths about cruising which can at least partially be blamed on the popular television show is that nearly everyone who cruises is young, single, glamorous, and independently wealthy," says Charlanne Fields Herring in *The Cruise Answer Book*. "Quite to the contrary," she continues, "the average age of passengers on many ships is over 50, and most are married and on vacation or retired from wellpaying, but demanding jobs."

What are the advantages of ocean cruising? According to Antoinette Deland, author of *Fielding's Worldwide Cruises*: "If the advantage of just one rate for everything and no hidden extras (except what you intend to spend for shopping, drinks, and tipping) appeals to you, you may also enjoy the fact that all the many details of when, where and what time things happen each day have already been solved by the ship lines. You not only leave the driving to them, but the food and entertainment decisions as well. They have even eliminated any language problems and you just sit on deck and relax."

Some people have avoided taking a cruise on the pretext that it would be a boring time. Charlanne Herring dispels that notion. "Just about the last thing anyone has ever been on a cruise is bored! If, however, you don't like to go to movies, play bingo or card games, exercise, shoot skeet, read, play trivia games, swim, play video games, gamble (on horses or in a casino), learn crafts, shop, talk to people, listen to music or dance, see beautiful scenery, snorkel or skindive, play golf or pingpong or tennis or pool games, visit new places, be entertained by comedians, singers, dancers, magicians, attend lectures on anything from time management to beauty, then you may be bored."

Choosing an Ocean Cruise

Type of ship, time of year, ports of call, and length of vacation time are all important factors to consider in choosing an ocean cruise. Several good books and magazines on cruising are available in bookstores and libraries that describe various cruise lines, their ships, and ports of call. The books are also good for general background information on cruising and details on dress, tipping, activities, menus, and so forth. (A list of cruise books of interest to mature travelers appears in Chapter 8.) Most cruise lines also produce marketing videos about their ships and cruises, available through travel agents or travel video outlets.

For current information, travel agents carry dozens of brochures on various cruise vacations. Travelers might also consider consulting copies of the *Official Steamship Guide International,* subscribed to by travel agents and available in many public libraries, or *Cruise Travel,* a bimonthly magazine. Both list prospective cruises, ships, and ports of call.

Ships

Vacation cruise ships range from as small as 200 passengers to over 2,500 passengers. In fact, some superships that will accommodate 4,000 passengers are currently being built. The larger ships tend to be more formal and offer more facilities, entertainment, and activities, while the smaller vessels are more intimate, friendlier, and can dock at a greater number of ports. The age of a ship generally is not an important factor, as they are refurbished frequently. Travel agents and other cruise information sources can identify when various ships were last upgraded or renovated. The nationality of the ship's crew will set the tone for the cruise, and in Europe will determine the official ship's language.

Cruises are "one-class" service. Everyone on board can use all of the ship's facilities.

In general, late fall and winter are excellent times to cruise in the Caribbean or South Pacific. However, the weather in these areas is almost always nice, and good deals are often available on cruises in off-peak season, i.e., when everyone else is not trying to escape cold weather. Transatlantic crossings during fall and winter are rough and bad weather is the norm. Late spring, summer, and early fall are ideal times to cruise the Mediterranean or the Baltic Sea or the coasts of Turkey and other Middle Eastern countries.

In addition to choosing favorite ports of call, mature travelers should also consider the ship's schedule for those ports. Does it allow adequate time to tour the area or merely a few hours for nearby shopping and sightseeing? Is visiting several ports a prime consideration or is it preferable to spend more time relaxing at sea?

Single Travelers

Many singles are attracted to cruises because of the camaraderie aboard most ships. Dinner is served at large tables, and many lines organize special parties for singles.

There are a number of groups that focus on single travelers. Some will help locate roommates or offer a newsletter with listings of other singles looking for travel partners. Others organize groups to travel together on a particular cruise. Often these groups will organize their own activities both on board and on shore excursions, while also offering plenty of time to meet fellow passengers.

Royal Cruise Lines was the first major cruise line to institute a "host" program for mature single women, who are the majority of its cruise passengers. Retired or semiretired gentlemen are offered free passage in exchange for socializing (within strict guidelines) with the single ladies, giving them an opportunity to dance or round out a table of cards, or have an escort on shore excursions.

Fares

Fares depend on a number of factors, including level of accommodation (see below), type of cruise, length of cruise, and ports of call. An appealing factor to many vacationers is that once the fare is established, no other charges will be assessed. There are no surprises as to how much the vacation will actually cost. The only additional money a cruise vacationer should need is for personal expenses such as drinks on board, shopping either on board or on shore excursions, and tipping. Each cruise line will explain tipping policies aboard their ship. Travel agents and the many good books available on cruising also explain tipping policies in detail.

Most cruise lines will not cash personal checks, but will advance money on a credit card. Ship personnel can provide information on how to change dollars to local currency in a foreign port.

Port charges are assessed by local port authorities and generally are included in the price of the cruise. They can change up to the day of embarkation and could be assessed even after the trip has begun.

"Air/sea" or "fly/cruise" packages include either free or reduced airfare along with the cruise ticket. These are available from most major North American cities and include transfers between the airport and ship as well as baggage handling. Some lines now even offer connecting flights from smaller regional airports as part of a package deal.

"Sail 'n' stay" programs have been added to some cruise lines in their attempt to appeal to even broader markets with more customized vacations. Sail 'n' stay packages work with hotels and resorts to allow passengers to disembark on a Caribbean island, for example, stay at a resort for a few days, and then reboard the ship on its return trip.

A good way to compare value and price when choosing a cruise is to calculate a per-day price based on the actual number of days on the ship, plus airfare if not included as part of an air/sea package.

Discounts

Discounts on cruise fares are available in a number of ways. First, substantial discounts are always available for early booking, that is, at least six months prior to sailing. Deposits are usually fully refundable up to 60 days before sailing. Any deposits or fares paid after that time would only be recoverable through trip cancellation insurance should the traveler need to cancel the trip.

Many lines offer at least a 10 percent discount to older travelers; each line's age requirements for eligibility may vary.

It is also possible to book passage through a cruise clearinghouse. These companies buy blocks of cabins in advance and then offer them at group rates to individual customers.

Cruise discount agencies offer last-minute bookings at substantial discounts when cruise lines are ready to accept any reasonable revenue for an otherwise unfilled cabin. Some intrepid and highly flexible travelers have even appeared at the dock just hours before sailing to negotiate a greatly reduced price for remaining cabins.

Health Care

All major cruise ships maintain a medical staff and full health facilities on board for treating problems from mild seasickness to a passenger death.

Seasickness is not a common problem on large ships or those with stabilizers, which overcome the roll of the sea. A number of medications for motion sickness are always available on ships. Additional solutions are the "Sea-Band," an elastic band worn on the wrist that activates acupressure points, and the Transderm Scop patch worn behind the ear that time-releases medication into the body. The patches are available by prescription only and may create mild side effects in some people.

Cruise vacationers should bring a complete supply of needed medications. Ship pharmacies may carry some standard items, but are not generally equipped to refill individual prescriptions. Cruise-ship doctors report that the two most common medical problems among cruise vacationers are sunburn and forgetting to bring prescription medications.

All cruise ships are accessible to any person in a wheelchair who has limited mobility and can walk behind the chair for support or walk with a walker, cane, or crutches, according to Tom Gilbert, president of OPT. In 1985, two cruise lines with four ships had cabins that could accommodate passengers who were completely confined to a wheelchair. According to Gilbert, there are now 13 lines with 22 ships. Several travel organizations for the disabled can help those with more limiting handicaps choose appropriate cruise vacations.

Accommodations

Vacationers should check cruise brochures for an illustration or description of the ship's deck plan delineating the size of each room, number of closets, dresser space, bathroom facilities, type of beds (single, double, or bunk), and general layouts. The majority of cabins are interior rooms with no portholes.

An outside stateroom with a porthole will run $100–$200 per person more than inside rooms. Luxury suites on newer ships now even offer private balconies with floor-to-ceiling windows.

In addition to size and location, pricing for a cabin depends on the type of beds (two lower beds cost more than bunk beds), whether it is booked during a heavy tourist or holiday season, and which deck it is on. The higher the deck, the higher the price. Lower deck cabins offer the advantage of less roll in heavy seas. Most forward rooms bear the brunt of sea motion, but those lower and more aft get vibration and noise from the ship's engines. Other considerations in choice of cabin might be proximity to elevators and stairwells, or to noisy discos or other public areas.

A third or fourth person can reduce the cost of any room. Children sharing a cabin with two full-fare adults pay half the minimum fare. Rates are much higher for single rooms than doubles. Cruise lines charge a "single supplement," or up to 200 percent of the cost of regular double occupancy, if only one person will occupy the space. Solo travelers can request a "guaranteed share" rate. This means the cruise company will either find a roommate to share the cabin or will guarantee the regular double-occupancy rate if no one can be found. A "guaranteed single" rate guarantees space and rate (at the "run-of-ship" rate) but does not specify a cabin until sailing time, when the single traveler is placed in any cabin still available— often a much higher priced room.

Other Considerations

DINING

Food is one of the main features of a cruise, with not only three meals served daily, but additional juice and consommé breaks, afternoon snacks, and midnight buffets—nearly nonstop opportunities to expand the waistline another inch before heading off to the ship's health club facilities.

Meals are served in two "sittings," approximately two hours apart. It is best to choose either the early or late sitting when booking the cruise, according to one's own preference for dining time.

Menus will often reflect the nationality of the line and its crew. Vacationers should check on sample menus in advance to be sure they will accommodate individual tastes. They should also inquire as to the availability of special diets such as kosher and HealthMark, or food that will appeal to children, if needed.

SERVICE

A cruise line's main product is service, but levels of service and attitude can vary widely. Travelers can check with travel agents or friends about their experience on various lines, or consult magazines that evaluate cruise lines on a regular basis.

FACILITIES

Facilities also vary greatly from ship to ship. Vacationers should compare the following for individual preferences: public rooms, swimming pools (number and size), deck areas, restaurant facilities, gymnasium, sauna, deck sports, library, elevators, movie theater, chapel, dance bands, bars, game rooms, hospital, cabins, bathrooms, and so forth.

ACTIVITIES

Most ships offer a wide range of activities, but many will specialize in certain areas, offering a jogging deck or golf range, for example. If traveling with grandchildren, vacationers will want to see if children's games and events are provided to allow for separate adult activities or free time. Some ships offer once-a-year special activities such as gourmet cooking classes and jazz or classical music festivals.

ENTERTAINMENT

Some ships offer big-name talent; others have audience-participation entertainment, dance music, or gambling, for example. With careful checking, vacationers will find exactly the desired activities for a fulfilling cruise experience.

SHORE EXCURSIONS

These are organized tours given by concessionaires at the different ports of call. Tickets are purchased on board, and ship personnel usually hold meetings to familiarize passengers with each excursion, along with a recommendation—either good or bad—about various trips. They also can help with self-guided explorations, including advice about normal cab fares, places to see, where to eat, etc.

Booking Passage

Ocean cruises should be booked from six months to one year ahead to guarantee full choice of ship, ports of call, accommodations, and scheduling. Cruises can be booked through cruise-only travel agents, general travel agents, or through the ship line itself. Travelers with scheduling flexibility and less concern for specific accommodations could check with cruise discounters for last-minute, reduced-rate bookings.

Freighter Cruises

Modern freighters may have accommodations for up to 80 passengers—often quite elegant, spacious staterooms compared to the more cramped quarters of vacation cruise ships. Meals are shared with the officers. Some freighters have even added such amenities as a swimming pool. Missing are a social director, nonstop planned activities, name entertainment, gambling, and planned shore excursions. Present are a quiet, uninterrupted enjoyment of the ocean, a chance to relate to the other passengers without outside intrusions, and a library with books and games brought along or left by other passengers. Freighter cruises also offer a chance to visit interesting, unusual, and sometimes off-the-beaten-path ports not usually visited by other cruise ships.

Freighter travel appeals to inquisitive, independent types, those who prefer not to travel as part of a large group. As Robert and Barbara Kane note in their book *Freighter Voyaging*: "Freighters are for people who are happy creating their own amusement. People who are comfortable not knowing exact itineraries, departure and arrival times. . . . People who read, who love the sea, who enjoy observing the activities of a working cargo ship. . . . There is time to relax, to converse, to feel the majesty of the ocean, to await one glorious sunset after another, to feel excitement when another ship comes into view, to watch for dolphin, flying fish, and to wait with anticipation for the first smudge on the horizon which heralds your ship's approach to its next landfall."

Since freighters do not carry a doctor as part of their regular staff, there are often upper age limits for those who may sail. Most lines accept passengers up to age 75, but generally will require a certificate of good health for those 65 and older.

Freighters generally cost one-half to one-third the amount of a popular cruise ship, but the number of days aboard may add up to the same overall total. Some lines now offer one-way passage, allowing passengers to remain in a foreign land to visit on their own and return home by alternate transportation.

Accommodations aboard freighters are generally better than even the high-priced staterooms aboard cruise ships. Most are spacious outside cabins high above the water with large windows instead of portholes, often resembling an average motel room rather than a tight cabin.

Meals aboard freighters are generous and tasty since passengers eat with the ship's officers. Meals are served at earlier hours than aboard cruise ships, to accommodate the crew's schedule. Additional snacks are often available during the day or in late evening.

Time available at ports of call will depend, of course, on cargo scheduling. Average time in a port for a cruise ship is 6 to 12 hours, which also is generally the shortest stopover for a freighter. Freighters may remain in port for days. Passengers can spend time on their own in port, or arrange a local tour or excursion. The ship remains home base, and food and lodging are guaranteed no matter how long the ship is in port.

Booking Passage

Freighter cruising has become so popular in recent years that booking passage well in advance is required. Most cruises will need to be booked at least one year in advance. Freighter cruise passengers also need to be flexible since departure dates may be advanced or postponed depending on cargo conditions. Passage can be booked through specialized agencies such as the TravLtips Cruise & Freighter Travel Association, cruise-only or general travel agents, or the freighter line.

Barge Cruises

Elegant hotel barges that carry from 8 to 24 passengers ply the canals and rivers of Europe to the delight of travelers who enjoy the slow, quiet enjoyment of unhurried waterways. Passengers often help pull the barges through locks or turn the control wheels to work the locks, or hop off for a few hours to hike or bicycle through the countryside and rejoin the boat at the next lock or at its evening mooring.

There are two basic types of barge travel, primarily in Europe and Great Britain. "Floating hotels" offer a captain and crew, and may range from old working canal boats with galley, bathroom, shower, beds, heating, and good headroom to luxurious canal barges with gourmet foods and wines. Another alternative is to charter a barge to self-pilot. Vacationers would need to check on local licensing regulations for piloting a boat or barge, if any, in the destination countries.

Meals are generally provided on board the barges or may be planned for local eateries on shore. Many barge trips are organized around the cuisine of a particular region and will feature locally grown produce or wines, for example.

Booking Passage

Advance booking time for barge cruises varies depending on seasonal demand. Vacationers should check with general travel agents or specialized companies such as Floating through Europe for complete information.

River Cruises and Ferries

Dozens of big passenger ships carry vehicles and are classed as ferries. According to Michael and Laura Murphy, authors of *Ferryliner Vacations in North America,* "The length of their routes and duration of their voyages . . . range from a few hours and a few miles up to several days and well over a thousand miles. They can carry vehicles and as many as 1500 passengers, and do so at reasonable cost, despite the fact that they offer not only cabins but fine dining and such amenities as lounges, bars, swimming pools, casinos, duty-free shops, solariums, and even discotheques, dance bands, saunas, and movie theaters."

Ferries are found all over the world, plying lakes, rivers, bays, and other areas of spectacular scenery. Ferry passengers book passage port to port, staying over as long as they choose at their destinations.

A particularly popular ferry trip among senior travelers is through Alaska's Inside Passage. Alaska's ferries in the Marine Highway System are part of one of the most unusual public transportation programs in the world. They were designed to provide convenient, year-round transportation for Alaskans living near the coast. Seniors over the age of 65 travel free on the ferries between October 1 and May 15. Regular fees apply for those wishing staterooms. Some travelers have found ferry travel even more alluring than the larger luxury ships that cruise the area in the summer because the smaller ferries can slip in and out of areas the larger ships can't reach, offering an even closer view of the area's wildlife and shoreline. The passage is protected by a chain of barrier islands, making the weather relatively mild even in the winter months.

Riverboat cruises are similar to ocean cruises in that they do not book port-to-port legs, although they may stop at several destinations for shore excursions, as do cruise ships. In the United States, Mississippi River steamboats offer a popular river cruise as they pass antebellum estates as well as modern industrial cities. Cruises up the Rhine or the Danube in Europe offer passengers spectacular views of castles atop high mountains as well as the busy industrial hubs of central Europe.

Booking Passage

Advance booking time for various ferry and riverboat cruises varies by seasonal and popular demand. At least one year advance booking is recommended for Alaskan ferries if one is also transporting a vehicle. Foot passengers can generally book immediate passage on local ferries at the dock. Riverboat cruises of several days' duration may require reservations many weeks or months in advance. Others, such as a day-trip on the Mississippi from the port of New Orleans, may be booked upon arrival at the dock. A travel agent can provide complete information.

Sailing

For those who prefer to experience the oceans and waterways of the world "up close and personal," a number of sailing schools and windjammer (tall ship) cruises offer travelers an opportunity for hands-on sailing experiences. According to Steve Colgate, Olympic sailor and founder of Offshore Sailing School, one of the largest sailing schools in the world, "Twenty years ago, learn-to-sail students in their 50s or 60s were unique. Today they comprise over 30% of our enrollment."

Unlike large cruise ships with organized activities, restricted to certain large ports, smaller vessels can explore coastlines more closely and enter small harbors. Most excursions do not require previous sailing experience, and offer instruction in sailing and navigation to the novice. Some do not require help from passengers; others are completely passenger-run.

Booking Passage

Advance booking time required for small sailing vessels varies according to seasonal and popular demand. Travel agents or individual suppliers should be contacted for booking information.

Chapter 6

Adventure and Special-Interest Travel

FACTS OF INTEREST

- There are 5.7 million travelers in the 55–64 age group.

- According to AARP statistics, older Americans account for 30 percent of all travel, and 80 percent of all leisure travel; 32 percent of all hotel/motel nights; 34 percent of all package tours overseas; and 44 percent of adult passports.

- Repeat trips accounted for 93 percent of overseas departures by older travelers in 1988, according to data from the U.S. Travel and Tourism Administration's Inflight Survey.

- When Elderhostel began in 1975, only 200 students took classes at five schools in New Hampshire. Recently, over 1,600 institutions in all 50 states and 40 foreign countries found over 165,000 seniors flocking to the varied classroom experiences.

- According to the U.S. Travel Data Center, the 55-plus market took four trips every year; 23 percent squeezed in seven trips annually.

- Forty-one percent of adults age 75 and older took a domestic trip last year and 12 percent went abroad, according to a Mediamark research study.

What are older adults doing at their vacation destinations? Increasingly, just seeing the sights pales by comparison to active participation in sports, physical activity, and mental stimulation. Mature travelers want to do, to learn, to participate, and to follow through on lifelong dreams, hobbies, and interests.

This chapter explores adventures with balloons and rafts and llamas and even camelback as more and more older travelers take off for a variety of adventure and special-interest travel holidays.

Although the terms "adventure" and "special-interest" travel are often used interchangeably, for the purposes of this book adventure travel generally refers to active participation in a sport or travel mode such as river rafting, dogsledding, or horseback riding. Special-interest travel is defined to include trips organized around hobbies and interests, volunteering, and learning programs, among others.

A host of interesting senior travel/transportation possibilities include bicycling, ballooning, canoeing/kayaking, diving, scuba/snorkeling, dogsledding, horse riding/packing/carriage tours, llama/mule/camel expeditions, river rafting, covered-wagon tours, and wildlife safaris. Older travelers simply need to choose an activity or interest, and a trip will probably already exist to fulfill that interest, or one can be created. Many times package tours can be arranged through local chapters of special-interest groups such as gardeners, bird-watchers, photographers, and so forth.

Adventure Travel

The following activities are some interesting examples of adventure travel experiences as recommended by mature participants. *Sobek's Adventure Vacations* and the Specialty Travel Index's *Adventure Vacation Catalog* are particularly good sources for adventure travel ideas. (See the specialty travel section under Books in Chapter 8.)

Ballooning

Hot-air balloons offer a soft, almost magical way to see the countryside below as they drift quietly, gently on the air currents. It's a time, some balloon enthusiasts have said, to count the cows below, to experience the flow of the wind aloft, to see firsthand both the exposed front and secluded backs of the neighborhood farms and homes, and to anticipate with relish the traditional champagne brunch upon landing. Most balloon flights are held in the early morning to catch the most favorable air currents, and are available almost anywhere in the United States and various parts of Europe. Hot-air balloons are regulated by the Federal Aviation Authority (FAA) in the United States, and pilots must be licensed. Check the appropriate credentials and experience of balloonists in foreign countries.

Bicycling

Bicycling has become one of the fastest growing means of "motorless transportation" among travelers. It's inexpensive, safe, quiet, and nonpolluting. A bicycle can be transported by plane for approximately $45, allowing the traveler an opportunity to put wheels down anywhere in the world to begin a leisurely (or more strenuous) up-close exploration of back roads and country lanes. Trips may range from one- to two-day explorations of one's own neighborhood to several-week cross-country tours of the United States, Europe, or China. Check with individual tour operators for a rating of difficulty as well as distance. Some trips will follow the group with a "sag wagon" to carry supplies as well as tired riders.

Canoeing and Kayaking

While ballooning offers silent observation from above, canoeing and kayaking offer the same opportunity to view nature and its wildlife from water-level vantage. Quietly plying the backwaters motorized boats can't reach, these craft have offered many a traveler an undisturbed look at native birds, animals, and plant life. Some wetland areas such as the Everglades can be properly observed only by canoe trips into its interior. In other areas, rivers cut through deep canyons accessible only to humans on the water. Many organized tours offer instruction for novices to navigate relatively gentle waterways, while others supply trained white-water experts to guide participants through difficult water courses.

Diving and Snorkeling

With over 75 percent of the world covered by water, one can hardly have seen the world without going into the water as well as over it. Scuba diving requires an air tank, which divers strap to their back, while skin diving requires only a mask, snorkel (breathing tube), and fins. Scuba diving requires instruction for certification; some places in the Caribbean, particularly, offer a three-hour "resort course," guided step by step by a qualified instructor, as a brief introduction to diving. Snorkelers stay on the surface, but may dive 20–30 feet by holding their breath. Both forms of diving offer spectacular views of underwater life and scenery.

Dogsledding

While lengthy dogsledding trips may be fairly arduous, and often involve snowshoeing and/or cross-country skiing as well, some one-day trips are now provided to simply ride and enjoy the quiet thrill of snowy scenery and winter wildlife. Participants on longer trips share in harnessing, feeding, and caring for the dogs.

Horse Packing and Trekking

Some fairly exotic areas can be visited on horseback—from the rim of a volcano in Hawaii to Indian cliff dwellings in the Arizona desert. Many horseback trips include spectacular back-country fishing; a Glacier National Park horseback trip offers both fishing and white-water rafting. Riding experience, general health, and physical conditioning requirements should be specified for each trip.

On horse packing trips, according to *The Adventure Vacation Catalog,* camping at night is under the stars or in outfitter-supplied tents. Trekking means riding each day to a different destination, such as a country inn, mountain lodge, or ranch.

Llama/Mule/Camel Expeditions

Hiking with a pack animal frees the humans to enjoy longer hikes with more amenities since the animals carry the supplies—and sometimes the humans too. Packing with animals can especially open up areas to children or those with less stamina who might not be able to enjoy a wilderness area with a backpack. And animals add an interesting kind of companionship. As *The Adventure Vacation Catalog* notes: "Each animal adds a different point of view to your trek: llamas . . . gentle, intelligent and inquisitive; downright nosy . . . camels, 'ships of the desert,' who are a lot jollier than their press notices would indicate . . . and patient, hard-working mules, more sure-footed in the mountains than any horse."

Mountaineering

Scaling the sheer rock face of a towering mountain, and then rappeling back down, may need to be saved for the young and extraordinarily healthy, but several mountaineering schools offer introductory courses, complete with needed equipment, for those who would like to enjoy the experience. For example, Outward Bound, the oldest and largest adventure education organization in the United States, conducts classes for various ages that emphasize personal growth, self-reliance, and teamwork, as well as basic outdoor skills.

On Foot

The one form of human transportation that literally knows no limits is, of course, to use one's own feet. Walking tours of an area, whether organized or self-determined, are a common and popular way to find the intimate nooks and crannies of a big city or to capture panoramic scenic vistas. Today, however, a number of trips specifically organized around walking, hiking, and backpacking entice travelers to many points of the globe.

Basic trips can be defined as walking tours, hiking/trekking, and backpacking expeditions. Walking tours generally last less than a day and no supplies are needed. On a hike or trek, someone or something else, such as a porter, a pack animal, or vehicle, carries equipment and supplies. On backpacking trips, each person is self-sufficient in carrying food and supplies. While some backpacking trips may require advanced climbing skills or excellent physical conditioning, many others offer more leisurely treks through areas with spectacular photographic opportunities or chances to study wildlife patterns in remote backcountry settings.

River Rafting

Whether paddled by the passengers, propelled by oars manned by the guide, or in a motorized raft, river rafting recently has attracted large numbers of participants, including ever-increasing numbers of older adults. Age and ability to swim are not a factor for anyone in reasonably good health who wants the excitement of "running the rapids," along with some extraordinary opportunities for viewing wildlife and nature in areas inaccessible to other forms of transportation. As *The Adventure Vacation Catalog* notes: "Rapids . . . can vary from short drops to half-mile-long chutes . . . wide boulder fields to narrow channels . . . run straight or corkscrewed. Whatever their idiosyncrasies, they're guaranteed to give you a whole new perspective on life. Rapids don't move all that fast—rarely above 10 miles per hour. But when you're catapulting through white frothing fury, you'll feel like you're on the roller coaster ride of a lifetime." River rafting excursions seem to exist on every river in the world, and definitely occupy the most listings in specialty travel directories.

Skiing

Skiing, whether downhill or cross-country, offers exciting possibilities for adults interested in winter vacation opportunities. Such groups as the Over-the-Hill Gang and the 70+ Ski Club exist entirely to organize trips for mature skiers who, like surfers seeking the "endless summer," plan ski trips year-round to take advantage of winter in both the northern and southern hemispheres.

Special-Interest Travel

The incredible success of Elderhostel probably best illustrates the eagerness of older adults to pursue learning experiences as a major travel focus. Elderhostel remains the biggest and certainly most popular special-interest travel experience for older adults.

When Elderhostel began in 1975, only 200 students took classes at five schools in New Hampshire. Recently, over 1,600 institutions in all 50 states and 40 foreign countries found over 165,000 seniors flocking to its varied classroom experiences.

Elderhostel offers short-term, noncredit, residential, academic (learning/adventure) programs at over 1,600 colleges, universities, environmental education centers, and folkcraft schools in the United States, Canada, and 40 countries overseas. Elderhostel is open to anyone age 60 or above, plus a younger companion or spouse accompanying a participant. Elderhostel is a learning adventure accessible to all older adults, regardless of income or formal educational level. Participants live on the campus for one to four weeks, take courses on a variety of liberal arts and sciences subjects, take field trips, and enjoy extracurricular activities and campus life. Costs average $245 for a week-long program in the United States or Canada, which includes all tuition, room and board, classes, field trips, recreational programs, and other activities. Overseas programs are considerably more expensive in order to cover the round-trip airfare as well as tuition, room and board, classes, field trips, and most other expenses. Scholarships are available for those who need financial assistance. Eight catalogs per year detailing Elderhostel programs are available free upon request or can be found in most public libraries.

The remainder of this chapter describes a very few of the other seemingly endless possibilities for senior travelers to enrich their lives while stimulating their minds and bodies. (A listing of specialty travel books of interest to mature adults can be found in Chapter 8.)

Archaeology

The study of ancient history through man's physical remains is a fascinating focus for many trips. Specialized archaeologic tours are available in many parts of the world from the Andes to Sri Lanka, from Egypt to Illinois, many of which include hands-on help with excavation, cataloging, and research. Others offer walk-throughs of archaeological digs with knowledgeable guides. College credits may be available for some trips.

Art and Architecture

Several specialized tours lead groups through a number of art history and art appreciation experiences that may also include a study of the magnificent museums or homes that house special collections. The focus may be on a particular period, school, or regional native art. College credits are available through some programs. Yet other programs offer the opportunity to learn or enhance one's own artistic skills.

Cooking and Gourmet Tours

With food such an important part of any travel experience, many trips are now planned specifically to focus on food. Tours may offer lessons with a renowned chef, visits and tastings at world-famous restaurants, or samplings from a particular region. Those interested in lessons should check to see if classes will be participatory or observation only. Ask if restaurant costs are included or must be handled individually.

Crafts

From Peruvian textile arts to Appalachian woodworking, crafts are an eternal key to civilizations and their folk art—and an increasingly popular theme for travel. Organized tours to China, for example, may forgo popular scenic or historic stops to visit textile factories, with lectures from local experts. Those who enjoy independent travel may find a driving tour of the Southwest enhanced by stops at local Indian pottery and jewelry shops.

Farm and Ranch Holidays

From working ranches in Montana to a wheat farm in England, farm vacations allow visitors to participate as much or as little as they'd like in regular farm and ranch chores. For those who may have plowed one too many furrows earlier in their life, the holidays allow quiet relaxation in pastoral serenity, and plenty of fresh air, good food, and family life.

Genealogy Trips

Many older adults, especially, plan entire itineraries to visit ancestral homes, track down old records, trace an immigrant's path to America, or otherwise add details to the family tree.

Murder Mystery Tours

A number of mystery specialty bookstores either sponsor or frequently publicize murder mystery tours. Some take place in old mansions or English manor houses; others re-create the opulent Orient Express in private railcars. Yet others book an entire hotel for a weekend or longer of murder mystery fantasy. An elaborate plot unfolds, clues are sprinkled about, and participants are asked to solve the mystery while donning costumes for and acting out various characters' parts.

Nature Trips

The environment has taken top billing these days, with many travelers organizing trips around a number of interests—from expanding on hobbies such as bird watching or gardening to exploring the ecology of exotic areas or observing and studying endangered species. Nature tours exist for almost any special interest, or can be designed independently. Travelers may take anything from Pacific whale-watching cruises to African safaris. There literally is no corner of the world that cannot be explored with an eye on nature. Besides the difficulty of choosing which to do first, only the difficulty of access to an area is a matter of concern.

Photography

While almost every traveler takes photographs, trips now exist specifically for photography and camera buffs. These types of excursions are usually accompanied by a photography instructor and are designed with itineraries and pacing to allow for outstanding photography. Tours may also be planned to coincide with the best time of day or season of the year, or may be planned specifically to photograph nature, wildlife, scenery, or people.

Religion

From studying the Buddhists in Tibet to the Passion Play in Oberammergau, trips centering on the religions of the world—their people, artifacts, and historic spiritual sites—have become a popular focus for tours and travel.

Research Expeditions

Research expeditions offer travelers extraordinary opportunities not only to visit unusual locales, but also to have hands-on experience in ongoing scientific research. Most of the groups are nonprofit, and the expenses of the trip may be tax-deductible since participants volunteer labor and skills. Earthwatch, for example, offers the chance to join more than 80 expeditions in over 30 countries. Projects include archaeology, animal behavior, marine sciences, and tropical forest ecology. Some projects may also offer academic credit.

Retirement Trips

Several tour companies have evolved in recent years to supply trips for older adults to explore potential retirement locations in such areas as Mexico, Central and South America, and Sun Belt areas in the United States. The vacations allow time to live for an extended period in the area, meet with other retirees, and explore the locale for shopping, medical facilities, churches, and other amenities before committing to a permanent move.

Other Possibilities

The list of other possibilities for special-interest travel is limited only by one's imagination and—as of this writing—by locations on this planet. Truly anything is possible for the mature traveler who is seeking enrichment and learning as the purpose for travel.

There are several places to start to find the trip of one's dreams. Specialty clubs such as square-dance groups or bonsai gardeners or church clubs will organize group tours based on their activities and interests. Many good directories of specialty travel possibilities and suppliers are available in libraries and bookstores. See Chapter 8 for listings of specialty travel books. Travel agents can also access information on a number of special-interest groups.

And finally, when absolutely no one seems able to find an organized group setting out to trace the path of the Black Plague across medieval Europe, for example, the dedicated mature traveler will simply do it himself. No doubt a chance conversation with another visitor perusing the records in an ancient French monastery will find a like-minded pilgrim—and voilà—another senior special-interest travel group is born!

Resources

Chapter 7

Directory of Organizations

General Travel Organizations

AeroTours International
William Robin Engel, President
36 E. 3rd Street
New York, NY 10003
(800) 223-4555; (212) 979-5000

> AeroTours provides custom-designed itineraries suited to each
> client's age, interests, time frame, and budget, especially older
> travelers who have unlimited time but limited budgets. Destina-
> tions include Australia, New Zealand, Fiji, Tahiti, Indonesia,
> Thailand, Malaysia, New Guinea, and the Philippines. Extended-
> stay options in economical apartments are available in some
> countries. There are also weekly departures for locally hosted
> tours in most of the destinations, plus several fully escorted
> group trips to Australia.

AJS Travel Consultants, Inc.
Max Mermelstein, President
177 Beach 116th Street
Rockaway Park, NY 11694
(718) 945-5900

> AJS Travel Consultants packages "50 Plus Club" custom-tai-
> lored travel vacations to Israel, Switzerland, and Italy for older
> adults. The vacation packages feature leisurely paced itineraries,
> carefully selected hotels, most meals, and the services of local
> hosts. The trip to Israel includes kosher meals.

American Association of Retired Persons (AARP)
Horace Deets, Executive Director
1909 K Street, NW
Washington, DC 20049
(202) 662-4850

AARP Travel Service
P.O. Box 38997
Los Angeles, CA 90038
(800) 227-7737

> The American Association of Retired Persons is a national membership organization of over 30 million people, open to anyone over the age of 50. Its purposes are to enhance the quality of life for older persons; to promote independence, dignity, and purpose for older persons; to lead in determining the role and place of older persons in society; and to improve the image of aging. AARP offers an extensive travel club with services for both group and independent travel. The AARP Travel Service offers group travel, escorted tours, hosted cruises, and hosted apartment living. The Purchase Privilege Program offers discounts on air transportation, lodging, car rentals, and sightseeing. The AARP Motoring Plan provides emergency road and towing services as well as trip routing and other road services.
>
> AARP TRAVEL BOOKS: *Travel Easy, Touring by Bus at Home and Abroad, On the Road in an RV,* and *Retirement Edens Abroad.*

American Automobile Association (AAA)
1000 AAA Drive
Heathrow, FL 32746-5063
(407) 444-7000

> The American Automobile Association is the pioneering and probably still most widely known and used automobile club in America. Among its services are emergency road service, trip planning, a credit card, traveler's checks, and insurance coverage. AAA also offers an extensive full-service travel agency for both independent and group travel arrangements. Other services include passport photos, International Driving Permits, travel insurance, and more. AAA also publishes popular travel guides, road atlases, and guides to roadside accommodations. Offices

are located in most major American cities. Check with a local office for fees and membership requirements.

American Bus Association (ABA)
George T. Snyder, Jr., Executive Vice-President and CEO
1015 15th Street, NW, Suite 250
Washington, DC 20005
(800) 283-2877; (202) 842-1645

> The ABA is a private, nonprofit association of private bus service companies in the United States. Members must have been in business at least a year, have Interstate Commerce Commission (ICC) certification, comply with ICC minimum insurance requirements of $5 million per vehicle, and adhere to the ABA's ethics code, including a dedication to public safety, and integrity, sincerity, and accuracy in financial and business affairs. Senior travel planners may want to be sure buses they book for group travel are members of the ABA. The organization does not supply any consumer information; it should be contacted only for serious problems concerning a member company once other resources have been exhausted.

American Society of Travel Agents (ASTA)
1101 King Street
Alexandria, VA 22314
(703) 739-2782

> ASTA is the principal trade association for travel agents and other travel companies such as airlines and cruise lines. It represents its members' interests with various government bureaus, but can act on behalf of consumers as well. Members displaying the ASTA seal must have been in business for three years and must subscribe to a strict code of ethics.

American Youth Hostels, Inc.
Richard Martyr, Executive Director
P.O. Box 37613
Washington, DC 20013-7613
(202) 783-6161

> American Youth Hostels, a nonprofit association that provides year-round opportunities for outdoor recreation and inexpensive educational travel, has passed the 50-year mark, as have many of

its participants. AYH is part of the larger International Youth Hostel Federation representing 70 nations and over four million hostelers worldwide. Hostels provide low-cost, dormitory-style accommodations, generally with self-service kitchen, dining area, and common room. Only an AYH membership card and sheet sleeping sack are required to stay in a hostel. AYH's World Adventure program offers a variety of trips worldwide, including some especially for people over age 50. Recent 50+ trips included bicycling in New England and Alaska, touring the Wisconsin cheese country, hiking San Francisco, and motor trips in North America and Europe. All trips are cooperative: Everyone pitches in to help with route planning, menus, daily agendas, and so forth. Annual membership fee: $15 for seniors (age 55+); lifetime fee: $250 (any age). Members receive the *AYH Hostel Handbook* with detailed listings of more than 200 AYH hostels in the United States; *Knapsack Magazine,* published biannually, with travel features and tips of hostelers; and *World Adventure Catalog,* detailing adventure trips around the world.

Canadian Hostelling Association
Len Brown, Executive Director
1600 James Naismith Drive, Suite 608
Gloucester, Ontario K1B 5N4
Canada
(613) 748-5638

The Canadian Hostelling Association seeks to promote travel for people of all ages primarily through the provision of low-cost accommodations, generally in dormitory-style facilities. CHA also sponsors planned outdoor recreational activities year-round such as cycling, hiking, canoeing, snowshoeing, skiing, and rock climbing. A $15 senior membership card offers: entry into more than 5,000 hostels in 75 different countries, reduced rates for hostel accommodation in Canada, reduced rates for entry into places of interest, reduced prices on the purchase of recreational equipment, and participation in local CHA recreational activities. CHA also provides some programs through Elderhostel Canada. Members receive a free directory of hostels in Canada.

Classic Tours International
625 North Michigan Avenue
Chicago, IL 60611
(800) 828-8222; (312) 642-2400

> Classic Tours has specialized for years in deluxe African safari tours, and has now added travel programs to Morocco, Egypt, and Turkey as well. The safaris include: 10- to 18-day "classic safaris," à la carte safaris such as gorilla trekking or an excursion to the Seychelles, foreign independent travel such as a private safari or tour of the continent by plane, and special-interest programs such as golf, fishing, and camel safaris. Group size is limited, ensuring a window seat in safari vehicles to every participant. A portion of the price of each tour program is donated to organizations dedicated to the preservation of historic sites and the conservation of wildlife. Tour cost also includes comprehensive travel insurance offering protection for trip cancellation, medical assistance, and emergency assistance or evacuation, if needed. Classic Tours also offers an extensive booklist of background reading for each area visited. All the titles can be ordered through the company.

Community College Tours
Joseph Jeppson, Coordinator
P.O. Box 620620
Woodside, CA 94062
(800) 527-3137 (California); (209) 477-2209

> Community College Tours organizes tours for mature adults in the company of college professors. Recent trips have included such areas as Oberammergau, Russia, and Scandinavia; Britain and Ireland; and Nile River and Aegean cruises. Predeparture parties and lectures are held in northern and southern California; plans are to enhance the stateside social aspects of the group's programs in the near future. Repeat participants receive $50 off current trips for each previous trip taken through this organization.

Evergreen Travel Service, Inc.
Jack J. Hoffman, President
Betty J. Hoffman, Chairman

19505 44th Avenue W
Lynnwood, WA 98036
(800) 435-2288; (206) 776-1184

> For over 30 years, Evergreen Travel has promoted and conducted travel arrangements and tours for disabled travelers. (See below under "Disabled Travel.") It also conducts "Evergreen Lazybones Tours" for those unable to keep up with standard tours and requiring slow-paced itineraries. As the owners assert, if the Eiffel Tower is there for those who leave the hotel at 6:30 A.M., it will probably still be there for those who leave at 9 A.M. Current tours include England, Russia, Italy, China, and the South Pacific, as well as various areas of the United States such as the Canadian Rockies; also offered is a Panama Canal cruise. All groups are small and personally escorted. Individual travel arrangements to any part of the world for any activity can also be arranged.

Federation of American Consumers and Travelers (FACT)
Barb Enloe, National Director
National Headquarters
1030 Fifteenth Street, NW
Washington, DC 20005

Membership Service Office
318 Hillsboro Avenue
Edwardsville, IL 62025
(800) USA-FACT; (618) 656-0454

> FACT describes itself as representing "Mainstream America" to ensure people from all walks of life a higher quality of life than they could obtain individually. It seeks services, merchandise, and other benefits for members that represent unusual value, and supports programs and other organizations whose purpose is to enlighten, enrich, and/or educate the American consumer. Members receive the newsletter *Factfinder,* containing a wide range of consumer information on health, travel, family life, and more. The newsletter is also available to nonmembers for $24 a year. Membership fee: $60/year.

Frommer's Dollarwise Travel Club, Inc.
Margaret Basalone, Business Manager

15 Columbus Circle, 15th Floor
New York, NY 10023
(212) 373-8125

> A division of Simon and Schuster Publishing Co., the Dollarwise Travel Club offers the following benefits: any two travel books (normal retail up to $15.95 each) and any one Frommer City Guide (normal retail up to $5.95); discounts off further travel books; and a year's subscription to *The Dollarwise Traveler*. The latter is a quarterly newspaper featuring a number of money-saving travel articles and features, travel tips, an international calendar of events, and travel questions and answers by and from readers. Additional columns list members' hospitality exchanges and travel companion requests. Membership fees: $18/year; inquire about a special rate for seniors.

Frontier Travel & Tours/Vistatours
David Lippincott, President and General Manager
1923 N. Carson Street, Suite 105
Carson City, NV 89701
(800) 648-0912; (702) 882-2100

> Frontier Travel and Vistatours offer senior citizen travel all over the United States and Mexico, as well as international group travel. They organize the largest single group tour to the annual Rose Parade in Pasadena, California. Also offered are specialized "Grandparents and Grandchildren" trips to such areas as South Dakota, a Texas dude ranch, and Washington, D.C./Williamsburg. All destinations are preinspected and approved; all tours include a professional escort/manager and 24-hour telephone contact. Clients receive the monthly publication *Frontier Trails* and the Vistatours catalog.

Golden Age Travellers
Carlos A. Afre, President
Pier 27, The Embarcadero
San Francisco, CA 94111
(800) 258-8880; (414) 296-0151

> Golden Age Travellers makes travel arrangements specifically for seniors, from day-trips to three-week programs in countries such as Portugal, Spain, Mexico, Costa Rica, and more. It offers up to 60 percent discounts on cruises, has a roommate matching

service, and also designs escorted land tours. Annual membership fee: $10 per person; $15 per couple. Members receive *Golden Age Travellers Newsletter,* published bimonthly with news of upcoming tours and cruises.

Golden Companions
Joanne R. Buteau, President
P.O. Box 754
Pullman, WA 99163-0754
(208) 883-5052

Golden Companions assists mature travelers in finding travel companions, either an individual or a small group. The organization provides a networking service for older people who want to travel, but not alone or not wanting to pay the high single supplement charged to single travelers. Members receive the complete, nationwide membership list of travelers, a free mail-exchange service for those who do not wish to publish their address, tour discounts, regional travel information from other members, vacation-home exchanges, and the opportunity to attend local get-togethers. Membership fee: $40 for 6 months; $60 for 12 months. Members receive *The Golden Traveler,* a bimonthly newsletter offering travel articles, discounts for seniors, home exchanges, and member information.

Grand Circle Travel
Alan E. Lewis, Chairman
347 Congress Street
Boston, MA 02210
(800) 248-3737; (617) 350-7500

Grand Circle Travel has designed and run international travel programs exclusively for mature Americans for 33 years. Aiming for 100 percent customer satisfaction, the company offers affordably priced cruise vacations, escorted tours, and also "extended vacations" of two weeks or longer in Yugoslavia, Mexico, Portugal, London, the Swiss Alps, and Spain's Costa del Sol. These feature apartment-style accommodations, social programs, and optional excursions. "Frequent traveler credits" earmark 3 percent of the cost of a trip toward a discount on a future Grand Circle vacation. An informative booklet, *Going Abroad: 101 Tips for Mature Travelers,* is available free upon request, as well as free catalogs of Grand Circle vacations and cruises.

Grandparents Travel Club (Ask Mr. Foster/Littleton Travel, Inc.)
Adonna L. Hipple, Executive Director
8039 S. Lincoln Street, Suite 102
Littleton, CO 80120
(303) 798-1386

> The Grandparents Travel Club was designed by a grandmother who enjoyed travel with her own grandchildren. The trips, planned around school vacations, provide educational and entertaining vacations for grandparents and grandchildren. Some include entire families. The agency also represents many tours for mature travelers.

Group Leaders of America
Charles Presley, President
P.O. Box 129
Salem, OH 44460
(800) 628-0993; (216) 337-1027

> Group Leaders of America serves travel leaders of senior clubs, organizations, recreation centers, and other senior groups with 20 trade shows a year across the Midwest and East Coast to connect them with travel suppliers, tour operators, and other travel services. A quarterly newspaper, "The GLAMER Traveler," contains features on senior group leaders, travel benefits, and industry news on new senior programs, plus tips on arranging better travel, choosing a bus company or tour operator, etc. Older adult travelers may call Group Leaders of America for information on local travel groups in their area.

International Pen Friends
Leslie Fox, Regional Representative
P.O. Box 290065, Homecrest Station
Brooklyn, NY 11229-0001

> International Pen Friends (IPF) seeks to promote friendship and goodwill in the world by matching members with penfriends of similar age and interests in countries of the member's choice. IPF has over 250,000 members in 153 countries, and holds rallies for members and their families and friends. Members often visit their penfriends when traveling abroad, or request new friends to write to in countries they plan to visit. Penfriend service can be provided in English, French, German, Portuguese, and Spanish. A partial service can be given in 18 other languages. Membership

fees (to receive a list of 14 names, plus have own name circulated to 14 other people): $16 for one person or $24 for two age 21–60; $12 for one person over 60. Members receive *People and Places,* a quarterly newsletter written by and for members about their countries and towns (available in English only).

Mayflower Tours
John P. Stachnik, President
1225 Warren Avenue
Downers Grove, IL 60515
(800) 323-7604; (708) 960-3430

Mayflower Tours provides escorted group tours throughout the continental United States, Hawaii, and Canada, originating from the Chicago area. Although not specifically advertised for older adults, the many photos of tour participants in its 80-page catalog overwhelmingly portray that age group.

Mile Hi Travel
Lynn Bradley or Bob Olmsted, Group Travel Coordinators
767 17th Street, Suite 120
Denver, CO 80202
(303) 297-3000

Mile Hi Travel offers specialized services for older adult travelers, especially mature single travelers. In addition to full-service trip planning for either escorted tours or independent travel by train, plane, or cruise ship, the company also offers day-trips originating from Denver, Colorado. Clients receive three travel brochures annually.

The National Association of Senior Travel Planners (NASTP)
The National Association of Senior Travelers
Joan Gasparello, Executive Director
44 Cushing Street
Hingham, MA 02043
(617) 740-1185

The travel planners association provides senior travel planners (either volunteer or paid planners working with public, private, social, religious, and fraternal senior clubs, organizations, and retiree groups) access to travel services and suppliers. The group sponsors 15 "Senior Travel Day" trade shows a year in 11 East

Coast states. The organization will provide the name of a local travel group to interested older travelers. Membership fees are $10 per club or $150 per supplier. Members receive a free annual directory, "NASTP Going Places," listing travel suppliers and travel advertising; also "The Seasoned Traveler," a newsletter three times annually, containing news of club activities from various members, calendar of events, travel tips, and popular travel suggestions. Members also receive a free travel journal. The National Association of Senior Travelers produces two programs for the Cable Travel Network, and offers travel information and education via a toll-free telephone line.

National Tour Association, Inc. (NTA)
Pete Anderson, President
546 E. Main Street
P.O. Box 3071
Lexington, KY 40596-3071
(800) NTA-8886 (U.S.); (800) 828-6999 (Canada)
(606) 253-1036

> The National Tour Association is the primary domestic tour industry association in North America, comprised of tour operators, suppliers (such as hotels, attractions, sightseeing services, etc.), and destination marketing organizations (state tourism offices, convention and visitors bureaus, and chambers of commerce). It serves as an advocate for consumers regarding the quality and pricing of group tours, and provides a consumer protection plan in case of a tour company bankruptcy.

> PUBLICATION: *Travel Together,* a basic introduction to group tours, including a listing of NTA operator companies; free upon request.

Partners-in-Travel
Miriam E. Tobolowsky, Executive Director
P.O. Box 491145
Los Angeles, CA 90049
(213) 476-4869

> Partners-in-Travel seeks to make travel a happier experience by providing information and opportunities for shared travel with a compatible companion. The service is designed for independent,

adventurous travelers, not those who prefer preplanned, circumscribed travel experiences. More than two-thirds of the membership is over age 55. The service operates via its newsletter and matching service. Partners-in-Travel also provides a vacation-home exchange program via its newsletter for those who wish to extend hospitality and/or accommodations to fellow members. Membership fees are based on a choice of services. Yearly members receive six issues of the newsletter and six listings for $45 per year. A limited six-month membership includes three listings and three issues for $30. A year's subscription to the bimonthly newsletter only is $35. "TravelMates" receive six listings for $20, plus a copy of the first newsletter in which their listing appears. Members receive *Partners-in-Travel Newsletter,* featuring a listing of members seeking travel companions, plus cost-cutting tips and information relating to the needs and interests of the traveler. *To Your Good Health,* offered free with any level of service or membership, is a 20-page pamphlet of practical tips and guidelines to ensure a safe, healthy, problem-free trip.

Saga Holidays
Jerry Foster, President
120 Boylston Street
Boston, MA 02116
(617) 451-6808

Saga Holidays is a tour operator that for more than 40 years has designed trips specifically for travelers over age 60. A companion age 50–59 is eligible to participate in their tours when accompanying an older traveler. Saga also plans and coordinates several Elderhostel programs. Saga holidays are fully escorted and include airfare, insurance, most meals, all accommodations, $100,000 flight insurance, and a liberal cancellation policy. Many tours are designed for singles or for grandparents traveling with their grandchildren. Clients receive six or more catalogs and three or more newsletters annually.

Senior Escorted Tours, Inc.
Gilbert R. Sinkway, President
P.O. Box 400
Cape May Court House, NJ 08210
(800) 222-1254

Senior Escorted Tours welcomes travelers of all ages who enjoy escorted tours, but designs tours especially for seniors. Recent trips included tours of the Catskill Mountains; Orlando, Florida; Australia and New Zealand; Cape May/Wildwood, New Jersey; Nova Scotia and Cape Cod; and the Passion Play in Germany.

Senior Travel and Recreation Activities Council (STRAC)
Alice Ward, Director
P.O. Box 1142
Redondo Beach, CA 90278
(213) 370-5094

The Senior Travel and Recreation Activities Council (STRAC) assists senior activities directors and coordinators in planning excursions and tours for their senior groups. Its *Leisure Time Directory* lists senior travel services and opportunities in California, Arizona, Nevada, Oregon, and Washington. Mature travelers may contact the organization for the names of attractions, hotels, resorts, and transportation companies that offer a STRAC discount to individuals as well as those traveling in groups. The STRAC SecondWind Travel Club offers a STRAC discount ID card, an annual directory of travel services and suppliers, and a regular newsletter outlining special travel promotions.

Senior Vacation Hotels
Peggy Puljanowski, Executive Director
7401 Central Avenue
St. Petersburg, FL 33710
(813) 345-8123

Senior Vacation Hotels provides Florida vacation packages for the budget-minded senior that include lodging, two full meals daily, and entertainment. Accommodations are in four historic, European-style hotels with large lobbies, ballrooms, game rooms, and so forth, in Lakeland, Bradenton/Sarasota, and St. Petersburg. Each location offers a full calendar of free events such as in-house parties, cocktail and theatre parties, live entertainment, dance bands, bingo and card parties, plus restaurant excursions and local beach and mall trips, at nominal charges.

Singleworld
Wendy Lowenstein, Director

401 Theodore Fremd Avenue
Rye, NY 10580
(914) 967-3334

> Singleworld organizes travel for single people, such as cruises in the Caribbean, Alaska, Tahiti, and the Mediterranean, and a variety of tours to various regions in Europe. All tours are fully escorted. Cruise accommodations offer double, triple, or quad occupancy to avoid single supplement charges. Membership fee: $25/year. Members receive a quarterly newsletter with news of upcoming trips and single travel tips.

Solo Flights
Betty Sobel, Executive Director
121 S. Campo Road
Westport, CT 06880
(203) 226-9993

> Solo Flights is a travel center specializing in vacations for single people of all ages. Travel arrangements are made entirely by phone and mail. Available are group tours and cruises, as well as advice on resorts. As specialists in single travel, the company can often arrange shared accommodations to avoid the extra fees for singles. There is no fee for its services. Clients receive a quarterly newsletter.

TourMasters World of Tours
Jack Bates, Owner
4401 Harlen Avenue
Waco, TX 76710
(817) 754-2027

> TourMasters provides travel services for both group and independent travel, including both escorted and unescorted tours worldwide. The company's specialty, however, is recreational vehicle travel, tours, and caravans in the United States, Canada, and Mexico.

Travel Buddy, Inc.
Dona M. Risdall, Executive Director
P.O. Box 31146
Minneapolis, MN 55431
(612) 881-5364

Travel Buddy supplies reputable travel companions for children or adults of all ages, or for travelers with slight handicaps. Teachers, nurses, and other professionals are available as travel companions. Fee per arrangement is $75 (nonmembers); $55 for members. Additional fees for extra or professional assistance depend on level of help needed and duration of trip. Clients provide round-trip transportation for the buddies, but buddies pay for their own lodging and meals. Travel Buddy can also help with travel arrangements at no additional charge. Annual membership fee: $25 for individuals, couples, or families. Members receive the monthly *Trip Tips* containing general travel information.

Travel Companion Exchange, Inc.
Jens Jurgen, Founder and President
P.O. Box 833
Amityville, NY 11701
(516) 454-0880

Travel Companion Exchange helps singles of all ages find another person of the same or opposite sex to share all kinds of travel experiences. The majority of TCE's members are over age 49. TCE requires an extensive personal profile questionnaire including preferences in accommodations, travel habits and preferences, why one is looking for a travel partner, how to share expenses, important characteristics in a companion, and so forth. Applicants also complete a brief, anonymous "minilisting" to appear in the bimonthly newsletter. A complete Profile Page is mailed to one free potential "match" each month and to other members at their request. The club also sponsors TCE's Hosting Exchange for members who have visited or hosted each other at their homes. There are several levels of membership fees. Associate membership (for those seeking a same-sex travel companion): $36 for six months, $60 for one year, $96 for two years. VIP membership (for those seeking opposite sex or both male and female partners): $66 for six months, $120 for one year, and $192 for two years. TCE sometimes offers free memberships to widowers 70 and over to balance supply and demand in this age group. Members receive one free Profile Page of a potential companion each month, plus additional profiles at $2 each. Members receive *Travel Companions,* a bimonthly newsletter containing minilistings of all new club members, listings of members' upcoming travel plans, and whom they are seeking to accompany them, plus several pages of travel tips, book reviews, and advice articles for singles.

United States Tour Operators Association (USTOA)
Robert E. Whitley, President
211 East 51st Street, Suite 12B
New York, NY 10022
(212) 944-5727

> The United States Tour Operators Association is a professional organization for tour operators. Members must have been in business at least three years, must furnish a minimum $250,000 indemnity bond or equivalent, and must adhere to a strict code of ethics regarding truth, accuracy, and clarity in advertising.
>
> PUBLICATIONS: *How To Select a Package Tour* is an informational brochure listing guidelines for choosing a tour, how to read a tour brochure, and a glossary of tour travel terms. Available free upon request from USTOA. *Guide to USTOA Members, Their Programs, Services and Destinations* lists current USTOA members and the types of programs offered. Free upon request from USTOA.

Worldwide Discount Travel Club
Ted Hankoff, President
1674 Meridian Avenue
P.O. Box 855
Miami Beach, FL 33119-0855
(305) 534-2082

> Worldwide Discount Travel is a nationwide membership organization founded in 1982. It operates as a travel clearinghouse to sell leftover or remnant space on cruises, airlines, and travel tours. Flexible travelers who are available to travel on short notice can achieve savings up to 50 percent to a number of destinations. Members receive *Travelog* bulletins every three weeks listing current discount travel opportunities. Departure cities vary and destinations change seasonally depending on what space has not been sold at that point. Travelers should do extensive background research on various cruise lines, ships, and destinations, as the bulletins do not include the specific information one would receive directly from the cruise companies or

travel agents. Membership fees: $50/one year; $80/two years; singles receive $10 off either choice of membership.

Specialty Travel Organizations

The following organizations provide out-of-the-ordinary or special-interest travel experiences organized around such activities as sports, study, volunteering, or traveling with grandchildren.

Alpine Autour
Warren Goodman, Tour Director
14 Forest Avenue
Caldwell, NJ 07006
(800) 443-7519; (201) 226-9107

Alpine Autour trips are unique three-week, 2,000-mile driving excursions for mature travelers through the Alpine regions of Yugoslavia, Austria, and Italy, with optional side tours to Germany and Switzerland. Most participants tour by motorcycle, while others drive rental cars. Average age of the motorcyclists is 55 plus. Participants are instructed each day on the route and the hotel booked for that evening, but they are free to explore on their own during each day. Groups are often invited to visit private homes, and European motorcycle club members frequently join the group for dinner and discussion. Personal motorcycles are shipped through special arrangements with Yugoslav Airlines. Trips are limited to 24 participants.

American Hiking Society
Susan Henley, Executive Director
1015 31st Street, NW
Washington, DC 20007
(202) 385-3252

The American Hiking Society is a nonprofit organization dedicated to protecting the interests of hikers and preserving America's footpaths. It encourages volunteerism in trail building and maintenance through work trips and volunteer vacations. It also maintains a public information service to provide hikers and other trail users with facts regarding facilities, organizations, and how to make best use of trails while protecting the environment.

Memberships begin at $15 for seniors and students. Members receive a subscription to the *American Hiker* quarterly magazine, eight issues of the American Hiker newsletter, and periodic legislative alerts on trails issues.

PUBLICATION: *American Hiker,* a quarterly magazine of hiking and the outdoors featuring volunteer opportunities, personal accounts, news, and camping/hiking product reviews.

American Sunbathing Association, Inc. (ASA)
Jack DePree, President
1703 N. Main Street
Kissimmee, FL 34744-9988
(407) 933-2064

The American Sunbathing Association, established in 1929 as the American League for Physical Culture, is the national association of 35,000 nudists who belong to 200 nudist clubs in North America. The group serves local clubs with legal representation against harassment while on ASA grounds, establishes a framework for standards of conduct, and distributes video tapes and printed materials to educate the public on the value of the nudist lifestyle. Membership includes discounts at ASA parks, the right to participate in various regional and the annual ASA conventions, and membership in the International Naturist Federation, a worldwide nudist organization. Some local clubs may also offer additional senior citizen discounts to visiting ASA members. Members receive *The Bulletin,* the ASA monthly newspaper with feature stories and news from clubs across the country.

PUBLICATION: The *Nudist Park Guide* is a complete directory of North American nudist parks and clubs. Available for $13 from ASA.

American Volksport Association (AVA)
Dr. Brenda S. Caldwell, Executive Director
1001 Pat Booker Road, No. 203
Universal City, TX 78148
(512) 659-2112

The American Volksport Association, a nonprofit organization, sponsors noncompetitive walking, swimming, and cross-country skiing events for individuals and families. Events are designed to allow participants to proceed at their own pace through scenic and/or historic sites. Participants may receive awards for the number of events and kilometers completed; a $1.50 fee covers the cost of the awards and includes liability insurance. Membership fees average $6–$10 for local clubs; there is no charge for participation in events. AVA represents the United States as one of 16 member countries in the International Federation of Popular Sports, which originated in Germany, Austria, Switzerland, and Liechtenstein. France, Belgium, Luxembourg, the Netherlands, England, and Canada are among the other member countries. The group also plans to add Eastern Bloc countries in the near future. The largest participation in events is by those age 35–74, and participants frequently take part in events in areas they are visiting.

Backroads Bicycle Touring
Tom Hale, Executive Director
1516 Fifth Street
Berkeley, CA 94710-1713
(415) 527-1555

Backroads provides preplanned, van-supported bicycling vacations ranging from 2 to 17 days in North America, Europe and the Pacific region. Trips are open to all ages and abilities, with both a short route and longer route offered each day. Vans carry equipment and provide lifts for tired cyclists. In addition, Backroads offers "Prime Time" tours for bicyclists age 50 or older that feature shorter and flatter routes than the average tour. Other special-interest tours include singles, family, and photography tours. Accommodations include southern plantation mansions, French châteaus, New England country inns, Italian villas. and historic western lodges. Free catalog available upon request.

Barvi Tours/Retire in Mexico
11658 Gateway Boulevard
Los Angeles, CA 90064
(800) 824-7102; (213) 474-4041

Barvi Tours organizes vacation tours to various areas in Mexico for those who are considering retirement living in Mexico and would like to familiarize themselves with the area. Included in the trips are informational seminars and get-togethers with retirees in the area, including visits to their homes. Several informational brochures about the tours are available, as well as advice and information on living in Mexico.

Earthwatch
Brian Rosborough, President
680 Mt. Auburn Street
P.O. Box 403
Watertown, MA 02272
(617) 926-8200

> Earthwatch sponsors scientists in the field who are researching in disciplines as varied as rain forest ecology, endangered species, animal behavior, archaeology, and public health care. It seeks volunteers to donate time and money to work with researchers at over 120 projects in 50 countries, year-round. Volunteers pay their own way for two- or three-week sessions; their tuition helps fund the research. Minimum age for participation is 16, but Earthwatch finds seniors particularly suited for many of the projects requiring patience and perseverance. A sampling of projects includes such varied interests as: Hawaii's forest birds, Poland's primeval forest, giant clams of Tonga, Hadrian's Wall, Iron Age Namibia, ancient agriculture in Japan, Canary Island dolphins, and saving cranes in Vietnam.

> PUBLICATION: *Earthwatch* magazine, published six times yearly, details each project, explaining its mission, staging area, costs, duties of volunteers, lodging and dining arrangements, and other pertinent details. Cost of the magazine is $25 per year for Earthwatch members.

Elderhostel, Inc.
William D. Berkeley, President
80 Boylston Street, Suite 400
Boston, MA 02116
(617) 426-7788

Elderhostel Canada
Dr. Robert H. Williston, Executive Director
33 Prince Arthur Avenue, Suite 300
Toronto, Ontario M5R 1B2
Canada

Elderhostel offers short-term, noncredit, residential, academic (learning/adventure) programs at over 1,600 colleges, universities, environmental education centers, and folkcraft schools in the United States, Canada, and 40 countries overseas. Elderhostel is open to anyone age 60 or above, plus a younger companion or spouse accompanying a participant. Elderhostel is a learning adventure accessible to all older adults, regardless of income or formal educational level. Participants live on the campus for one to four weeks, take courses on a variety of liberal arts and sciences subjects, take field trips, and enjoy extracurricular activities and campus life. Costs average $245 for a week-long program in the United States or Canada, which includes all tuition, room and board, classes, field trips, recreational programs, and other activities. Overseas programs cost considerably more in order to cover round-trip airfare as well as tuition, room and board, classes, field trips, and most other expenses. Scholarships are available for those who need financial assistance. Eight catalogs per year detailing Elderhostel programs are available free upon request or can be found in most public libraries.

Galaxy Tours
Hal F. Ryder, President
P.O. Box 234
Wayne, PA 19087
(800) 523-7287; (215) 964-8010

Galaxy Tours has conducted custom-designed military tours for veterans and other interested travelers since 1960. Tours visit 49 countries all over the world, and combine comprehensive sightseeing of popular tourist areas and attractions along with the historic background of military action and precise routes of military service in each area, personalized for veterans on the tour. Special events are also organized to commemorate anniversaries of historic occasions. The quarterly newsletter *Galaxy Gazette,* targeted specifically to the mature traveler, is available free upon request.

Global Volunteers
Burnham Philbrook, President
2000 American National Bank Building
St. Paul, MN 55101
(612) 228-9751

Global Volunteers takes teams of volunteers on two- or three-week personal learning and work experiences in rural villages in Mexico, Jamaica, Guatemala, Western Samoa, India, and Tanzania. Participants help in such projects as building schools and community centers, teaching, and some agricultural work such as reforestation. Volunteers' ages have ranged from 20 to 73 on past projects. Volunteers share their skills, energy, and labor while discovering firsthand the culture, lifestyle, and hopes and joys of a village people. Participants pay all expenses, which range from $1,065 to $3,000, including air travel from a gateway city, and all living and meal accommodations on the site. All trip-related expenses are tax-deductible. Volunteers participate in training through manuals, video tapes, and on-site meetings. Some language training may be provided for non–English-speaking countries. Participants receive a quarterly newsletter focusing on a specific site and its team members.

Golf Card International Corp.
1137 East 2100 South
P.O. Box 526439
Salt Lake City, UT 84152-6439
(800) 453-4260; (801) 486-9391

This golfing membership group offers members complimentary greens fees for two rounds of golf at 1,750 affiliated courses and country clubs across the United States and in Canada, the U.S. Virgin Islands, and Jamaica. Members also receive discounts on golf and lodging at 350 resorts nationwide. Average age of the membership is 61. Annual membership fees: $75 for an individual; $120 for husband and wife. Members receive the bimonthly *Golf Traveler* magazine featuring golf tips, personality profiles, stories about great golf courses, and the most current listings of Golf Card courses and resorts, plus *The Golf Traveler Atlas* to help plan golfing vacations.

Grandparents and Grandchildren Summer Camp
Bev Bridger, Executive Director
John Friauf, Adirondack Program Director
Sagamore Lodge and Conference Center
Sagamore Road
Raquette Lake, NY 13436
(315) 354-5311

The Sagamore Institute and the Foundation for Grandparenting cosponsor a unique one-week summer camp experience for grandparents and grandchildren with a full range of summer camp activities such as nature walks, crafts, and games. The Sagamore Institute is a not-for-profit educational organization devoted to responsible use of the environment, regional history, traditional crafts, personal growth, and positive social change. The Foundation for Grandparenting is dedicated to exploring and enhancing grandparent-grandchild relationships.

Grandtravel (A division of The Ticket Counter)
Helena T. Koenig, Owner
6900 Wisconsin Avenue
Chevy Chase, MD 20815
(800) 247-7651; (301) 986-0790

Grandtravel provides fully escorted, all-inclusive vacations for grandparents and grandchildren traveling together. Its programs have been developed by a team of teachers, psychologists, leisure counselors, and educators, giving special attention to current interests, historical sites, and natural attractions. Predeparture counseling is available from Grandtravel to help grandparents and grandchildren understand each other's needs.

Heartland Bicycle Tours
Catherine Lloyd, Executive Director
1 Orchard Circle
Washington, IA 52353
(319) 653-2277

Heartland Tours offers two- to four-day bicycle tours to scenic areas of Iowa, Illinois, and Wisconsin. Tours are rated beginner to advanced, and are supported by vans to carry luggage and provide snacks and lifts to tired bikers. Accommodations are provided at country inns and bed & breakfast facilities, when available. Participants are given maps for the day's travel and then proceed at an individual pace. Over 20 percent of recent participants have been over the age of 50; discounts are available to those over the age of 60.

Institute for Success over 60
Greg McCombs, Executive Director

P.O. Box 160
Aspen, CO 81612-0160
(303) 925-1900

> Although not a travel organization, this institute for personal growth and development sponsors a "Fit over Fifty" travel program offering summer hiking and river rafting, and a winter program in alpine and cross-country skiing. The trips are designed for participants to "learn to risk" in order to become less afraid to experience change and challenges in life.

Institute of International Education
809 United Nations Plaza
New York, NY 10017-3580
(212) 883-8200

> A nonprofit organization with over 600 U.S. college and university members, the Institute of International Education has provided information on educational exchange to higher education and the public for 70 years. Its annual *Vacation Study Abroad* provides a complete guide to over 1,300 vacation study programs around the world.

Interhostel
University of New Hampshire
6 Garrison Avenue
Durham, NH 03824
(800) 733-9753; (603) 862-1147

> Interhostel is an intensive study/travel program for adults 50 and over at host universities abroad. Each program's unique presentations are led by experts on topics such as the region's history, politics, natural environment, economics, literature, arts, and music. Excursions to sites of historic or cultural significance enhance learning in the classroom. Most programs are two weeks long. Prices published in any of the three catalogs per year are guaranteed in U.S. dollars and include the following: all group educational activities; admissions to galleries, museums, or performances listed in the program; ground transportation for programmed excursions; tuition; lodging; three meals daily; and round-trip transfers to the airport for group flights. Airfare is not included. An average of 35 participants stay in multiunit residence halls with shared baths or in modest hotels, some with

shared baths. Most meals are served in the institution's dining facilities and occasionally in local restaurants.

Lampert Tours/National Retirement Concepts
Janet Lampert, President
1454 N. Wieland Court
Chicago, IL 60610
(312) 951-2866

Lampert Tours operates tours geared to those age 50 to 70 to explore retirement communities in various Sun Belt states. Tours currently visit Arizona, Florida, North and South Carolina, Arkansas, and New Mexico. The trips combine a vacation with on-site education on relocating for retirement. Both singles and couples are welcome. The program is not connected with real estate sales.

League of American Wheelmen
John Cornelison, Executive Director
6707 Whitestone Road, Suite 209
Baltimore, MD 21797-4106
(301) 944-3399

The League of American Wheelmen, founded in 1880, is an advocacy and information association for bicyclists. It also works to promote bicycling for recreation, transportation, and fitness. Discounts on airfares, hotels, sporting equipment, and airline bike boarding passes are available to members. Annual membership fees: $25, individual; $30, family. Members receive the magazine *Bicycle USA* (eight issues per year); *Tourfinder*, worldwide bicycle tour listings; and *Almanac*, with state-by-state details on major rides, events, and local clubs.

Lifestyle Explorations
Jane Parker, Director
P.O. Box 576487
Modesto, CA 95355
(209) 577-4081

Lifestyle Explorations (formerly called Retirement Explorations) provides preretirement vacations in foreign retirement areas that have met 12 quality-of-life criteria. Countries currently visited are Costa Rica, Spain, Portugal, Argentina, and Uruguay. To avoid expensive mistakes, tour participants first complete a Retirement Values Inventory, trying to match their desires for retirement with the location of the tour. On the trip, participants meet with American retirees living in the area, attend informational seminars, and meet various medical, legal, business, and real estate professionals as local contacts for further information. Both singles and couples are welcome.

Mountain Travel, The Adventure Company
Leo Le Bon, Founder and President
6420 Fairmount Avenue
El Cerrito, Ca 94530
(800) 227-2384; (415) 527-8100

This 22-year-old specialty travel group describes its philosophy thus: "Mountain Travel is a continuing experiment in discovery: of new territories, of extraordinary people and cultures, and of wildlife far from our usual experience. We feel that the best way to discover new things about nature, this world and ourselves, is by traveling in small parties—on foot, wherever possible— enjoying firsthand the boundless beauty and variety of our small planet." Participants venture all over the world: on adventure cruises to remote regions, trekking into areas unavailable to vehicles, on four-wheel-drive-vehicle overland journeys, inn-to-inn hikes, ski adventures, camel/elephant safaris, wildlife and natural history safaris, and adventure tours by vehicle to offbeat locations with optional hiking. Maximum group size is 15. Trips are graded from easy to strenuous. The catalog, beautifully illustrated with outstanding photos from previous trips, could be enough to delight the armchair traveler for hours. Forty-one percent of Mountain Travel's clients are over age 50, with 5 percent of those in the 70–75 age range. Many of the trip leaders, as well as the company's copartners, also fall into the older adult category.

National Senior Sports Association (NSSA)
Lloyd Wright, Executive Director
10560 Main Street
Fairfax, VA 22030
(703) 385-7540

The National Senior Sports Association provides sports vacations for men and women over the age of 50. It organizes and conducts recreational and competitive tournaments in golf, tennis, and bowling at resorts around the world, using group purchasing and off-season scheduling for economical rates. Rates vary according to resort and season. Participants are grouped by skill levels, with activities planned for nonplayers as well. NSSA also sponsors a "Sports Holiday Abroad" program to golf courses in Scotland and Ireland, as well as Bermuda, the Bahamas, and Acapulco. Membership includes some discounts on sports apparel and equipment, car rental, and assistance with flight plans. Membership fee (single or couple): $25 for one year; $65 for three years; $150 lifetime. Members receive *Senior Sports News,* a monthly newsletter listing upcoming events plus news and winners of previous trips and tournaments.

OmniTours
1 Northfield Plaza
Northfield, IL 60093
(800) 962-0060

> OmniTours offers escorted tours exclusively for seniors on Amtrak trains. The tours begin in Chicago and visit all regions of the country. It offers one tour combining rail travel with a Mississippi steamboat cruise, and other varied travel excursions.

Outdoor Vacations for Women over 40
Marion Stoddart, Executive Director
P.O. Box 200
Groton, MA 01450
(508) 448-3331

> Outdoor Vacations for Women over 40 provides outdoor adventure vacations to older women, from one-day and weekend trips to six-night or more vacations. Day and weekend trips are arranged for such activities as hiking, canoeing, animal tracking, cross-country skiing, and bicycling. Longer vacations may combine any of those activities, plus rafting, sailing, and other activities in such locations as Greece and Turkey, Switzerland and France, the San Juan Islands and Olympic Peninsula, or the Grand Canyon. On-site instruction is provided for each activity; no experience or particular skill levels are required. Program

guides are women who have gained experience as rangers, naturalists, and instructors for the Professional Ski Instructors of America, Outward Bound, National Outdoor Leadership School, American Canoe Association, and the American Red Cross.

Outward Bound USA

John F. Raynolds III, President
384 Field Point Road
Greenwich, CT 06830
(800) 243-8520; (203) 661-0797

Outward Bound, a nonprofit organization, is the largest and oldest adventure-based education program in the United States, conducting wilderness programs through its five schools in Colorado, Maine, Minnesota, North Carolina, and Oregon. Instruction in dogsledding and winter camping, canoeing, canyoneering, mountaineering, sailing, cycling, rafting, backpacking, and trekking are designed to foster personal growth and fulfill human potential. The programs are meant to develop an individual's self-confidence, leadership skills, and ability to cooperate with others. No previous experience is required. There is no upper age limit, although groups are often organized by age. In addition, special groups have been organized for cancer patients and their family members, as well as groups for women only and for couples. Financial aid is available according to need. Course catalogs available free upon request.

Over the Hill Gang International

Earl Clark, President
13791 E. Rice Place
Aurora, CO 80015
(303) 699-6404

With the theme "Once you're over the hill, you pick up speed!" the Over the Hill Gang organized originally to promote regular ski trips for older adults. It has now expanded to promote an active, adventurous way of life, with recreational and social activities for people over 50. Current activities include biking, sailing, tennis and golf, rafting, hiking, camping, and fishing. Ski trips visit such areas as Switzerland, Austria, France, and Italy; also there's an annual seniors week at major Colorado ski resorts. Local chapters across the country hold social activities and off–ski-season recreational events. Membership includes discounts at various ski resorts, and on clothing and equipment. Members receive the quarterly newsletter *The Legend,* containing news of benefits and discounts, upcoming trips, and news from local chapters. Membership fees: Local Gang (includes international), $50 individual, $80 with spouse; International/at-large only, $25 individual, $40 with spouse.

Rainbow Adventures
Susan L. Eckert, President
1308 Sherman Avenue
Evanston, IL 60201
(708) 864-4570

Rainbow Adventures provides worldwide adventure travel and active vacations for women over 30; the average age of most groups is 50 or older. Small groups of 10 to 20 women explore the world on such trips as horseback riding in Ireland; a cruise down the Nile, ending in snorkeling and swimming in the Red Sea; trekking through the Swiss Alps, the Colorado Rockles, or the Himalayas; and cross-country skiing or snowmobiling in Yellowstone. Vacations offered are as diverse as tent safaris in Africa to covered-wagon treks in Wyoming. Trips are rated anywhere from "ridiculously easy" to moderate. Four brochures a year, all targeted at the mature woman traveler, are available upon request.

Rascals in Paradise
Deborah Baratta, Executive Director
650 Fifth Street, Suite 505
San Francisco, CA 94107
(800) U-RASCAL; (415) 978-9800

Rascals in Paradise arranges family vacations suitable for grandparents and grandchildren and extended families. Fees include accommodations, meals, activities, tax, and service charges. Babysitters are also supplied to allow time for adults-only activities. Several programs are teacher-escorted and encourage involvement in local culture, games, schools, churches, and villages.

Seniors Abroad
Evelyn Zivetz, Director

12533 Pacato Circle North
San Diego, CA 92128
(619) 485-1696

> Seniors Abroad provides opportunities to learn about family and community life of older persons through three different homestays with senior hosts in Japan, Scandinavia, and New Zealand/ Australia. The group arranges homestays only for guests and hosts over age 50. Participants pay the full cost of their travel, but hospitality is voluntary on the part of the host, at no cost to the guest. Homestays are also arranged in the United States for visitors from those countries. No membership fee.

70+ Ski Club™
Lloyd T. Lambert, Founder
104 Eastside Drive
Ballston Lake, NY 12019
(518) 399-5458

> The 70+ Ski Club is a nonprofit group organized to promote skiing for active downhill skiers over the age of 70. Over 5,000 members worldwide enjoy free or reduced-cost skiing at numerous ski areas. Domestic get-togethers are held in New York, New Hampshire, and Vermont. Overseas ski trips have gone to Switzerland, Austria, and Italy, plus a U.S. summer-season trip to New Zealand (in its winter season). Applicants must supply proof of age. Members receive an identifying club jacket patch and a ten-page listing of free or reduced-fee ski areas. The club is registered with the patent office to ensure it remains nonprofit. It has no paid staff, and any proceeds from club memberships are donated to the U.S. Ski Team. Membership fees: $5 for lifetime membership (U.S. residents); overseas membership is $15 to cover added postage costs. Members receive biannual newsletters (June and November) describing club activities and upcoming trips.

Society Expeditions Cruises, Inc.
3131 Elliot Avenue, Suite 700
Seattle, WA 98121
(800) 426-7794; (206) 285-9400

> Fifteen-year-old Society Expeditions Cruises offers more than 50 adventures to exotic and unique destinations. The company's

two ships sail to destinations around the world, with special emphasis on Antarctica, the Amazon, Australia, New Zealand, Greenland, the South Pacific, Indonesia, South America, and Canada's Arctic. All programs feature up-close culture, wildlife and scenery study, on-board lectures, hands-on experiences, and deluxe accommodations. Inland pre- or postcruise tours are available for travelers who wish to explore a region further. Conservation is a central theme on all expeditions. Lecturers are chosen for their expertise in such areas as marine biology, ornithology, history, anthropology, geology, archaeology, and glaciology. Land excursions are led by expert naturalists.

Spa-Finders Travel Arrangements, Ltd.
Jeffrey Joseph, President
784 Broadway
New York, NY 10003
(800) 255-7727; (212) 475-1000

Spa-Finders is a travel service specializing in health, fitness, and spa vacations worldwide, including all travel arrangements and reservations. Types of spas include: fitness and beauty, luxury, or weight-loss, plus new-age retreats and mineral springs. The full-color, 132-page *Spa Finder* catalog is available for $4.95, price refundable with a vacation booking through the firm.

Suddenly Single Tours, Ltd.
Tillie Simon, Executive Director
161 Dreiser Loop
New York, NY 10475
(212) 379-8800

Suddenly Single Tours provides upscale deluxe tours with private rooms for individual travelers who share similar interests and a desire to begin new friendships. The tours provide exciting environments, five-star hotels, custom selected restaurants, and security while traveling with a diverse group of peers. Destinations include the U.S. national parks, the South Pacific, Egypt and Spain, Singapore, Budapest and Vienna, and Holland and Germany. Also offered are an opera tour to northern Italy and a barge-cruise tour through France.

United States Masters Swimming, Inc.
Dorothy Donnelly, Executive Secretary

2 Peter Avenue
Rutland, MA 01543
(508) 886-6631

> Masters Swimming is an organized program of swimming, offering swimming workouts, training for competition, and lap and fitness swimming. It is open to any adult over age 19, and includes some members age 90+. There are 54 local committees, located in all 50 states. Although not a travel organization, the group produces a booklet, *Places To Swim in the United States* (available for $2), that lets travelers know where swimming opportunities are available. A $12 registration fee includes secondary accident/medical coverage and a regular newsletter.

United States Servas Committee, Inc.
Rita Alexander, Executive Director
11 John Street, No. 706
New York, NY 10038
(212) 267-0252

> Servas is an international cooperative system of hosts and travelers established to help build world peace, goodwill, and understanding by providing opportunities for deeper, more personal contacts among people of diverse cultures and backgrounds. The name "Servas" comes from the Esperanto word meaning "serve," to denote the spirit of international mutual service that characterizes the movement. Travelers can plan visits with hosts in every region of the United States and in over 100 foreign countries. Stays are generally two days. Servas requests a $45-per-year, per-traveler, tax-deductible contribution, plus a refundable $15 deposit for the host lists when borrowed. Two reference letters and an interview are required for participation.

Valor Tours, Ltd.
Robert F. Reynolds, President
10 Liberty Ship Way
Sausalito, CA 94965
(415) 332-7850

> Valor Tours plans and operates custom tours for veterans to World War II European and Pacific battle sites. Trips may be organized for anniversary visits, in connection with the dedica-

tion of a memorial or monument, or at the request of various unit or division associations. Videos on various Pacific battle site locations are also available. The organization also helps military associations with monument and memorial site selection, construction, and dedication. Available free upon request are the company's informational brochure, *Thanks for the Memories,* and the semiannual *Color Guard* newsletter with information about tours; listings of books, videos, and computer games of interest to military buffs; and other related news.

Woodswomen
Denise Mitten, Executive Director
25 W. Diamond Lake Road
Minneapolis, MN 55419
(612) 822-3809

Woodswomen provides outdoor educational living experiences for women, and for women and children. Although designed for women of all ages and skill levels, the average age range for trip participants is 35–65 years. Trips focus on canoeing and rafting, hiking, skiing, trekking, and bicycling in such areas as Minnesota and the upper Midwest, the Northwest mountains, and Alaska. Overseas destinations include the Galapagos, New Zealand, Nepal, Mexico, and the Alps, among others. Some trips use a base camp, hotel, or cruise ship. The *Yearly Trip Calendar,* listing upcoming trips and detailed information about the organization, is available free. Memberships are available but not required for trip participation. Members receive *Woodswomen News,* a quarterly newsletter (available to non-members for a $2 donation).

Foreign Government Tourist Offices

The following foreign government tourist offices are a good place to start for travelers planning visits to foreign countries. They offer a wide array of maps, plus information on attractions, accommodations, transportation, language, currency restrictions, weather conditions, vaccination requirements, and other important travel details.

Arab Information Center
747 Third Avenue
New York, NY 10017
(212) 838-8700

Australian Tourist Commission
489 Fifth Avenue
New York, NY 10016
(212) 687-6300

Austrian National Tourist Office
500 Fifth Avenue
New York, NY 10017
(212) 944-6880

Bahamas Tourist Office
150 E. 52nd Street
New York, NY 10027
(212) 758-2777

Barbados Board of Tourism
800 Second Avenue
New York, NY 10017
(212) 986-6516

Belgian National Tourist Office
745 Fifth Avenue
New York, NY 10151
(212) 758-8130

Bermuda Department of Tourism
310 Madison Avenue
New York, NY 10117
(212) 818-4800

Bhutan Travel Company
120 E. 56th Street
New York, NY 10022
(212) 838-6382

Consulate General of Bolivia
211 E. 43rd Street
New York, NY 10017
(212) 687-0530

Bonaire Tourist Bureau
275 Seventh Avenue
New York, NY 10010
(212) 242-7707

Brazilian Tourism Board (Embratur)
551 Fifth Avenue
New York, NY 10017
(212) 286-9600

British Tourist Authority
40 W. 57th Street
New York, NY 10019
(212) 581-4708

British Virgin Island Tourist Board
370 Lexington Avenue
New York, NY 10017
(212) 646-0400

Canadian Government Office of
   Tourism
1251 Avenue of the Americas
New York, NY 10020
(212) 581-2280; (212) 768-2442

Caribbean Tourism Organization
20 E. 46th Street
New York, NY 10017
(212) 682-0435

Eastern Caribbean Tourist Association
220 E. 42nd Street
New York, NY 10017
(212) 986-9370

Colombian Government Tourist Office
140 E. 57th Street
New York, NY 10022
(212) 688-0151

Cook Island Tourist Authority
7833 Haskell Avenue
Van Nuys, CA 91406
(213) 988-6898

Costa Rica Tourist Board
200 S.E. 1st Street
Miami, FL 33131
(800) 327-7033; (305) 358-2150

Cyprus Trade Center and Tourism
13 E. 40th Street
New York, NY 10016
(212) 213-9100

CEDOK-Czechoslovak Travel Bureau
10 E. 40th Street
New York, NY 10016
(212) 689-9720

Danish Tourist Board
655 Third Avenue
New York, NY 10017
(212) 449-2333

Dominican Tourist Information Center
485 Madison Avenue
New York, NY 10022
(212) 826-0750

Egyptian Government Tourist Office
630 Fifth Avenue
New York, NY 10111
(212) 246-6960

Tourist Information Section
Fiji Mission to the United Nations
One United National Plaza
New York, NY 10017
(212) 355-7316

Finland Tourist Board
655 Third Avenue
New York, NY 10017
(212) 449-2333

French Government Tourist Office
610 Fifth Avenue
New York, NY 10020
(212) 757-1125

German National Tourist Office
747 Third Avenue
New York, NY 10017
(212) 308-3300

Ghana Tourist Office
445 Park Avenue
New York, NY 10022
(212) 832-1300

Greek Nation Tourist Information
574 Fifth Avenue
New York, NY 10036
(212) 221-3927

Grenada Mission & Information Office
141 E. 44th Street
New York, NY 10017
(212) 687-4554

Guatemala Tourist Commission
P.O. Box 523850
Miami, FL 33152
(305) 358-5110

Haiti Tourist Office
488 Madison Avenue
New York, NY 10022
(212) 751-6442

Hong Kong Tourist Association
590 Fifth Avenue
New York, NY 10036
(212) 869-5008

Hungarian Travel Bureau
1603 Second Avenue
New York, NY 10029
(212) 249-9342

Government of India Tourist Office
30 Rockefeller Plaza
New York, NY 10012
(212) 586-4901

Indonesian Tourist Promotion Board
323 Geary Street
San Francisco, CA 94102
(415) 981-3585

Irish Tourist Board
757 Third Avenue
New York, NY 10022
(212) 418-0800

Israel Government Tourist Office
350 Fifth Avenue
New York, NY 10018
(212) 560-0650

Italian Government Tourist Office
  (E.N.I.T.)
630 Fifth Avenue
New York, NY 10111
(212) 245-4822

Ivory Coast Embassy
Visa Tourist Office
117 East 55th Street
New York, NY 10022
(212) 355-6975

Jamaica Tourist Board
2 Dag Hammarskjold Plaza
New York, NY 10017
(212) 688-7650

Japan National Tourist Organization
630 Fifth Avenue
New York, NY 10111
(212) 757-5640

Kenya Tourist Office
424 Madison Avenue
New York, NY 10017
(212) 486-1300

Mexican Government Tourist Office
405 Park Avenue
New York, NY 10022
(212) 755-7212

Moroccan National Tourist Office
20 E. 46th Street
New York, NY 10017
(212) 557-2520

Netherlands Board of Tourism
355 Lexington Avenue
New York, NY 10016
(212) 370-7360

New Zealand Consulate General
   Tourist Information
630 Fifth Avenue
New York, NY 10022
(212) 698-4680

Consulate General of Nigeria
575 Lexington Avenue
New York, NY 10022
(212) 935-6100

Norwegian-Swedish National Tourist
   Office
75 Rockefeller Plaza
New York, NY 10019
(212) 582-2802

Pacific Area Travel Association
228 Grant Avenue
San Francisco, CA 94108
(415) 986-4646

Panama Government Tourist Bureau
19 W. 44th Street
New York, NY 10036
(212) 246-5841

Peruvian Tourism Promotion Board
7833 Haskell Avenue
Van Nuys, CA 91406
(213) 902-0726

Philippines Tourism
556 Fifth Avenue
New York, NY 10036
(212) 575-7915

Portuguese National Tourist Office
590 Fifth Avenue
New York, NY 10022
(212) 354-4403

Puerto Rico Tourism Company
1290 Avenue of the Americas
New York, NY 10104
(212) 541-6630

Romanian National Tourist Office
573 Third Avenue
New York, NY 10016
(212) 697-6971

Republic of Seychelles Permanent
   Mission to the UN
820 Second Avenue
New York, NY 10017
(212) 687-9766

Singapore Tourist Promotion Board
590 Fifth Avenue
New York, NY 10022
(212) 302-4861

South Africa Tourist Corporation
743 Third Avenue
New York, NY 10020
(212) 838-8841

Spanish National Tourist Office
665 Fifth Avenue
New York, NY 10022
(212) 759-8822

Sri Lanka Tourist Board
609 Fifth Avenue
New York, NY 10017
(212) 935-0369

Swiss National Tourist Office
608 Fifth Avenue
New York, NY 10020
(212) 757-5944

Tahiti Tourist Board
366 Madison Avenue
New York, NY 10017
(212) 989-0360

Taiwan Visitors Association
210 Post Street
San Francisco, CA 94108
(415) 989-8677

Tanzania Tourist Information
205 E. 42nd Street
New York, NY 10017
(212) 472-9160

Thailand Tourist Office
5 World Trade Center
New York, NY 10048
(212) 432-0433

Togo Information Service
1625 K Street, NW
Washington, DC 20006
(202) 659-4330

Trinidad and Tobago Tourist Board
118-35 Queens Boulevard
New York, NY 11435
(718) 575-3909

Turkish Tourism & Information Office
821 United Nations Plaza
New York, NY 10036
(212) 687-2194

U.S. Virgin Islands Government
    Tourism Office
1270 Avenue of the Americas
New York, NY 10020
(212) 582-4520

U.S.S.R. Company for Foreign Travel
630 Fifth Avenue
New York, NY 10111
(212) 757-3884

Venezuela Government Tourist Bureau
450 Park Avenue
New York, NY 10022
(212) 355-1101

Yugoslav National Tourist Office
630 Fifth Avenue
New York, NY 10022
(212) 757-2801

Zambia National Tourist Board
237 E. 52nd Street
New York, NY 10155
(212) 308-2155

Zimbabwe Tourist Board
35 E. Wacker Drive
Chicago, IL 60601
(800) 621-2381; (312) 332-2601

State Tourist Offices

Free maps and tourist information about various attractions, accommodations, campgrounds, climate, and other important travel information can be obtained from the following state tourism offices.

Alabama Bureau of Tourism & Travel
532 S. Perry Street
Montgomery, AL 36130
(800) 392-8096 (Alabama)
(800) 252-2262; (205) 261-4169

Alaska Department of Commerce &
    Economic Development
Division of Tourism
Department RD, Pouch E
Juneau, AK 99811
(907) 465-2010

Arizona Office of Tourism
1480 E. Bethany Home Road
Phoenix, AZ 85014
(602) 255-3618

Arkansas Department of Tourism
1 Capitol Mall
Little Rock, AR 72201
(800) 482-8999 (Arkansas)
(800) 643-8383; (501) 371-7777

California Office of Tourism
1121 L Street, Suite 103
Sacramento, CA 95814
(800) 862-2542; (916) 322-1396

Colorado Tourism Board
5500 S. Syracuse Circle, Suite 267
Englewood, CO 80111
(800) 433-2656; (303) 592-5410

Connecticut Department of Economic
    Development
210 Washington Street
Hartford, CT 06106
(800) 842-7492 (Connecticut)
(800) 243-1685; (203) 566-3948

Delaware State Travel Service
99 Kings Highway, Box 1401
Dover, DE 19901
(800) 282-8667 (Delaware)
(800) 441-8846; (302) 736-4271

Washington, D.C., Convention and
    Visitors' Association
1575 I Street, NW
Washington, DC 20005
(202) 789-7000

Florida Division of Tourism
107 W. Gaines Street
Tallahassee, FL 32301
(904) 487-1462

Georgia Tourist Division
Georgia Department of Industry and
    Trade
Box 1776
Atlanta, GA 30301
(404) 656-3590

Hawaii Visitors Bureau
2270 Kalakaua Avenue, Suite 801
Honolulu, HA 96815
(808) 923-1811

441 Lexington Avenue, Room 1407
New York, NY 10017
(212) 986-9203

3440 Wilshire Boulevard, Suite 502
Los Angeles, CA 90010
(213) 385-5301

50 California Street, No. 450
San Francisco, CA 94111
(415) 392-8173

Idaho Travel Council
Idaho Department of Commerce
State Capitol Building, Room 108
Boise, ID 83720
(800) 635-7820; (208) 334-2470

Illinois Office of Tourism
310 S. Michigan Avenue, Suite 108
Chicago, IL 60640
(800) 359-9299 (Illinois)
(800) 595-7300; (312) 793-2094

Indiana Tourism Development Division
1 North Capitol, Suite 700
Indianapolis, IN 46204-2288
(800) 2-WANDER; (317) 232-8860

Iowa Development Commission
Visitors Group
200 E. Grand
Des Moines, IA 50309-2882
(515) 281-3679

Kansas Department of Economic
    Development
Travel and Tourism Division
400 W. 8th Street, Fifth Floor
Topeka, KS 66603
(913) 296-2009

Kentucky Department of Travel
    Development
22nd Floor, Capitol Plaza Tower
Frankfort, KY 40601
(800) 225-8747; (502) 564-4930

Louisiana Office of Tourism
Inquiry Department
P.O. Box 44291
Baton Rouge, LA 70804-9291
(800) 339-8626; (504) 925-3860

Maine Publicity Bureau
97 Winthrop Street
Hallowell, ME 04347
(207) 289-2423

Maryland Office of Tourist
    Development
45 Calvert Street
Annapolis, MD 21401
(301) 269-3517

Massachusetts Division of Tourism
Department of Commerce and
    Development
100 Cambridge Street, 13th Floor
Boston, MA 02202
(800) 942-MASS; (617) 727-3201

Michigan Travel Bureau
Department of Commerce
P.O. Box 30226
Lansing, MI 48909
(800) 543-2-YES; (517) 373-1195

Minnesota Tourist Information Center
240 Bremer Building
419 N. Robert Street
St. Paul, MN 55101
(800) 652-9747 (Minnesota)
(800) 328-1461; (612) 296-5029

Mississippi Division of Tourism
P.O. Box 22825
Jackson, MS 39205
(800) 962-2346 (Mississippi)
(800) 647-2290; (601) 359-3414

Missouri Division of Tourism
P.O. Box 1055
Jefferson City, MO 65102
(314) 751-4133

Montana Promotion Division
1424 9th Avenue
Helena, MT 59620
(800) 548-3390; (406) 444-2654

Nebraska Division of Travel and
    Tourism
P.O. Box 94666
Lincoln, NE 68509
(800) 228-4307; (402) 471-3796

Nevada Commission on Tourism
Capitol Complex
Carson City, NV 89701
(800) 237-0774; (702) 885-4322

New Hampshire Office of Vacation
    Travel
P.O. Box 856
Concord, NH 03301
(800) 258-3608; (603) 271-2343

New Jersey Division of Travel and
    Tourism
CN 826
Trenton, NJ 08625
(609) 292-2470

New Mexico Travel Division
Joseph Montoya Building
1100 St. Francis Drive
Santa Fe, NM 87503
(800) 545-2040; (505) 827-0291

New York State Division of Tourism
1 Commerce Plaza
Albany, NY 12245
(800) 225-5697; (517) 474-4116

North Carolina Travel and Tourism
  Division
430 North Salisbury Street
Raleigh, NC 27611
(800) VISIT-NC; (919) 733-4171

North Dakota Tourism Promotion
State Capitol Grounds
Bismarck, ND 58505
(800) 472-2100 (North Dakota)
(800) 437-2077; (701) 224-2525

Ohio Office of Tourism
P.O. Box 1001
Columbus, OH 43266-0101
(800) BUCKEYE; (614) 466-8844

Oklahoma Division of Tourism
215 NE 28th Street
Oklahoma City, OK 73015
(800) 652-6552; (405) 521-2409

Oregon Economic Development
  Tourism Division
595 Cottage Street, NE
Salem, OR 97310
(800) 233-3306 (Oregon)
(800) 547-7842; (503) 378-3451

Pennsylvania Bureau of Travel
  Development
Department of Commerce
416 Forum Building
Harrisburg, PA 17120
(800) VISIT-PA; (717) 787-5453

Rhode Island Department of Economic
  Development
Tourism and Promotion Division
7 Jackson Walkway
Providence, RI 02903
(800) 556-2484; (401) 277-2601

South Carolina Division of Tourism
1205 Pendleton Street
Columbia, SC 29201
(803) 734-0127

South Dakota Division of Tourism
Capitol Lake Plaza
711 Wells Avenue
Pierre, SD 57501
(800) 843-1930; (605) 773-3301

Tennessee Tourist Development
P.O. Box 23170
Nashville, TN 37202
(615) 741-2158

Texas Tourist Development
P.O. Box 12008
Capitol Station
Austin, TX 78711
(512) 463-7400

Utah Travel Council
Council Hall
Capitol Hill
Salt Lake City, UT 84114
(801) 538-1030

Vermont Travel Division
134 State Street
Montpelier, VT 05602
(802) 828-3236

Virginia Division of Tourism
202 N. 9th Street, Suite 500
Richmond, VA 23219
(804) 786-4484

Washington Tourism Promotion and
  Development
101 General Administration Building
Olympia, WA 98504
(800) 544-1800; (206) 753-5600

Travel West Virginia
West Virginia Department of
   Commerce
State Capitol
Charleston, WV 25305
(800) CALL WVA; (304) 348-2286

Wisconsin Division of Tourism
P.O. Box 7606
Madison, WI 53707
(800) 372-2737; (608) 266-2161

Wyoming Travel Commission
Frank Norris Jr. Travel Center
Cheyenne, WY 82002
(800) 225-5996; (307) 777-7777

Accommodations

Travel accommodations for mature travelers can vary from minimal accommodations in youth hostels or campus residence halls to the most upscale resort. The following groups offer information on a number of different travel accommodations.

American Youth Hostels, Inc. (AYH)
Richard Martyr, Executive Director
P.O. Box 37613
Washington, DC 20013-7613
(202) 783-6161

American Youth Hostels, a nonprofit association that provides year-round opportunities for outdoor recreation and inexpensive educational travel, has passed the 50-year mark, as have many of its participants. AYH is part of the larger International Youth Hostel Federation representing 70 nations and over four million hostelers worldwide. Hostels provide low-cost, dormitory-style accommodations, generally with self-service kitchen, dining area, and common room. Only an AYH membership card and sheet sleeping sack are required to stay in a hostel. AYH's World Adventure program offers a variety of trips worldwide, including some especially for people over age 50. Recent 50+ trips included bicycling in New England and Alaska, touring the Wisconsin cheese country, hiking San Francisco, and motor trips in North America and Europe. All trips are cooperative: Everyone pitches in to help with route planning, menus, daily agendas, and so forth. Annual membership fee: $15 for seniors (age 55+); lifetime fee: $250 (any age). Members receive the *AYH Hostel*

Handbook with detailed listings of more 200 AYH hostels in the United States.

PUBLICATIONS: *Knapsack Magazine,* published biannually, with travel features and tips of hostelers; and the *World Adventure Catalog,* detailing adventure trips around the world.

Canadian Hostelling Association (CHA)
1600 James Naismith Drive, Suite 608
Gloucester, Ontario K1B 5N4
Canada
(613) 748-5638

The Canadian Hostelling Association seeks to promote travel for people of all ages primarily through the provision of low-cost accommodations, generally in dormitory-style facilities. CHA also sponsors planned outdoor recreational activities year-round such as cycling, hiking, canoeing, snowshoeing, skiing, and rock climbing. A $15 senior membership card offers: entry into more than 5,000 hostels in 75 different countries, reduced rates for hostel accommodation in Canada, reduced rates for entry into places of interest, reduced prices on the purchase of recreational equipment, and participation in local CHA recreational activities. CHA also provides some programs through Elderhostel Canada. Members receive a free directory of hostels in Canada.

Hideaways International
Michael F. Thiel, President
15 Goldsmith Street
P.O. Box 1270
Littleton, MA 01460
(800) 843-4433; (508) 486-8955

Hideaways is a travel club specializing in villa and condominium vacations, as well as yacht charters, special cruises, and intimate inns and resorts in both popular and off-the-beaten-path locations. Some of the private homes are listed for exchange as well as for rent. The company also offers regular travel-agency services. Membership fees: $19 for a four-month trial membership; $75 for a full year. Members receive the current issue of *Hideaways Guide* detailing current offers, and quarterly newsletters.

Idyll, Ltd.
Harold E. Taussig, President
Box 405
Media, PA 19063
(215) 565-5242

> Called "Untours," Idyll arranges do-it-yourself vacations combining reasonably priced apartment and chalet rentals with orientation programs and suggestions or arrangements for day-trips, special events, and attractions in the following countries: Switzerland, Austria, Germany, Wales, Scotland, and Ireland, and also in London (April to October). It has a similar program in New Zealand during the United States' winter months. A new program, Glasnost, includes similar accommodations and services in Budapest and Vienna. Children are welcome. Field staff are on duty in each country to meet travelers at the airport and to offer assistance when needed.

United States Servas Committee, Inc.
11 John Street, No. 706
New York, NY 10038
(212) 267-0252

> Servas is an international cooperative system of hosts and travelers established to help build world peace, goodwill, and understanding by providing opportunities for deeper, more personal contacts among people of diverse cultures and backgrounds. The name "Servas" comes from the Esperanto word meaning "serve," to denote the spirit of international mutual service that characterizes the movement. Travelers can plan visits with hosts in every region of the United States and in over 100 foreign countries. Stays are generally two days. Servas requests a $45 per-year, per-traveler, tax-deductible contribution plus a refundable $15 deposit for the host lists when borrowed. Two reference letters and an interview are required for participation.

Home/RV Exchange and Rental Services

> The following are some of the most established home and RV exchange services. Some focus on rentals in addition to

exchange, while others deal completely with free home exchanging. Subscription rates, listing fees, and geographic areas covered vary from company to company.

Agency Alpha
11789 Montana Avenue, Suite 13
Los Angeles, CA 90049
(213) 472-7216

> Home leasing in France and England. Registration fee $65; $45 for seniors over age 60.

At Home Abroad, Inc.
405 East 56th Street, 6H
New York, NY 10022
(212) 421-9165

> Rentals only of private homes in the Caribbean, Mexico, and Europe. Registration fee $50. Periodic newsletters with updated listings; packet of color photos of properties available upon request when planning a trip.

Creative Leisure
951 Transport Way
Petaluma, CA 94954
(800) 426-6367; (707) 778-1800

> Condo rentals in Hawaii and Mexico, and manor homes and hotels in Europe. No fees. Brochures available upon request featuring available condos.

Hideaways International
15 Goldsmith Street
P.O. Box 1270
Littleton, MA 01460
(800) 843-4433; (508) 486-8955

> A $75 membership fee provides the semiannual *Hideaways Guide,* featuring rental opportunities for villas, condos, yacht charters, intimate cruises, etc., worldwide. Members also receive quarterly newsletters, travel discounts, and personalized vacation planning.

International Camper Exchange
14226 442 Avenue SE
North Bend, WA 98045
(206) 888-9382

> An informal RV exchange program for travelers overseas and in the United States. No membership fees, but donations are welcomed. Requires two self-addressed stamped envelopes, including one with overseas postage, for listings and information.

International Home Exchange/INTERVAC U.S.
P.O. Box 190070
San Francisco, CA 94119
(415) 435-3497

> Offers 7,300 home-exchange listings worldwide. Membership fee of $35, with a 10 percent discount for those 62 and older; currently over a third of the membership are age 50 plus. Members receive three publications annually with updated home-exchange listings, plus some rental opportunities of members' homes.

Vacation Exchange Club
P.O. Box 820
Haleiwa, HI 96712
(800) 638-3841; (808) 638-8747

> Home exchanges worldwide. Membership fee $50. Members receive two books annually with complete listings available.

Moderate Hotels and Motels

> The following moderately priced hotels and motels offer a range of senior discounts on their accommodations. Discounts may be based on age, or on proof of membership in a national retirement organization such as the American Association of Retired Persons (AARP). Some hotel and motel chains also sponsor their own senior "clubs" (shown in parentheses below), which offer discounts on such travel services as food, lodging, car rentals, and admissions to nearby attractions.

Allstar Inns
(805) 687-3383

Aston Hotels and Resorts, in Hawaii
only
(800) 922-7866

Best Western
(800) 528-1234

Budget Host Inns
(800) 835-7424

Budgetel Inns
(800) 428-3438

Colony Hotels and Resorts, in Hawaii
   only
(800) 367-6046

Compri Hotels
(800) 426-6774

Country Hearth
(800) 848-5767

Days Inns (September Days)
(800) 325-2525

Downtowner/Passport Motor Inns
(800) 238-6161

Doubletree Hotels (Silver Leaf)
(800) 528-0444

Drury Inns
(800) 325-8300

Embassy Suites Hotels
(800) 326-2779

Econo Lodges
(800) 446-6900

Economy Inns of America
(800) 826-0778

Exel Inns
(800) 365-8013

E-Z 8 Motels
(619) 291-4824

Fairfield Inns
(800) 228-2800

Friendship Inns
(800) 453-4511

Guest Quarters
(800) 424-2900

Hampton Inns
(800) HAMPTON

Hilton Hotels (Senior HHonors)
(800) 445-8667

Holiday Inns
(800) HOLIDAY

Howard Johnson (Road Rally Program)
(800) 634-3464

Hyatt
(800) 233-1234

Imperial 400 Inns
(800) 368-4400

Independent Motels of America
(800) 341-8000

Inn Suites
(800) 842-4242

Knights Inns/Arborgate Inns
(800) 722-7220

La Quinta Motor Inns (Senior Class
   Club)
(800) 531-5900

LK Motels
(800) 848-5767

Luxury Budget Inns
(800) 441-4479

McIntosh Motor Inns
(215) 279-6000

Marriott (Leisure Life)
(800) 638-6707

Motel 6
(214) 386-6161

Nendels Motor Inns
(800) 547-0106

Omni International
(800) 228-2121

Prime Rate Motels
(800) 356-3004

Quality Inns
Comfort Inns
Clarion Hotels and Resorts
(800) 228-5150

Radisson Hotels
(800) 228-9822

Ramada Inns (Ramada Best Years)
(800) 228-2828

Red Carpet Inns
Master Host Inns
Scottish Inns
(800) 251-1962

Red Lion Inns
Thunderbird Motor Inns
(Prime Rate Program)
(800) 547-8010

Red Roof Inns (Ready Card Plus 60)
(800) THE ROOF

Regal 8 Inns
(800) 851-8888

Relax Inns
(800) 661-9563

Residence Inns
(800) 331-3131

Rodeway Inns (55-Plus Travel Saver
Coupons)
(800) 228-2000

Sandman Hotels and Inns
(800) 663-6900

Sheraton
(800) 325-3535

Shoney's Inns
(800) 222-2222

Stouffer (Great Years)
(800) 468-3571

Super 8 Motels
(800) 843-1991

Susse Chalet
(800) 258-1980

Travelodge/Viscount (Classic Travel
Club)
(800) 255-3050

Treadway Inns
(800) 631-0182

Vagabond Inns (Club 55 Program)
(800) 522-1555

Westin Hotels
(800) 228-3000

Transportation

Getting to a destination, and getting around once there, is an important part of any travel experience. The following resources offer travel discounts to older adults. However, prices and conditions change overnight in these industries, so travelers should check with specific companies regarding individual circumstances.

Airlines

The following domestic airlines currently offer at least a 10 percent discount to those over age 62; some also offer a discount to a companion of any age traveling the same itinerary as the senior passenger. Some also cater to mature travelers with coupon-book offers (each coupon good for a one-way trip) or nearly unlimited travel for a set, prepaid fee. Airline offers change frequently, so research is strongly advised.

Air Canada
(800) 422-6232

Alaska Airlines
(800) 426-0333

Aloha Airlines
(800) 367-5250

American Airlines
(800) 433-7300

Continental
(800) 525-0280

Delta
(800) 221-1212

Hawaiian Air
(800) 367-5320

Mexicana
(800) 531-7921

Midwest Express
(800) 452-2022

Northwest Airlines
(800) 225-2525

Pan American
(800) 221-1111

Piedmont
(800) 251-5720

TWA
(800) 221-2000

United
(800) 628-2868

USAir
(800) 428-4322

Trains

American Rail Tours
Alan Beck, President
124 E. 27th Street
New York, NY 10016
(212) 764-6266

> American Rail Tours provides railroad touring services to 500 destinations nationwide on any line used by Amtrak. The company's American Zephyr luxury dining car and tavern/lounge observation car, each renovated in deco '40s style, are available for group charter. Additional railroad equipment can be leased for especially large groups. Individuals can participate in murder mystery trips between Washington, D.C., and New York City.

Amtrak Distribution Center
P.O. Box 7717
Itasca, IL 60143
(800) 872-7245

The center provides informational brochures about Amtrak, its national timetable, escorted rail tours, and discounted hotel and sightseeing packages to travel agents. Consumers should call the toll-free number for information and reservations. Senior discounts are available on some fares and services.

BritRail Travel International, Inc.
Colin M. Hall, President
1500 Broadway
New York, NY 10036
(212) 599-5400

BritRail Travel International promotes, markets, and sells travel on British Rail via special rail passes and other tourist-oriented travel products such as day-trips by train, guided tours, and combination ferry and automobile tours. Combination rail passes for Britain and France, including round-trip Hovercraft fare across the Channel, are also featured. Special first-class, senior-citizen BritRail passes are available for travelers age 60+. The organization also offers a 25-minute video, "Great Britain by Train: Legendary Journeys." *Go BritRail 1990* (U.S. edition), a catalog of information, itineraries, and prices, is available upon request.

Buses

Greyhound-Trailways, Inc.
901 Main Street, Suite 2500
Dallas, TX 75202
(800) 752-4841 (handicapped reservations); (214) 744-6500

Greyhound-Trailways offers a 10 percent senior discount on travel between Monday and Thursday, and 5 percent Friday through Sunday. Reservations for special assistance, if needed, must be made 48 hours in advance.

Car-Rental Agencies

These major national car-rental agencies often offer discounts to senior travelers, in addition to various seasonal or geographic special-price promotions. Although upper age limits to rent cars are virtually nonexistent in the United States, age limits are common in foreign countries. Mature travelers are advised to call ahead to see what may apply in individual situations, and to check on the possibility of senior discounts through local car-rental agencies.

Alamo
(800) 327-9633

American International
(800) 527-0202

Avis
(800) 331-1800

Budget/Sears Rent-a-Car
(800) 527-0700

Dollar
(800) 421-6868

General Rent-a-Car
(800) 327-7607

Hertz
(800) 654-3131

National
(800) 328-5800

Thrifty Rent-a-Car
(800) FOR-CARS

Camping and Recreational Vehicles (RVs)

The following organizations provide a wide range of camping and RV travel information, services, and social opportunities. With the extreme popularity of RV travel and camping among older adults, most of these groups boast of more than 50 percent membership or participation by people over 50.

American Camping Association (ACA)
John Miller, Executive Vice-President
Bradford Woods
5000 State Road 67 North
Martinsville, IN 46151
(317) 342-8456

The American Camping Association is a nonprofit organization dedicated to accrediting camps and maintaining high camp standards. ACA conducts a camp standards and accreditation program, and an education/certification program for camp directors. Accredited camp members offer year-round camping opportunities for seniors; session length, activities offered, and costs vary from camp to camp.

PUBLICATION: *Guide To Accredited Camps,* updated each January, lists over 1,900 camps nationwide that offer a quality camping

experience. A special section lists camps with senior-based programs. $9.95. Available in bookstores and libraries or from ACA.

Escapees, Inc. (SKP)
Joe Peterson, President
Route 5, Box 310
Livingston, TX 77351
(409) 327-8873

>   Escapees, Inc., is a support network for those who live and travel
>   via an RV for long periods. The majority of its more than 13,000
>   members are 60 and over. Membership benefits include free
>   camping (no hookups) at Escapee campground retreats, oppor-
>   tunities to attend rallies and seminars, mail forwarding and mes-
>   sage service (additional fees), and, if desired, eligibility to become
>   a co-owner in one of the group's nonprofit co-op RV parks.
>   Several books on RVing and related subjects can be ordered
>   through the organization. Membership fees: $5 to join, plus $40
>   annual dues. Members receive a 52-page bimonthly newsletter
>   containing information and money-saving articles that deal with
>   extensive and full-time RVing, plus members' personal travel
>   experiences.

Family Motor Coach Association (FMCA)
8291 Clough Pike
Cincinnati, OH 45244
(800) 543-3622; (513) 474-3622

>   The Family Motor Coach Association is an international, non-
>   profit association of families who own, use, or live in motor-
>   homes; RV dealers, manufacturers, and component suppliers
>   also belong. FMCA's purpose is to organize social activities,
>   exchange motorcoach information, and provide group benefits.
>   The group also works politically in support of recreational pro-
>   grams and the legal rights of RV owners. The group holds two
>   annual international conventions. Local chapters organize rallies
>   and other events throughout the year. FMCA benefits include:
>   reduced motor coach insurance rates, emergency message ser-
>   vice, trip routing, mail forwarding, free classified advertising, an
>   antitheft program, special caravans and tours, and a legal action
>   program regarding RV ordinances. Members receive *Family
>   Motor Coaching,* a monthly magazine with travel articles, technical

information, motorhome housekeeping, RV products and accessories and display and classified advertising, emergency help resources, and addresses of members who offer accommodations to fellow members.

Good Sam RV Owners Club
29901 Agoura Road
P.O. Box 500
Agoura, CA 91301
(800) 234-3450 (customer service); (818) 991-4980

Good Sam Club is a comprehensive RV organization that seeks to promote RV travel, and to provide benefits and services that enhance RV travel. Services offered (fees vary) include trip routing, mail forwarding, telephone message service, RV financing, traveler's checks, a discount phone card, insurance, credit-card protection, lost-key and lost-pet service, and emergency road service. Members receive discounts at over 1,500 RV parks and campgrounds, and on RV accessories and service and LP gas at various locations. Over 2,000 local Good Sam chapters across the country hold regular outings, meetings, campouts, and community projects. The organization also holds RV rallies, offers discounts on various tours and cruises, and operates Good Sam-Tours, a full-service travel agency with a specialty in arranging RV vacations with discount RV rentals worldwide. Members receive the monthly magazine *Highways* with RV news and travel tips.

PUBLICATIONS: *Trailer Life* ($18/year) and *MotorHome* ($20/year), by subscription only.

International Camper Exchange
John (Bill) Topping, Executive Director
14226 442 Avenue SE
North Bend, WA 98045
(206) 888-9382

International Camper Exchange has extended the concept of home exchanging to campers and RVs as a way to promote budget travel and meet people in foreign countries. The company maintains a list of available exchanges in various countries and offers advice on setting up an exchange, but participants are responsible for arranging their own exchanges. There are no membership fees; donations are accepted. Interested RV travelers need to send a stamped, self-addressed envelope for an application, plus a second stamped for overseas mailing.

Loners of America, Inc. (LOA)
Enola Echols, President
Rt. 2, Box 85E
Ellsinore, MO 63937
(314) 322-5548

> Loners of America is a not-for-profit, member-owned and operated RV club for mature, single men and women who enjoy traveling and camping. Most members are retirees. Members organize chapters, which, in turn, arrange campouts, rallies, and caravans for the benefit of all members. LOA is not a matchmaking organization; men and women may not attend club events in the same RV. Annual dues: $20, plus a one-time processing fee of $5. Chapter dues at the option of each chapter. Members receive an annual membership directory and a monthly newsletter listing upcoming events throughout the United States, reports of past events, RV news, and news from and about members.

Loners on Wheels (LoW)
Dick March, President
P.O. Box 1355-CM
Poplar Bluff, MO 63901
(314) 785-2420

> Loners on Wheels is a 20-year-old social club designed primarily for mature singles who enjoy the outdoors, camping, and travel. The group currently has over 3,200 members with 50 active chapters. Local groups hold frequent low- or no-cost outings at primitive state and federal campgrounds for walking, talking, campfires, and dancing, if space is available. Larger get-togethers (average cost $5–$7) are held approximately 12 times a year for lectures, travel films or slides, tours, dancing, and entertainment. This group is not designed as a dating or matchmaking service; those who do marry or travel together are dropped from the group. Annual membership fee: $24. Members receive a membership directory listing members' addresses, hobbies, interests, etc., and a monthly newsletter listing events, news from members, helpful hints, and RV mechanical and service tips.

National Campers and Hikers Association (NCHA)
Lyndon Mayer, President
4804 Transit Road, Building 2
Depew, New York 14043
(716) 668-6242

> The National Campers and Hikers Association provides opportunities to camp with a group in a family setting, offers services and benefits to members, and educates its members and the public on the environment, conservation, and campers' interests. It also organizes rallies, campouts, "travelong" caravans, and other camping activities. Membership numbers over 30,000 families, with thousands of local chapters in the United States, Canada, and several foreign countries. Seventy-five percent of the membership is age 55+; the majority of those own RVs. An annual retiree rally is held in February; individual chapters organize local retiree activities throughout the year. Other programs and services include: discounts, educational materials and workshops, insurance, and mail forwarding. Membership fee: $16 first year; $13 each year thereafter. Members receive *Camping Today,* the membership magazine.

National RV Owners Club (NRVOC)
K. W. Stephens, National Director
P.O. Drawer 17148
Pensacola, FL 32522
(904) 477-2123

> The National RV Owners Club is a camping and travel network of members who own or have access to a recreational vehicle. Sponsored by the International Family Recreation Association, NRVOC's purpose is to organize RV events and activities, exchange lifestyle information, and provide group benefits such as discount car rentals, a film-development club, RV and self-help books, and a discount catalog. The club also has interests in legislative action and legal rights of RV owners. Its events and activities include rallies, tours, caravans, safaris, and cruises. Benefits include membership identification, emergency message service, mail-forwarding service, group discounts, and classified exchange. Family membership fees: $15 for one year; $28 for two years; $40 for three years. Members receive NRVOC's

newsletter, *The Recreation Advisor,* containing useful information and advice for RV owners and users.

Recreation Vehicle Industry Association (RVIA)
David Humphreys, President
P.O. Box 2999
1896 Preston White Drive
Reston, VA 22090
(703) 620-6003

> The Recreation Vehicle Industry Association represents RV manufacturers and component parts suppliers. It serves as the industry voice with government and as a chief source for shipment statistics, market research, and technical data. It also promotes RV travel by providing information to the media and general public. RVIA sponsors an annual, week-long, public RV show at Dodger Stadium in Los Angeles with a special entrance-fee discount for seniors.

> PUBLICATIONS: RVIA offers a free comprehensive catalog of publications about the RV lifestyle. *Who's Who in RV Rentals* is a handy vacation-planning guide listing RV rental dealers in the United States and Canada. Rental dealers are listed by state and city. Each listing includes the dealership's name, address, and phone number, plus the type(s) of RVs for rent, how many people the RV sleeps, the unit's length, approximate rental rates, minimum number of rental days, and the deposit required to reserve the unit. It also lists any additional services such as one-way rentals, airport pickup, and livability packages (linens, utensils, etc). Cost: $5 (U.S. funds) postpaid for delivery in the United States and Canada; $7 (U.S. funds) postpaid if mailed overseas.

> Available free are nine separate resource lists for the RV buyer/owner who seeks further information about the RV lifestyle: *RV Shows, RV Rental Sources, Campground Information, State Campground Associations, Camping Clubs, RV Trade and Related Associations, Publications for Campers and RV Owners, RV Accessibility for the Handicapped,* and *RV Trade Publications.*

Special Military Active-Retired Travel Club (SMART)
Roy H. Allen, National Executive Secretary
P.O. Box 730
Fallbrook, CA 92028
(619) 723-2463

SMART brings together people with military backgrounds who are interested in the RV lifestyle. Members must be either active or retired military personnel; the majority of the current membership is retired. Members receive FAMCAMP (military family camps) maps and current updates, and the newsletter *The Smart Traveler*. SMART also offers discounted rates on RV caravan trips, which always provide special facilities and planning for handicapped RVers.

Vacations and Senior Centers Association, Inc. (VASCA)
Maureen F. Curley, Executive Director
275 7th Avenue, 18th Floor
New York, NY 10001
(212) 645-6590

Vacations and Senior Centers Association is an association of 16 nonprofit, camping vacation programs for older adults. The camps are located in New York, New Jersey, Pennsylvania, and Connecticut, and primarily serve New York City residents, although seniors from other areas may also attend. The VASCA network provides a safe, educational, and recreational experience designed for individuals who are not able to take more traditional vacations due to social, physical, or financial limitations. A schedule of programs, camps, locations, and fees is free upon request.

Brand-Name RV Owners Clubs

In addition to the camping clubs listed above, there are also a number of brand-name RV clubs. Only owners of particular brands of RVs may belong to these clubs. All these groups publish general RV travel information as well as technical information for their RV models, and often organize RV rallies and caravans for members. Information about specific clubs can be found at RV dealers and service centers.

RV Rally and Caravan Operators

These companies organize and operate RV rallies and caravans worldwide. Rallies bring campers together in one spot for special events, such as the Rose Bowl, for example, and for socializing, local tours, and sightseeing. Caravans consist of a number of . participants traveling together to tour a particular area. Most caravans travel with "wagonmasters," who act as tour organizers/escorts, and with mechanics to assist with problems. Caravan participants generally travel from point to point at their own speed, reuniting with the group at prearranged locations.

Compass RV Tours
20 S. Lafayette Street
Greenville, MI 48838
(800) 346-7572; (616) 754-2251

Creative World Rallies and Caravans
606 N. Carrollton Avenue
New Orleans, LA 70119
(800) 732-8337; (504) 486-7259

Point South RV Tours
11313 Edmonson Avenue
Moreno Valley, CA 92360
(714) 247-1222

TourMasters World of Tours
4401 Harlen Avenue
Waco, TX 76710
(817) 754-2027

Tracks to Adventure
2811 Jackson, Suite K
El Paso, TX 79930
(915) 565-9627

RV Resorts

RV resorts provide a wide range of activities beyond regular campground facilities. These may include golf, tennis, racquetball, fishing, saunas, spas, fitness centers, and more. Many operate as membership campgrounds, charging an initial fee to guarantee space both at a "home base" resort and free or discounted sites at affiliated clubs around the country.

ACI Parks
12301 NE 10th Place
P.O. Box 1888
Bellevue, WA 98009
(206) 455-3155

Camp Coast to Coast
1000 16th Street, NW, Suite 840
Washington, DC 20036
(202) 293-8000

Camper Ranch Club of America
P.O. Box 328
Conroe, TX 77305-0328
(409) 756-3328

Escapee Club's nonprofit co-op parks
Route 5, Box 310
Livingston, TX 77351
(409) 327-8873

Leisure Systems, Inc.
30 N. 18th Avenue, No. 9
Sturgeon Bay, WI 54235
(414) 743-6586

Outdoor Resorts of America
2400 Crestmoor Road
Nashville, TN 37215
(614) 244-5237

Resort Vacations International, Inc.
P.O. Box 7738
Long Beach, CA 90807
(213) 595-8818

U.S. Vacation Resorts, Inc.
3250 Ocean Park Boulevard, Suite 210
Santa Monica, CA 90405
(213) 399-5007

Thousand Trails
4800 S. 188th Way
Seattle, WA 98188
(206) 455-3155

Mail and Message Services

Mail and message services help keep travelers in touch with the world while away from home for extended periods. Used primarily by RV travelers, these services are also useful for those living on boats or traveling for extended periods of time. All of the mail services require a postage deposit.

Cascade Mail Service
P.O. Box 839
Canby, OR 97013
(503) 266-2931

Complete mail service; forwards mail weekly, bimonthly, monthly. Fee: $60/year plus postage and handling.

Family Motor Coach Association (FMCA)
8291 Clough Pike
P.O. Box 44209
Cincinnati, OH 45244
(800) 543-3622; (513) 474-3622

Free mail-forwarding and message service. Fee: $25/year for membership (limited to owners of motorhomes), plus postage. No handling charges.

Good Sam Club
Susan Bray, Executive Director
29901 Agoura Road
P.O. Box 500
Agoura, CA 91301
(800) 234-3450 (customer service); (818) 991-4980

Mail forwarding weekly of first- and second-class mail for members only. No message service. Fee: $15/year membership; $100/year or $25/quarter plus postage.

Home Base
Box 65656
Lubbock, TX 79464
(800) 422-HOME

> Complete mail-forwarding and message service. Fee: $25/month (mail and message service), plus postage. Message service only, $20/month. No charge per call.

Mail and Credit Card Association (MCCA)
P.O. Box 2870
Estes Park, CO 80517
(800) 525-5304

> Complete mail-forwarding and message service on customer-selected dates. Fee: $100/year plus postage and envelopes. Message fee: $2 per message.

National Association of Trailer Owners (NATO)
P.O. Box 1418
Sarasota, FL 33578
(800) 237-NATO; (800) 222-NATO (Florida)

> Mail forwarding twice a week to members. Fee: $11/year for membership, plus postage and handling (25 percent of postage).

SKP (Escapees) Mail and Message Service
Route 5, Box 310
Livingston, TX 77351
(409) 327-2870; (409) 327-8873

> Complete mail-forwarding and message service for members on customer-selected dates. Toll-free number for address changes and messages. Fee: $52/year membership, plus postage and envelopes. Message service: $25/year.

Travelers Mail Express
Box 1816
Roseburg, OR 97470
(800) 843-7282; (503) 672-8056

> Complete mail and message service on customer-selected dates. Fee: $13.50 registration; $84/year.

Travelers Overnight Mail Association (TOMA)
Box 2010
Sparks, NV 89431
(702) 331-1500

> Daily mail-forwarding service. Fees begin at $25/year and vary upward according to mail volume.

Travelers Remail Association (TRA)
710 W. Main Street, Suite 1
Arlington, TX 76013
(800) 872-6710; (817) 275-6710

> Mail-forwarding and message service on customer-selected dates. Fee: $50/year plus activity fee based on 50 percent of postage fee. Message service only: $20/year plus $1 for each two minutes.

Wanderers Mail Service
507 Third Avenue
Seattle, WA 98104
(206) 441-5678

> Mail and message service. Fee: $48/year plus all forwarding costs. Message service: $12/year plus 50 cents per call.

Federal Government Campground Offices

> The following government sources offer maps, visitors' guides, and campground information.

National Parks
National Park Service
18th and C Street, NW
Washington, DC 20240

National Forests
National Forest Service
U.S. Department of Agriculture
Office of Information
P.O. Box 2417
Washington, DC 20013

National Refuges
U.S. Fish and Wildlife Service
Public Affairs Office
Washington, DC 20240

Bureau of Land Management Sites
Bureau of Land Management
Public Affairs Office
1800 C Street, NW
Washington, DC 20240

U.S. Army Corps Projects
U.S. Army Corps of Engineers
20 Massachusetts Avenue, NW
Washington, DC 20314
Attn: Public Affairs Office

State Campground/Tourist Information

Free or low-cost camping information can be requested from these state campground associations or from the state tourist offices listed earlier in this chapter.

Arizona RV & Campers Association
221 W. Linger Drive
Phoenix, AZ 85021

California Travel Parks Association
P.O. Box 5648
Auburn, CA 95604
($2 for postage and handling)

Colorado Campground Association
5101 Pennsylvania Avenue
Boulder, CO 80303

Connecticut Campground Owners
    Association
14 Rumford Street
West Hartford, CT 06107

Florida Campgrounds Association
1638 North Plaza Drive
Tallahassee, FL 32308-5323

Georgia Campground Association
I-75 and Arabi Road
Arabi, GA 31712

Idaho Campground Owners
    Association
Route 1
Eden, ID 83325

Association of Illinois Rural Recreation
    Enterprises (AIRRE)
2057 W. Southmoor Road
Morris, IL 60450

Recreation Vehicle Indiana Council
3210 Rand Road
Indianapolis, IN 46241

Iowa Association of Private
    Campgrounds
Box 264
Monticello, IA 52310

Kansas Campground Association
RR 1, Box 97
Goodland, KS 67735

Campground Owners of Kentucky
Pioneer Playhouse
Danville, KY 40422

Louisiana Campground Owners
    Association
7676 Chef Menteur Highway
New Orleans, LA 70126

Maine Campground Owners Association
655 Main Street
Lewiston, ME 04240

Maryland Association of Campgrounds
9530 Rosehill Avenue
College Park, MD 20740

Massachusetts Association of
    Campground Owners
P.O. Box 100
Charlton Depot, MA 01509

Michigan Association of Private
    Campground Owners
P.O. Box 3384
Ann Arbor, MI 48106

Minnesota Association of Campground
    Operators
1000 E. 146th Street, Suite 121
Burnsville, MN 55337

Mississippi Campground Owners
    Association
8220 Oaklawn Road
Biloxi, MS 39532

Missouri Campground Owners
    Association
145½ N. Steward Road
Liberty, MO 64068

Campground Owners Association of
Montana
Box 215
West Glacier, MT 59936

New Hampshire Campground Owners
Association
P.O. Box 141
Twin Mountain, NH 03595

New Jersey Campground Association
29 Hand Avenue Extension
Cape May Court House, NJ 08210

New Mexico Campground Owners
Association
P.O. Box 694
Chimayo, NM 87522

Campground Owners of New York
P.O. Box 143
Dansville, NY 14437

North Carolina Campground Owners
Association
1027 Highway 70 W
Garner, NC 27529

Ohio Campground Owners Association
3386 Snouffer Road, Suite A
Worthington, OH 43085

Oregon Travel Park Association
60801 Brosterhous Road
Bend, OR 97702

Pennsylvania Campground Owners
Association
P.O. Box 147
Elmenton, PA 16373
($1 for postage and handling)

South Carolina Campground Owners
Association
RR Box 1, Box 52H
Yemassee, SC 29945

South Dakota Campground Owners
Association
Route 1, Box 4729
Blackhawk, SD 57718
(Send 25-cent, self-addressed, stamped,
long envelope)

Tennessee Campground Owners
Association
3070 Summer Avenue
Memphis, TN 38112

Texas Association of Campground
Owners
6900 Oak Leaf Drive
Orange, TX 77630

Utah Campground Owners Association
1370 North Temple
Salt Lake City, UT 84116

Vermont Association of Private
Campground Owners
RFD #3
St. Johnsbury, VT 05819

Virginia Campground Association
300 W. Franklin Street
Richmond, VA 23220

Washington Resorts & Private Parks
Association
12405 Tiley Road
Olympia, WA 98502

Wisconsin Association of Campground
Owners
P.O. Box 1770
Eau Claire, WI 54702

Wyoming Campground Owners
Association
1458 McCue
Laramie, WY 82070

Cruising

Alaska Marine Highway System
Pouch R
Juneau, AK 99811
(800) 642-0066

> The Alaska Marine Highway System operates the ferry system in Alaska, a main public-transportation system for many Alaskans and a popular tourist attraction, especially during the summer months. Seniors can travel Alaskan ferries at no charge between October and April (staterooms and car transportation extra).

Cruise Lines International Association (CLIA)
James G. Godsman, President
500 Fifth Avenue, Suite 1407
New York, NY 10110
(212) 921-0066

> Cruise Lines International Association is a trade organization representing nearly 20,000 travel agents and 36 cruise lines. CLIA publishes *Cruising—Answers to Your Most Asked Questions* and *101 Reasons To Take a Cruise*, free brochures available from travel agents.

Floating through Europe
Jennifer Ogilvie, President
271 Madison Avenue
New York, NY 10016
(800) 221-3140; (212) 685-5600 (New York)

> This organization offers luxury hotel-barge cruises that "discover the romantic waterways of Europe," according to its catalog. Cruises are available in England, Holland, or France, and include gourmet meals, guided excursions on shore to museums, homes, vineyards, and craft centers, and, on occasion, tickets to the theatre and hot-air balloon rides.

Freighter Travel Club of America
Leland J. Pledger, Editor
3524 Harts Lake Road
Roy, WA 98580

The Freighter Travel Club, founded in 1958, publishes *Freighter Travel News,* a monthly magazine of firsthand stories about freighter travel, tips on where to go, what to do while there, where to eat, stay, etc. Also included are news updates, book reviews, and comments/questions from members. The club is not connected with any travel agency and does not sell tickets or book passage, but will supply information and answer specific questions about freighter travel, steamship lines, and travel agencies. Membership fees: $18 for one year; $32 for two years.

International Cruise Passengers Association (ICPA)
Douglas Ward, Executive Director
Box 886
FDR Station
New York, NY 10150-0886
(212) 486-8482

The International Cruise Passengers Association was formed in 1980 to provide members with a centralized information source concerning cruise ships and the cruise industry. It conducts formal and informal inspections, evaluations, and ratings of cruise ships; provides a consumer "watchdog" role; and works to resolve serious complaints from ICPA members and subscribers regarding cruise vacations. It also provides information and support for the handicapped cruise passenger, and works to establish guidelines for the provision of shipboard support facilities for disabled travelers. ICPA does not book cruises. Membership fees are $25 per year and include six issues of *Cruise Digest Reports,* offering in-depth, no-nonsense reports on cruise ships and the cruise industry.

PUBLICATION: *Berlitz Complete Handbook to Cruising,* a handbook about cruising, with ratings and evaluations of cruise ships, revised every 18 months.

Last Minute Cruise Club
Molly Robertshaw, Owner
870 9th Street
San Pedro, CA 90731
(213) 519-1717

The Last Minute Cruise Club purchases unfilled cabins on four- and five-star-rated cruise ships for sale to travelers from two weeks to three months prior to departure. Prices are up to 50 percent off regular fares. There is no charge for membership. Members receive newsletters as discounts become available.

National Association of Cruise Only Agents
Ron Bitting, President
P.O. Box 7209
Freeport, NY 11520
(516) 378-8006

> Founded in 1985, this trade organization represents agencies (cruise consultants) that specialize in cruise travel.

Offshore Sailing School
Box 08130
16731 McGregor Boulevard
Ft. Myers, FL 33908
(800) 221-4326; (813) 454-1700

> Offshore Sailing School offers sailing classes for everyone from complete novices to advanced sailors. Over 30 percent of its enrollment are older adults.

Royal Cruise Line
Richard Revnes, President
One Maritime Plaza, Suite 1400
San Francisco, CA 94111
(415) 956-7200

> Royal Cruise Line caters to mature passengers with deluxe air/ sea cruises to worldwide destinations. In addition to typical cruise amenities and activities, Royal includes these special programs for older travelers: American Heart Association alternative entrées at all meals, the New Beginnings series of motivation lectures, fitness programs geared to older adults, and the Host Program, providing selected retired or semiretired gentlemen hosts to mingle and socialize with single women travelers. The company provides annual and semiannual cruise brochures, plus a pamphlet describing the Host Program and an information booklet, "Dine to Your Heart's Content," from the American Heart Association.

Society Expeditions Cruises, Inc.
3131 Elliot Avenue, Suite 700
Seattle, WA 98121
(800) 426-7794; (206) 285-9400

> Fifteen-year-old Society Expeditions Cruises offers more than 50 adventures to exotic and unique destinations. The company's two ships sail to destinations around the world, with special emphasis on Antarctica, the Amazon, Australia, New Zealand, Greenland, the South Pacific, Indonesia, South America, and Canada's Arctic. All programs feature up-close culture, wildlife and scenery study, on-board lectures, hands-on experiences, and deluxe accommodations. Inland pre- or postcruise tours are available for travelers who wish to explore a region further. Conservation is a central theme on all expeditions. Lecturers are chosen for their expertise in such areas as marine biology, ornithology, history, anthropology, geology, archaeology, and glaciology. Land excursions are led by expert naturalists.

South Florida Cruises, Inc.
Jim Bone, President
3561 NW 53rd Court
Ft. Lauderdale, FL 33309
(800) 327-7447; (305) 739-7447

> South Florida Cruises is a cruise clearinghouse company that buys sizable blocks of cabins from all the major cruise lines. It then offers substantial discounts to cruise vacationers on both last-minute and advance bookings through its group rates. The company can also make travel arrangements for individuals or groups, family reunions, class reunions, singles programs, travel with children, theme cruises, or other special needs.

TravLtips Cruise & Freighter Travel Association
Ed Kirk, President
163-07 Depot Road
P.O. Box 188
Flushing, NY 11358
(800) 872-8584; (800) 548-7823 (Canada); (718) 939-2400

> TravLtips is an information source and booking service for unusual sea travel, such as expedition voyages to remote environments,

and unusual itineraries on traditional ocean liners. Their particular specialty is travel aboard passenger-carrying freighters and cargo liners. Although not targeted specifically at seniors, most of the current 27,000 members are older adults. Members receive the bimonthly magazine *TravLtips,* containing first-person accounts of trips by members, plus freighter departures, rates, and itineraries from all over the world. They also receive the annual *Roam the World by Freighter,* featuring the best or most informative articles of the previous year, and *Cruise & Freighter Hotline,* a newsletter with updates of programs currently being offered by TravLtips. Membership fees: $15 per year; $25 for two years.

Health and Safety

These organizations offer some or all of the following travel services: medical assistance and/or medical insurance, trip cancellation or interruption coverage, help and information for those with disabilities or handicaps, and other health-related information. It is important to remember that Medicare coverage does not extend to foreign countries. Travelers with medical coverage other than Medicare should check personal policies for appropriate coverage.

Access America, Inc.
Ed Schulman, President
600 Third Avenue
Box 807
New York, NY 10163
(800) 284-8300; (212) 490-5345

Access America, a subsidiary of Blue Cross and Blue Shield of the National Capital Area and Empire Blue Cross and Blue Shield, provides travel insurance and assistance to Americans traveling away from home. The program offers supplemental health insurance to cover costs that Medicare or other health insurance does not cover while traveling away from home. Also available is insurance for cancellation or interruption of a trip due to serious illness or injury. In addition, Access America provides a 24-hour hotline to help in locating a local medical provider, altering travel plans due to emergencies, and arranging and paying for air evacuation if needed.

American Society of Tropical Medicine

Dr. Leonard Marcus, Consultant in Tropical Medicine and
Travelers Health
148 Highland Avenue
Newton, MA 02165
(617) 527-4003

> This organization provides lists of more than 70 doctors across the country who are familiar with the prevention and treatment of exotic diseases encountered by travelers.

The Berkely Group

Carefree Travel Insurance
ARM Coverage, Inc.
P.O. Box 310
Mineola, NY 11501
(800) 645-2424; (516) 294-0220

> Carefree Travel Insurance offers both a basic and deluxe plan of coverage for trip cancellation, trip interruption, baggage loss, accident and sickness, emergency evacuation, and accidental death and dismemberment. The company also offers 24-hour worldwide telephone emergency assistance. Fees depend on amount and duration of coverage.

Centers for Disease Control

Center for Prevention Services
Division of Quarantine
Atlanta, GA 30333
(404) 332-4559 (international travelers information)
(404) 332-4555 (general health and malaria information)

> The Centers for Disease Control offers two up-to-date health information lines explaining vaccinations needed for international travel, plus information on food and water, illnesses including traveler's diarrhea, and health information for specific areas of the world.

The Citizens Emergency Center
U.S. Department of State
Bureau of Consular Affairs
2201 C Street, NW, Room 5807
Washington, DC 20520
(202) 647-5225 (Monday through Saturday, and 24-hour
travel advisories)
(202) 647-4000 (Sundays and holidays)

> The Citizens Emergency Center deals with emergencies involving Americans abroad who die, become destitute, get sick, disappear, have accidents, or get arrested. The center works with U.S. consuls abroad to assist Americans who become physically or mentally ill while traveling by locating family members, assisting in transmitting private funds, and arranging travel to the United States by commercial carrier if necessary. When an American dies abroad, a consular officer notifies the American's family and informs them about options and costs for disposition of remains. It also offers advice and information to Americans who are arrested abroad, and helps track travelers who need to be notified about an emergency at home. The center also maintains a 24-hour travel-advisory hotline describing such risks as physical dangers, serious health hazards, or arbitrary detentions in countries around the world.

International Association for Medical Assistance to Travelers (IAMAT)
417 Center Street
Lewiston, NY 14092
(716) 754-4883

> IAMAT is a 25-year-old nonprofit organization that provides medical services to members all over the world. There is no charge for membership but donations are accepted. Members receive a directory listing IAMAT medical centers in 450 cities in 120 countries, along with names and addresses of English-speaking physicians who have had training in Europe or North America. Other information available includes climate charts on 1,440 cities worldwide, plus information on sanitary conditions of water, milk, and food.

International SOS Assistance, Inc.
One Neshaminy Interplex, Suite 310
Trevose, PA 19047
(800) 523-8930; (215) 244-2207

> International SOS Assistance offers travelers professional help worldwide in any medical or personal emergency. Services include telephone evaluation and advice by an SOS medical center and referral to English-speaking doctors, emergency evacuation, hospital admission deposits, emergency cash, emergency message transmission, and access to interpreters. It also covers medically supervised repatriation, transportation to join a disabled member, and repatriation of remains. Unlike medical insurance, there are no preexisting exclusions or age limits. Fees start at $25 for days 1–14, $2.50 each additional day; or $50/month or $195/annual membership. Members receive the *SOS Signal* newsletter containing membership news and travel tips.

Medical Data Banc, Inc.
7920 Ward Parkway, Suite 209
Kansas City, MO 64114
(816) 333-2080

> Medical Data Banc provides a complete emergency medical identification system on microfilm, sufficient for hospital admittance, treatment and surgical authorization, and authorization to treat minor children if parents or guardian cannot be reached. EKG cards are also available. Three-year membership rates are $18 for individuals, $36 for families.

Medic Alert Foundation International
Turlock, CA 95381-1009
(209) 668-3333

> Medic Alert is a nonprofit organization, founded in 1956, that offers a lifetime emergency medical ID service. Members receive a bracelet individually engraved with the member's primary medical information and identification number, and Medic Alert's 24-hour hotline telephone number. Medic Alert also supplies an annually updated wallet card bearing additional personal and medical information. Members can call the organization at any time to update their computerized medical records.

A one-time fee of $25 covers all services; medically indigent patients are enrolled without charge at the request of physicians.

NEAR Services
Richard Swinehart, Executive Director
450 Prairie Avenue, Suite 101
P.O. Box 1339
Calumet City, IL 60409
(800) 654-6700; (708) 868-6700 (Illinois)

> NEAR offers a wide range of services, including payment for the trip home, in case of serious illness, injury, or death anywhere in the world when traveling outside the local area of residence. Additional foreign hospitalization coverage is also available for an extra charge. A sample of services includes: emergency messages and tracing; lost-and-found service; emergency cash, credit card, or passport services; physician referral; rapid customs clearance in case of emergency; and in case of death, undertaker arrangements—embalming or cremation, and preparation and transportation home of the body, plus coordination of preparing and issuing a death certificate. Members receive a quarterly newsletter containing travel and health tips. Membership fees: $150/individual or $220/family annually; semiannual, $100/individual, $140/family; or $5 per person per day for short-term memberships (includes foreign hospitalization insurance).

Travel Assistance International
Pierre Volpert, President
1133 15th Street, NW, Suite 400
Washington, DC 20005
(800) 821-2828; (202) 347-2025

> Travel Assistance International, founded in 1963, offers medical, legal, and personal assistance services and primary insurance benefits for travelers. For medical problems, TAI will locate physicians, dentists, and medical facilities; replace prescriptions; provide coverage for medical expenses outside the United States; and arrange and pay for emergency medical transportation. Multilingual agents in 480 offices in 211 nations and territories offer additional services such as: advancing cash; relaying emergency messages; locating lost luggage, documents, or personal possessions; making emergency travel arrangements; and

providing telephone translation or locating local interpreters. Subscription fees depend on length and degree of coverage and number of individuals covered. Subscribers have access to a toll-free number for up-to-the-minute information about their destination, such as travel advisories, currency exchange rates, special events, immunization requirements, etc. Subscribers also receive "TAI LINES," a quarterly newsletter.

Travel Insurance Programs Corporation (TIPCO)
Tom St. Denis, Sr., President
1220 U.S. Highway #1
North Palm Beach, FL 33408
(800) 334-3367; (407) 627-4404

TIPCO markets and administers a variety of travel insurance plans for domestic and international travel. Its various plans cover trip cancellation/curtailment charges, accident and sickness expenses (including medical evacuation and repatriation), and baggage loss. It utilizes the Medex travel-assistance program for medical emergencies abroad. Note: while there is no change in premium for older adults up to age 75, reduced benefits and higher deductibles apply to those age 76–84. A separate policy is issued for those over age 85. Occasional newsletters are available to clients.

Traveling Nurses Network
Helen Hecker, Executive Director
P.O. Box 129
Vancouver, WA 98666
(206) 694-2462

The Traveling Nurses Network provides registered nurses for any traveler, regardless of disability, or for those wanting the reassurance of a professionally trained companion. The agency consists of registered nurses with expertise in all medical areas, including diabetes, dialysis, cardiology, respiratory disease, spinal-cord injury, blindness or vision impairment, deafness or hearing impairment, developmental disability, and psychiatry. The network specializes in assisting wheelchair travelers and also works with various travel resources, including arranging oxygen or respiratory equipment, equipment rental, specially equipped vans, accessible accommodations, and group tours.

TravMed/Medex
Linda Reems, Manager
P.O. Box 10623
Towson, MD 21204
(800) 732-5309; (301) 296-5225 (Maryland)

> TravMed offers major medical insurance and a travel-assistance services program for overseas travelers, through the International Travelers Assistance Association. Medex's multilingual assistants help clients abroad find medical services with English-speaking doctors, or help find translators as needed; provide contact to family; and arrange for emergency evacuation if medically necessary. Insurance coverage includes specified dental, physician, and hospital services; emergency medical evacuation; and expenses for repatriation of remains.

U.S. Department of State
Bureau of Consular Affairs
2201 C Street, NW, Room 5807
Washington, DC 20520
(202) 647-1488

> The Department of State provides a number of informational pamphlets to assist U.S. travelers abroad, such as *Travel Tips for Older Americans, A Safe Trip Abroad,* and the *Travel Tips* series, which outline important information for travelers to various regions of the world, including some current political or social "hot spots." A handy booklet, *Handbook and Directory of Consular Services,* lists information on governmental citizens services overseas, passport services, visa services, and telephone listings for related government agencies. In addition, the State Department provides an assistance hotline at the Citizens Emergency Center for U.S. travelers who need to deal with medical emergencies, death, arrest, or other major problems while abroad.

Disabled Travel

Amtrak
Special Services Desk
(800) USA-RAIL

Amtrak provides a number of special services and accommodations for disabled travelers, from accessible sleeping rooms and bathrooms to wheelchair lifts to food service for those unable to move freely about the train. Advance notice is required up to 72 hours prior to departure.

Eastern Paralyzed Veterans Association (EPVA)
James J. Peters, Executive Director
75-20 Astoria Boulevard
Jackson Heights, NY 11370-1178
(718) 803-EPVA

The Eastern Paralyzed Veterans Association is a nonprofit group organized to provide veterans service and to ensure access for all disabled and aging persons. It provides travel and accessibility information free of charge for the disabled of any age.

PUBLICATIONS: *Ten Questions and Answers about Air Travel for Wheelchair Users* and *The Guide to Riding Wheelchair-Accessible Buses in NYC.*

Evergreen Travel Service, Inc.
Jack J. Hoffman, President
Betty J. Hoffman, Chairman
19505 44th Avenue W
Lynnwood, WA 98036
(800) 435-2288; (206) 776-1184

For over 30 years, Evergreen Travel has promoted travel and conducted tours for the handicapped. Various programs include: Wings on Wheels Tours (for the wheelchair disabled), White Cane Tours (for the visually impaired and blind), Flying Fingers Tours (for the deaf and hearing impaired), Happy Tours (for the developmentally disabled), and finally, Lazybones Tours for those unable to keep up with standard tours and requiring slow-paced itineraries. In addition to tours and cruises worldwide, Evergreen can arrange individual itineraries almost anywhere to do almost any activity. Working by its motto, "We made the world accessible!" this company has arranged such travel opportunities as trekking in the Himalayas by sedan chair for quadraplegics and elephantback sightseeing in India for wheelchair travelers. Tour groups are small and are fully escorted.

Flying Wheels Travel, Inc.
Judd Jacobson and Barbara Jacobson, Directors
143 W. Bridge Street
P.O. Box 382
Owatonna, MN 55060
(800) 657-4446; (800) 722-9351

> Flying Wheels Travel, founded in 1970, arranges group tours and independent travel for the physically handicapped and their friends and relatives. Recent tours have visited areas all over the world and have included ocean cruises. Travelers who need personal assistance are requested to bring a traveling companion with them, or Flying Wheels will attempt to find one, if needed. Groups are limited to 25 participants, including the tour escort, who is trained to assist with daily medical and physical needs.

Greyhound-Trailways, Inc.
Helping Hand Service for the Handicapped
901 Main Street, Suite 2500
Dallas, TX 75202
(800) 752-4841 (handicapped reservations); (214) 744-6500

> Greyhound-Trailways' Helping Hand Service allows free travel on the same itinerary for a handicapped passenger's companion or assistant, and transports wheelchairs, walkers, or other required equipment outside of normal baggage allotments. Specially trained personnel at bus depots help lift passengers on and off the bus, and necessary equipment will be unloaded at each stop if needed. In addition, Greyhound offers a 10 percent senior discount on travel between Monday and Thursday, and 5 percent Friday through Sunday. Reservations for special assistance must be made 48 hours in advance.

International Cruise Passengers Association (ICPA)
Box 886
FDR Station
New York, NY 10150-0886
(212) 486-8482

> The International Cruise Passengers Association was formed in 1980 to provide members with a centralized information source concerning cruise ships and the cruise industry. It conducts

formal and informal inspections, evaluations, and ratings of cruise ships; provides a consumer "watchdog" role; and works to resolve serious complaints from ICPA members and subscribers regarding cruise vacations. It also provides information and support for the handicapped cruise passenger, and works to establish guidelines for the provision of shipboard support facilities for disabled travelers. ICPA does not book cruises. Membership fees are $25 per year and include six issues of *Cruise Digest Reports,* offering in-depth, no-nonsense reports on cruise ships and the cruise industry.

PUBLICATION: *Berlitz Complete Handbook to Cruising,* a handbook about cruising, with ratings and evaluations of cruise ships, revised every 18 months.

Organization for the Promotion of Access and Travel for the Handicapped (OPT)
Tom Gilbert, President
P.O. Box 15777
Tampa, FL 33684
(813) 932-0916

OPT is a nonprofit organization providing free services and information to persons with disabilities or handicaps, and to the travel industry to promote understanding and facilitate access and travel for all individuals. OPT publishes a complete list of cruise ships with cabins for wheelchair users who are quadriplegics, triplegics, or paraplegics with no lower extremity mobility. OPT has devised an extensive questionnaire for use by travel agents and tour operators to help them serve handicapped clients. It also publishes an occasional newsletter with updated travel information and tips, free to members. Annual membership fees are: $10/nonprofit organizations; $15/individuals; $25/businesses.

Society for the Advancement of Travel for the Handicapped (SATH)
Mark T. R. Shaw-Lawrence, Development Director
26 Court Street
Brooklyn, NY 11242
(718) 858-5483

SATH disseminates information concerning travel and tourism for the handicapped population to handicapped organizations,

the travel industry, and national and international tourism organizations. SATH offers its members information on a wide range
of specialized services available to the handicapped traveler,
publications and services available to them, and listings of tour
operators who specialize in tours and travel arrangements for the
disabled in the United States and abroad. Annual membership
fee: $40; $25 for handicapped persons over age 65. Members
receive *SATH News,* a quarterly travel newsletter.

PUBLICATIONS: *The United States Welcomes Handicapped
Visitors,* informational travel sheets.

Travel Buddy, Inc.
Dona M. Risdall, Executive Director
P.O. Box 31146
Minneapolis, MN 55431
(612) 881-5364

Travel Buddy supplies reputable travel companions for children
or adults of all ages, or for travelers with slight handicaps. Teachers, nurses, and other professionals are available as travel companions. Fee per arrangement is $75 for nonmembers, $55 for
members. Additional fees for extra or professional assistance
depend on the level of help needed and the duration of the trip.
Clients provide round-trip transportation for the buddies, but
buddies pay for their own lodging and meals. Travel Buddy can
also help with travel arrangements at no additional charge.
Annual membership fee: $25 for individuals, couples, or
families. Members receive the monthly *Trip Tips* containing general travel information.

Travel Information Service (TIS)
Moss Rehabilitation Hospital
12th Street and Tabor Road
Philadelphia, PA 19141
(215) 456-9600 (voice); (215) 456-9602 (TDD)

The Travel Information Service provides information on handicap-accessible travel from material in its files. Coverage includes
accessibility information on transportation, accommodations,
cruises, restaurants, and other tips for travel in the United States
and abroad. TIS does not make travel arrangements, but refers
requesters by telephone, mail, or in person to travel agencies,

airlines, and other resources offering special services to disabled people. A nominal fee is charged to cover postage and handling for information packages that are mailed.

Traveling Nurses Network
Helen Hecker, Executive Director
P.O. Box 129
Vancouver, WA 98666
(206) 694-2462

The Traveling Nurses Network provides registered nurses for any traveler, regardless of disability, or for those wanting the reassurance of a professionally trained companion. The agency consists of registered nurses with expertise in all medical areas, including diabetes, dialysis, cardiology, respiratory disease, spinal-cord injury, blindness or vision impairment, deafness or hearing impairment, developmental disability, and psychiatry. The network specializes in assisting wheelchair travelers and also works with various travel resources, including arranging oxygen or respiratory equipment, equipment rental, specially equipped vans, accessible accommodations, and group tours.

Travel Information Sources

Book Passage
Elaine Petrocelli, President
51 Tamal Vista Boulevard
Corte Madera, CA 94925
(800) 321-9785; (415) 927-0960

Book Passage is a travel-specialty bookstore, with a large inventory of travel books for seniors. Books can be ordered by mail or at the bookstore itself. Book Passage also offers free lectures by travel authors and travel experts, as well as classes for writers and travelers. Some classes have a fee. The Book Passage catalog is free upon request.

Forsyth Travel Library, Inc.
Stephen F. Forsyth, President
9154 W. 57th Street
P.O. Box 2975
Shawnee Mission, KS 66201-1375
(800) 367-7984; (913) 384-3440

The Forsyth Travel Library operates both a warehouse store and mail-order business, distributing a wide range of travel information and supplies. Its inventory includes books, maps, guides, travel videos, language cassettes, travel reference materials, and travel accessories such as money belts and electrical adapters. It also accepts applications for American Youth Hostels and serves as a tour agent for British and European rail passes. Free catalogs upon request. Forsyth publishes occasional newsletters with up-to-date travel information and tips.

The Literate Traveller
Nancy A. Heck, President
8306 Wilshire Boulevard, Suite 591
Beverly Hills, CA 90211
(213) 398-8781

The Literate Traveller is a mail-order house with a unique selection of guidebooks and travel literature. Its catalog displays an uncommon and eclectic mix of travel books, from Hemingway's *Moveable Feast* to traditional guidebook series, from nineteenth-century travel chronicles by Mary Wilson to Dian Fossey's *Gorillas in the Mist*. The selection covers guidebooks and travel books emphasizing culture, art, and history; adventure narratives, both classic and contemporary; and practical books for independent, group, or even armchair travelers. Books are grouped by geographic area, with additional sections covering anthologies and special guides, tips on choosing a travel guide, and complete lists of guidebook series. From the look of the catalog's cover, depicting an old-fashioned, cherished personal diary, to the well-written reviews of each book, the catalog alone offers a unique trip through the literature of travel. *The Literate Traveller* catalog is available for $2 through the publisher. A free newsletter, published three times annually, features current travel news and recommended reading on related topics, plus new travel titles.

Money Exchange

Travel advisers suggest having at least two days' incidental expense money in the currency used in the destination country. Currency can be exchanged through travel agents (generally requires 48 hours), through some large American banks, or through the company listed below.

Deak International
29 Broadway
New York, NY 10006
(212) 820-2470

> Deak International, with offices in several major cities throughout North America and worldwide, provides foreign currency exchange to travelers over the counter or through travel agents. They also offer traveler's checks in dollars or foreign currency and will cash foreign checks.

Consumer Information and Complaints

The following government offices and travel trade organizations can help consumers with information and advice in resolving complaints or problems. The trade organizations help maintain professional standards of practice among their members; many also offer helpful information for travelers to avoid problems in advance. Complete information on each of these organizations is given elsewhere in this book.

American Bus Association (ABA)
1015 15th Street, NW, Suite 250
Washington, DC 20005
(800) 422-1400; (202) 842-1645

American Camping Association
Bradford Woods
5000 State Road 67 North
Martinsville, IN 46151
(317) 342-8456

American Society of Travel Agents
1101 King Street
Alexandria, VA 22314
(703) 739-2782

American Sunbathing Association, Inc.
1703 N. Main Street
Kissimmee, FL 34744-9988
(407) 933-2064

Cruise Lines International Association
500 Fifth Avenue, Suite 1407
New York, NY 10110
(212) 921-0066

Family Motor Coach Association
8291 Clough Pike
Cincinnati, OH 45244
(800) 543-3622; (513) 474-3622

International Cruise Passengers
  Association
Box 886
FDR Station
New York, NY 10150-0886
(212) 486-8482

National Association of Cruise Only
  Agents
P.O. Box 7209
Freeport, NY 11520
(516) 378-8006

National Tour Association, Inc.
546 E. Main Street
P.O. Box 3071
Lexington, KY 40596-3071
(800) NTA-8886 (U.S.)
(800) 828-6999 (Canada)
(606) 253-1036

Recreation Vehicle Industry Association
  (RVIA)
P.O. Box 2999
1896 Preston White Drive
Reston, VA 22090
(703) 620-6003

United States Department of
  Transportation
400 7th Street, SW
Washington, DC 20590
(202) 366-2220
(Handles airline complaints)

United States Tour Operators
  Association (USTOA)
211 East 51st Street, Suite 12B
New York, NY 10022
(212) 944-5727

Legal Assistance

American travelers who face legal problems while abroad can
find help from the following public and private organizations.

The Citizens Emergency Center
U.S. Department of State
Bureau of Consular Affairs
2201 C Street, NW, Room 5807
Washington, DC 20520
(202) 647-5225 (Monday through Saturday, and 24-hour
travel advisories)
(202) 647-4000 (Sundays and holidays)

The Citizens Emergency Center deals with emergencies involving
Americans abroad who die, become destitute, get sick, disap-
pear, have accidents, or get arrested. The center works with U.S.
consuls abroad to assist Americans who become physically or
mentally ill while traveling by locating family members, assisting
in transmitting private funds, and arranging travel to the United
States by commercial carrier if necessary. When an American
dies abroad, a consular officer notifies the American's family and

informs them about options and costs for disposition of remains. It also offers advice and information to Americans who are arrested abroad, and helps track travelers who need to be notified about an emergency at home. The center also maintains a 24-hour travel-advisory hotline describing such risks as physical dangers, serious health hazards, or arbitrary detentions in countries around the world.

International Legal Defense Counsel (ILDC)
Robert L. Pisani, Executive Director
111 S. 15th Street
Philadelphia, PA 19102
(215) 977-9982

The International Legal Defense Counsel is a private U.S. organization that specializes in defending Americans arrested in foreign countries.

Chapter 8

Reference Materials

Books

General Travel

Blinder, Martin. *Smart Travel.* Bedford, MA: Mills & Sanderson, 1986.
124p. $9.95 (paperback). ISBN 0-938179-02-0.

> Subtitled "Trade Secrets for Getting There in Style at Little Cost
> or Effort," this book should be required reading for the dedi-
> cated traveler who knows there's always a better deal—without
> necessarily sacrificing the quality expected—but doesn't know
> how to find it. Now that traveler can know—and find it—as
> Blinder shares priceless insider tips on everything from avoiding
> haggling with cab drivers over foreign currency to arranging
> special menus on airplanes. This is the book to use to get more
> than one's money's worth from hotels, restaurants, airlines,
> cruise lines, trains, and rental-car services. Blinder strongly rec-
> ommends using a travel agent, but after absorbing the informa-
> tion in this book, readers will understand how the travel industry
> works and be capable of getting even more value from that
> agent. Also included are strong recommendations for keeping
> valuables safe, travel tips for women traveling alone, and sound
> principles of packing. The book concludes with the author's
> recommendations for singular hotels and distinctive trips.

Brosnahan, Tom. *Frommer's Beat the High Cost of Travel: Travel More,
Travel Better.* New York: Prentice-Hall, 1988. 435p. $6.95 (paperback).
ISBN 0-13-402132-0.

This outstanding addition to Frommer travel books is based on four simple laws, the author's "rules of the road," that created a way, as he says, "to put waiters completely at my service, to make hotel clerks do what I asked, and to find out true bargain fares from reservation agents or travel agents." This is not the usual discount guide pointing readers to specific companies or outlets. Instead, it teaches travelers to think creatively about travel products and services, and includes insider information on what companies need so both consumers and companies can benefit. One section of the book deals specifically with senior discounts.

Carlson, Raymond, and Maria Maiorino, eds. *National Directory of Free Tourist Attractions*. Babylon, NY: Pilot Books, 1987. 78p. $3.95 (paperback). ISBN 0-87576-131-3.

Pilot Books specializes in succinct, easy-to-use information for travelers. This compact volume offers over 1,150 listings of attractions such as museums, botanical gardens, restored villages, ships, and other presentations of history, science, and folk art. Items are listed within states by city, name and type of attraction, address, times of operation, and telephone number.

Carlson, Raymond, ed. *Directory of Free Vacation and Travel Information*. Babylon, NY: Pilot Books, 1988. $3.95 (paperback). ISBN 0-87576-120-8.

This compact directory lists over 700 sources from which to obtain free brochures, maps, events calendars, and other useful travel information covering recreational areas, landmarks, and other tourist attractions in the United States and Canada. Also listed are the addresses of 106 foreign tourist offices located in the United States to contact for information.

————. *1990–1991 National Directory of Budget Motels*. Babylon, NY: Pilot Books. 80p. $3.95 plus $1 postage and handling (paperback). (Available from the publisher only.) ISBN 0-87576-051-1.

This compact directory contains listings for over 2,200 budget motels in the United States and Canada. It includes the headquarters for 26 of the chains, most with free "800" numbers for reservations and information. Also detailed are family, senior citizen, military, group, and other discounts, and special facilities for the disabled.

Carpenter, Patricia. *Away for the Holiday*. Minneapolis: PCA
Publishing, 1988. 365p. $12.95 (paperback). ISBN 0-944283-01-2.

> There are a number of reasons older adults will find this a useful
> resource book for ideas on where to go and what to do for the
> Christmas holidays. More older people live in smaller homes or
> retirement communities that do not accommodate large family
> gatherings; some don't want to be in the same place they cele-
> brated when a spouse was alive; families are scattered all over
> the country; they're single and don't want to intrude on others'
> family celebrations; or everyone wants to enjoy being with one
> another rather than preparing food or washing the dishes. What-
> ever the reason, Carpenter's directory of inns, hotels, resorts,
> spas, holiday tours, holiday cruises, and city and community
> celebrations is chock-full of helpful suggestions for holiday
> travel. It even includes a refresher course on holiday traditions
> around the world—from the United States to the Far East, from
> Africa to South America, and the European community.

Frommer, Arthur. *The New World of Travel 1988*. New York:
Prentice-Hall, 1988. 366p. $12.95 (paperback). ISBN 0-13-048886-0.

> Among Arthur Frommer's many excellent travel books, this one
> particularly is outstanding in its focus on "vacations that cater to
> your mind, your spirit and your sense of thrift." The book is a
> very good read, with wide-ranging topics that "reveal a thousand
> life-enhancing secrets of the travel trade." Chapter IX, "Travel
> Opportunities for the Older American—What's Helpful, What
> Isn't," is especially noteworthy for older travelers. Examples of
> the types of lists found in the appendix include: 21 of America's
> Foremost Discount Travel Agencies; 19 of the Nation's Leading
> Discount Cruise Agencies; 42 of America's Foremost Bed-and-
> Breakfast Reservations Organizations. This book should be
> required reading for any traveler looking for new ideas and
> sound travel information.

Grimes, Paul. *The New York Times Practical Traveler*. New York:
Random House, 1985. 411p. $10.95 (paperback). ISBN 0-8129-1152-0.

> Culled from his "Practical Traveler" column for *The New York
> Times,* this book offers a wealth of information for any traveler.
> As the cover of the book notes, the author discusses all you need

to know about hotels, insurance, travel agents, car rentals, luggage, passports, charters, foreign currency, cruises, traveling with kids, customs, medical emergencies, special diets, traveling with pets, railroad passes, tours, special discounts, etc. Those topics are only the beginning as the author goes on to cover such items as guidebooks, travel gadgets, complaints and legal recourse, plus special information about traveling in South America, Africa, China, and the Soviet Bloc. One chapter deals specifically with discounts for older travelers. The narrative is explicit, easily readable, and full of interesting anecdotal material.

Harris, Robert W. *Gypsying after 40: A Guide to Adventure & Self-Discovery*. Santa Fe: John Muir Publications, 1987. 253p. $12.95 (paperback). ISBN 0-912528-71-0.

Warning: For the true traveler—as opposed to the occasional tourist—this outstanding, charming treatise on later-life "gypsying" may become dog-eared and worn before its time as one turns to it over and over again for travel insights and personal discoveries. As Harris notes in his introduction, this book is for those who "suffer from living with unfinished business, curiosity about distant places, fascination with exotic people, passion to see what's on the other side of the mountain and the lust to satisfy these urges. In this book we want to feed that passion and tell you how to fulfill your dreams." And he does so, with a flair for describing the magic of new places, while incorporating a wealth of pragmatic details. He alternates between astonishingly practical advice never even needed by most visitors to an area (i.e., which kind of high rubber boots to wear in Mideastern bathrooms) to lyrical ruminations on the glory of personal growth and discovery encountered when people travel to truly fulfill their dreams. *Gypsying after 40* is an excellent sourcebook for opening one's mind to travel possibilities regardless of one's preferred travel style.

Ledray, Linda E. *The Single Woman's Vacation Guide*. New York: Fawcett Columbine, 1988. 506p. $9.95 (paperback). ISBN 0-499-90210-2.

Many single women, especially older women, may have reservations about traveling alone. Although not aimed specifically at any age group, this book could be valuable to any woman who has never traveled alone. The author offers basic travel information for the novice traveler, along with abundant inspiration to give it a try. A section detailing over 20 vacation spots includes the author's rating of the general ambience, social climate, and activities of each. Also covered are contacts for tour information, tips for trip preparation and getting there, treasures to purchase, exploring the area, where to stay, where to eat, and interesting side trips.

McGraw Publications. *The Traveler's Handbook*. Edison, NJ: Hunter Publishing, Inc., 1988. 112p. $8.95 (paperback). ISBN 1-55650-169-2.

The Traveler's Handbook is a quick-reading, easy-reference book of travel tips ranging from protecting one's money to correct social behavior in various countries. Although oriented primarily to the business traveler, the book is worth a quick perusal by any international traveler. Especially useful are charts and diagrams for currency regulations, time zones and time comparisons (i.e., hours ahead or behind Greenwich Mean Time), world weather, world holidays, type of electrical current by country, international airports, airport terminal signs, and international highway signs.

McNair, Sylvia. *Vacation Places Rated*. New York: Rand McNally & Company, 1986. 218p. $12.95 (paperback). ISBN 0-528-88012-8.

Vacation Places Rated offers an interesting, comprehensive overview of 107 popular vacation destinations in every state except Iowa, Nebraska, and North Dakota. An introductory chart lists attributes for each area including: area in square miles, population, bright lights (contains one or more cities over 500,000 population), warm winters (average temperatures of 60 degrees Fahrenheit in December and January), seacoast, lakes, mountains, plenty of snow, open space (fewer than 40 persons per square mile), and special attractions. Subsequent chapters rank, and explain in detail, areas that offer the following: "blessings of nature"; sports and recreation; lodging, food and transportation; historical landmarks and museums; entertainment; and finally, a ranking combining all the former factors. A final section allows readers to rank various destinations according to their own criteria.

Malott, Gene, and Adele Malott. *Get Up and Go: A Guide for the Mature Traveler.* San Francisco: Gateway Books, 1989. 325p. $10.95 (paperback). ISBN 0-933-469-06-3.

> This very readable book is designed to take both the hassle and high cost out of travel. Recognizing that older people want comfort and security as well as economy when they travel, the Malotts deal extensively with questions of health and safety. There are chapters on plane, train, bus, ship, automobile, RV, and even "armchair" travel. Tips include how to choose a travel agent, obtain the best accommodations at the lowest rates, get a passport, protect one's home while away, and bring home travel memories on film. Appendixes list hundreds of phone numbers for gathering information, making reservations, and securing special deals available to seniors. Also included are explanations of travel terms, work sheets, currency tables, and translations.

Massow, Rosalind, *Travel Easy—The Practical Guide for People over 50.* (An AARP book.) Glenview, IL: Scott Foresman & Co., 1985. 272p. $8.95 (paperback). ISBN 0-673-24817-8.

> In this valuable handbook published by the American Association of Retired Persons, veteran traveler Rosalind Massow presents clearly written, practical information and travel tips especially for the older traveler. It explains much a novice or experienced traveler needs to know to plan a trip, and how to get the most for the time and money spent. The book includes maps of major tourist areas worldwide, highlighting countries and capitals; lists of state and national tourist and travel offices; and information on overseas travel—from passports and visas to shopping, customs, and handling foreign currency. Massow also includes interesting "insider" information such as why some hotels overbook, why an airline may not accept a ticket from another airline when a flight has been canceled—and what to do about it, or at least how to be prepared for it. Two additional helpful sections on medical and dental first aid and how to find medical help are offered by Norton M. Luger, M.D., and Lyonel S. Hildes, D.D.S.

Miller, Saul. *Super Traveler.* New York: Holt, Rinehart and Winston, 1980. 367p. $14.95 (hardbound). ISBN 0-03-049571-7.

Subtitled "The Complete Handbook of Essential Facts, Regulations, Rights, and Remedies for Trouble-free International Travel," this book provides a useful overview of various legal, medical, and consumer problems a traveler might encounter while abroad. Although seriously out of date in certain areas due to rapidly changing political conditions and domestic deregulation of recent years, the book nevertheless points out important issues to investigate. In the absence of updated information in print, a traveler is forewarned to ask at appropriate government offices or travel information sources as to current regulations on such matters as legal rights of redress from airlines, hotels, and tour operators; current requirements for passports, visas, and vaccinations; and taking personal property into and out of various countries. Legal rights involving accidents, lost or stolen items, and other misunderstandings are also discussed.

Palder, Edward L. *The Retirement Sourcebook*. Kensington, MD: Woodbine House, Inc., 1989. 521p. $14.95 (paperback). ISBN 0-933149-24-7.

The Retirement Sourcebook is a comprehensive reference guide to every topic of concern or interest to today's retiree. Part One covers consumer information such as banks and credit unions, insurance, investments, and legal services; Part Two covers home and family life; and Part Three details travel and leisure opportunities. The travel section lists toll-free hotlines, brochures, pamphlets, books, and organizations of interest to the older traveler, including information on transportation, domestic and foreign travel, and travel for the handicapped.

Palmer, Paige. *The Senior Citizen's Guide to Budget Travel in Europe*. Babylon, NY: Pilot Books, 1990. $3.95 (paperback).

The Senior Citizen's Guide is an abbreviated but useful guide to some aspects of travel planning: bargain hunting in accommodations and fares, passports, insurance, health and fitness, medical records, money matters, sightseeing, and local transportation. Additional sections cover gift buying, packing checklists, and a listing of European government tourist offices located in major cities of the United States and Canada.

————. *The Senior Citizen's Guide to Budget Travel in the United States and Canada.* Babylon, NY: Pilot Books, 1989. Rev. ed. 64p. $3.95 (paperback). ISBN 0-87576-103-8.

> This compact guide lists motel and restaurant chains in the United States and Canada offering senior discounts, budget chain motel headquarters, and where to write for selected rail, air, or camping discounts. It also catalogs state tourism offices, along with a capsulized list of each state's major attractions.

Philcox, Phil, and Beverly Boe, comps. *Toll-Free Travel and Vacation Information Directory.* Babylon, NY: Pilot Books, 1988. 39p. $3.95 (paperback). ISBN 0-87576-135-6.

> Unless a traveler has unlimited time and inclination to browse through a national directory of toll-free telephone listings for travel information sources, this directory can be indispensable for anyone planning a vacation, looking for the best buys, or needing any other travel information. Listed are toll-free numbers for airlines, apartment and condominium rentals, cruise lines, discount travel services, hotel and motel chains, medical and travel insurance, senior citizen and student travel sources, tour operators, domestic and foreign tourist information offices, and other useful numbers.

Seales, John Baldwin. *An Insider's Guide to the Travel Game.* Leucadia, CA: Rand Editions, 1983. 178p. $7.95 (paperback). ISBN 0-914488-28-7.

> Subtitled "How To Get the Most for Your Travel Dollar," this outstanding book offers several valuable suggestions for achieving that goal. Since the travel industry is so complex and changes so rapidly, Seales focuses on what questions to ask, how to get them answered, and how to evaluate the answers given. His valuable guidelines should help keep travelers from falling prey to less than forthright claims, and teach them to constantly search for value rather than judge a product or service on price alone. The book also includes a section on unique special-interest tours.

Weaver, Frances. *Last Year I Went around the World . . . This Year I Plan To Go Elsewhere.* Golden, CO: Fulcrum, Inc., 1989. 102p. $9.95 (paperback). ISBN 1-55591-032-7.

This charming little book is highly recommended for any traveler, but mainly the mature woman traveler, especially if she is single. As described on the book's jacket, the author is "a 64-year-old mother of four and grandmother of eight who writes, lectures and travels in a one-woman crusade against the loneliness and boredom of aging." This lighthearted guide offers a wide range of valuable travel advice and ideas, liberally sprinkled with entertaining and informative anecdotes from Weaver's own travel experiences, and a big dose of inspiration to quit fussing and get moving. Her upbeat, encouraging attitude may best be summed up in her conclusion to Chapter 2: "Ready? All you need is an open mind and a big map."

Webster, Harriet. *Trips for Those over 50.* Dublin, NH: Yankee Publishing, 1988. 175p. $9.95 (paperback). ISBN 0-89909-158-X.

This charming guidebook from *Yankee Magazine* details numerous interesting and historic areas and attractions in New England of particular interest to older travelers. The trips cover a number of different subjects, interests, and lifestyles, arranged by region within the six New England states. A helpful chart provides a quick reference to the many categories the author has covered for each trip: park/nature areas, "old-fashioned" fun, water sports, extended stays, year-round spots, local transportation, one-stop attractions, nonwalking tours, off-season specials, and handicap accessibility. Also included are several encouraging travel hints for single travelers, for those who prefer not to drive, and for those who would like to "go back to school" while enjoying a pleasurable vacation.

Weintz, Caroline, and Walter Weintz. *The Discount Guide for Travelers over 55.* New York: E. P. Dutton, Inc., 1983. 278p. $7.95 (paperback). ISBN 0-525-93281-X.

Although prices listed in this extensive discount guide are by now out of date, *The Discount Guide* provides some good starting points for mature travelers to seek discounts for hotels and motels; plane, train, and bus travel; sightseeing attractions; and car rentals. Those listed in this book are organized by state or county and city in the United States, Canada, Europe, Mexico, and the Caribbean.

Specialty Travel

The term "specialty travel" encompasses a wide range of out-of-the-ordinary or special-interest travel experiences organized around sports, study, volunteering, and traveling with grandchildren, for example. Numerous travel books focus on specialty vacation activities such as skiing, photography, museums, food and wine, gardens, festivals, and more. The following are a sampling of what is available, as recommended and used by a number of senior travelers.

American Hiking Society. *Helping Out in the Outdoors*. Washington, DC. 96p. $6 (paperback).

An annual directory listing volunteer jobs and internships available in national parks and forests and other public lands. Positions include such jobs as campground hosts, trail crews, fire lookouts, historical researchers, wildlife observers, and wilderness/backcountry rangers. Listings are arranged by states or regions, and describe the types of volunteer positions available, requirements for the positions, and benefits available. Contact: American Hiking Society, 1015 31st Sreet, NW, Washington, DC 20007; (703) 385-3252.

American Sunbathing Association. *The Nudist Park Guide*. 200p. $13.

A complete directory of North American nudist parks and clubs. The guide includes maps, information about facilities, directions, and phone numbers of more than 200 nudist parks and clubs in the United States and Canada. Outstanding, tasteful photographs illustrate people and families of all ages who are members of the various clubs. Most parks offer overnight accommodations, from tent and RV camping to motel-type rooms or apartments, plus full use of recreational and sports facilities. Contact: American Sunbathing Association, 1703 N. Main Street, Kissimmee, FL 34744-9988; (407) 933-2064.

Campbell, James. *Senior Guide: Day-Hiking in the Southwestern National Parks and Monuments*. Gold Hill, OR: WestPark Books, 1986. 220p. $11.95 (paperback). ISBN 0-936205-11-3.

Dr. James Campbell, an ecologist and former park ranger, has taught outdoor skills and natural history for many years. In this book he uses his considerable expertise to define safe and rewarding day-hiking for seniors. His humorous, animated style makes the book a pleasure to read even if the reader never plans to don hiking boots and backpack for a day on the trail. Part I offers full details on choosing a trail; clothing; equipment; special considerations for older hikers such as weather, altitude, and other hazards; and numerous safety hints. Part II describes 20 magnificent day-hikes in various southwestern locations. Each description includes pertinent information on where to find the trailhead, distance, elevation, difficulty of grade, ranger station location, best seasons to hike, common plants and animals, and cautionary notes on water, lightning, loose rock, etc. Each factual outline is accompanied by a fascinating little travelogue detailing what to look for on the trail, along with bits of historical and ecological information.

Crawford, J. *Directory of Low-Cost Vacations with a Difference.* Babylon, NY: Pilot Books, 1989. 68p. $5.95 (paperback). ISBN 0-87576-122-4.

> This handy directory is a worldwide guide to over 300 fascinating alternatives to the ordinary vacation. It covers bed & breakfast or farm vacations, home exchanges, people-to-people programs, senior citizen programs, student exchanges, study groups, and vacation work programs. The names, addresses, and a brief description of organizations offering these unusual vacations are listed.

Hyman, Mildred. *Elderhostels: The Student's Choice.* Santa Fe: John Muir Publications, 1989. 253p. $12.95 (paperback). ISBN 0-945465-28-9.

> Over 1,200 Elderhostel programs in the United States and abroad have attracted hundreds of thousands of older adults each year. Author Mildred Hyman noticed, however, that the course offerings, lodgings, food service, and access varied widely from place to place. This book is a result of interviewing hundreds of veteran hostelers as to the best and the worst of 100 of the most popular programs both at home and abroad. Each listing evaluates the instructors, environment, housing, food, programs, admittance requirements, and available transportation, plus information on the host institution's unique attributes

and shortcomings. As many hostelers remarked, there is no "worst" program, but many could use improvement. This guide fills in the important, albeit subjective, gaps left by the brief descriptions in the Elderhostel catalog about details such as a hilly campus or lack of shower facilities, or poor organization of field trips, or whether a private car is a necessity. This book is especially recommended for novice Elderhostelers.

Institute of International Education. *Vacation Study Abroad 1990*. New York: Institute of International Education, 1989. 223p. $24.95 (paperback). ISBN 0-87206-173-6.

For the eternal student searching for a learning vacation, this directory is a gold mine of information on over 1,300 study programs and short courses geared to all levels of postsecondary education: undergraduate, graduate, adult, and professional. The programs listed are offered by U.S. colleges and universities, foreign universities and language schools, and by nonprofit and proprietary educational organizations. Although final and complete information must be obtained directly from program sponsors, this directory provides a good introduction to available courses by listing the program sponsor and name, location, dates, subjects, credit, eligibility, program highlights, housing, and costs. A useful introductory chapter helps newcomers to foreign study plan ahead and avoid common mistakes.

League of American Wheelmen. *Bicycle USA TourFinder*. 48p. $25 (paperback; includes organizational membership).

A comprehensive catalog of bicycle tours and touring services in the United States and 40 foreign countries. It lists where operators run their tours, miles ridden per day and per tour, and services and accommodations provided by the operators. The 1990 edition includes a number of feature articles about various tours, plus two profiles of senior members: a 71-year-old man who set a new record for bicycling at the Third World Senior Games, and a 73-year-old woman with 61 years of riding experience about to embark on a 3,200-mile "Across America" ride from Los Angeles to Boston. *TourFinder* is available for $5 from: League of American Wheelmen, 6707 Whitestone Rd., Suite 209PR, Baltimore, MD 21207.

McMillon, Bill. *Volunteer Vacations*. Chicago: Chicago Review Press, 1987. 175p. $11.95 (paperback). ISBN 1-55652-002-6.

> This directory of volunteer vacations contains two main sections. The first is an alphabetical listing of organizations such as Earthwatch, the Sierra Club, and the Cousteau Society, as well as projects run by religious groups, social services agencies, universities, and other special-interest groups—both in the United States and abroad—that recruit volunteers to assist them on short-term working vacations. The types of projects the organizations offer; their location, cost, and time of year they operate; and requirements for volunteers are included. The second section contains a number of handy cross-referenced indexes to define the types of volunteer projects available and which organizations offer such projects. The indexes include: project type (scientific, ecological, social action, and other special interests), cost, location, season, and length of stay.

O'Byrne, Robert. *Senior Golf*. La Fox, IL: Winchester Press, 1977. 174p. $8.95 (paperback). ISBN 0-87691-231-5.

> A "senior golfer" is defined by the United States Golf Association as a man over 55 or a woman over 50. This book provides senior golfers with extensive information on golf vacations in the United States and abroad, arranged by region and then within each state. Famous golf resorts are enumerated, as well as those that, in the author's opinion, offer good value and pleasure. A final section indicates which resorts offer good retirement possibilities.

Sobek's International Explorers Society. *Sobek's Adventure Vacations*. 4th ed. Philadelphia: Running Press, 1986. 140p. $12.95 (paperback). ISBN 0-89471-428-7.

> *Sobek's Adventure Vacations'* exquisite prose and outstanding photographs make it a captivating armchair travelogue for those with wilderness fantasies. For those who want to indulge those fantasies, the book offers specific descriptions, itineraries, activities, rank of difficulty or skill level, and an indication of moderate to premium pricing per trip. Chapters are organized by world region: Africa, Asia, Europe, Oceania, North and South America, and the Poles. An activity index helps a reader find that

bicycling tours are available only in India, China, Japan, Switzerland, France, eastern Europe, and Tasmania, while rafting trips span the globe from the Colorado River to the Ganges. The index is not complete, however, as dogsledding is listed as an activity and a dogsledding trip is offered, but that topic is not shown in the index. Access to the listed tour operators or access to further trip information is offered only through Sobek's Expeditions in Angels Camp, California.

Specialty Travel Index. *The Adventure Vacation Catalog.* New York: Simon and Schuster, 1984. 382p. $14.95 (paperback). ISBN 0-671-50770-2.

> *The Adventure Vacation Catalog* is a comprehensive sourcebook of adventure travel and special-interest travel opportunities throughout the world. It lists almost 400 tour operators and 600 different activities from archaeology to yacht charter. In between are such travel possibilities as ballooning, bird watching, caving, gourmet cooking and folklore tours, language study, llama/mule/camel expeditions, railway trips, research expeditions, and covered-wagon trips. All the trips in the book are guided adventure vacations under skilled leadership. Trips are open to all ages, but may specify certain skill levels. Chapters are organized by activity. Each includes descriptions and requirements of various trips, tour operators who offer them, and important questions to ask. Extensive indexes also list foreign and state tourism offices, clubs and associations, tour operators, and trips by category or geographic area.

————. *Specialty Travel Index.* 132p. $5 individually; $8 for one-year subscription (two issues) (paperback).

> A directory listing thousands of special-interest trips. Activities range from archaeology and ballooning to health and fitness trips, opera, photography, river rafting, safaris, train trips, and many more. The directory is indexed by activity (i.e., art history, jungle expeditions, seniors/retired) and the countries offering such opportunities. The next section reverses the order and indexes by country and the activities available in each. The final section lists tour providers and descriptions of their programs, locations, costs, etc. Contact: Specialty Travel Index, 305 San Anselmo Avenue, Suite 217, San Anselmo, CA 94960; (415) 459-4900.

Transitions Abroad. *Educational Travel Directory*. 64p. $6.95 (paperback).

> Published annually, the directory contains country-by-country listings and descriptions of publications and organizations that offer jobs, study/travel programs, special-interest travel opportunities, and home and hospitality exchanges. Contact: Transitions Abroad, P.O. Box 344, Amherst, MA 01004; (413) 256-0373.

Accommodations

> A number of excellent books listing accommodations from bed & breakfast lodging to deluxe resorts are accessible for use by the mature traveler. The following have been recommended and used by a number of older travelers, but are only a sampling of what is available.

Beerbower, Albert C., and Verna E. Beerbower. *Swap and Go: Home Exchanging Made Easy*. New York: Frommer/Pasmantier (a division of Simon & Schuster), 1986. 250p. $10.95 (paperback). ISBN 0-671-60228-4.

> The Beerbowers are veteran home exchangers who explain in detail all the money-saving benefits of a home exchange, and precisely how to do it. Instructions cover how to advertise one's home, write introductory letters, and nail down specific dates and arrangements, with additional hints on being a good guest in someone else's home. The book also includes information on home rentals, plus various tips on low-cost travel. Helpful appendixes list vacation home–exchange agencies, foreign and local tourist offices, and U.S. consular offices abroad.

Campus Travel Service. *U.S. and Worldwide Travel Accommodations Guide*. Laguna Beach, CA: Campus Travel Service, 1989. $11.95. ISBN 0-945499-00-0.

> The *U.S. and Worldwide Travel Accommodations Guide* is an outstanding sourcebook for inexpensive lodging at over 600 colleges and universities in the United States, Canada, Europe, New Zealand, and Australia. Prices range from $12–$24 a day for well-managed, safe, clean, comfortable dormitory lodgings available by the day, week, or month. They vary from single and

double rooms to bedroom apartments and suites with kitchens. Most are open during the summer, some year-round. The guide indicates price per person, meals (if included), available dates, and other information such as age restrictions, plus nearby activities and attractions. Also included are 20 special reports such as how to save on travel expenses, helpful hints for overseas travelers, free sources of vacation planning information, bed & breakfast reservation services, home-exchange services, and U.S. and foreign tourist offices. The only flaw in this excellent guide is some inattention to proofreading; readers should be prepared to double-check addresses, phone numbers, and other information that may have figures transposed or contain other inaccuracies.

Lanier, Pamela. *The Complete Guide to Bed & Breakfasts, Inns & Guesthouses in the United States and Canada.* Santa Fe: John Muir Publications, 1990. 485p. $15.95 (paperback). ISBN 0-945465-43-2.

Voted the best guidebook by innkeepers across the country, this information-packed volume is valuable for those who enjoy the personal service and unique atmosphere of a bed & breakfast (B&B) inn or guest home, often at less cost than impersonal hotels or motels. Comprehensive information is offered on over 5,500 inns, listed by city and state, including such items as: type of accommodation, type of breakfast and/or other meals, prices, credit cards accepted, bathrooms, and reservations information. Listed are restrictions, if any, on children, pets, or smoking, as well as accessibility for the handicapped. Also included are hundreds of reservation service organizations that will book rooms in inexpensive guest houses or private homes. An intriguing finale to the book lists B&Bs with special features such as antiques, distinctive decor, fishing, gardens, golf, and gourmet or vegetarian meals.

Soule, Sandra W. *America's Wonderful Little Hotels and Inns, The West Coast, 1990.* New York: St. Martin's Press, 1990. 354p. $12.95 (paperback). ISBN 0-312-03282-X.

This book is representative of an entire series of *America's Wonderful Little Hotels and Inns* guides, which are organized by region: the United States and Canada, New England, the Middle Atlantic, the West Coast, and the South. Another similar series covers Europe and Great Britain/Ireland. Chapters begin with a brief description and history of the area, followed by listings of specific accommodations by city. Information includes number of rooms and amenities; facilities such as lounge or parlor areas, parking, swimming, etc.; location; credit cards accepted; rates; and available extras such as handicap accessibility, cribs, pet accommodations, and foreign languages spoken. No money is charged or accepted for a lodging to be included in the guide. Helpful additions to each listing are descriptions, comments, and evaluations from travelers who have stayed at the inns.

Airlines

Barbare, Richard, and Linda Hafendorfer. *Traveler's Guide to Major U.S. Airports.* Atlanta: Peachtree Publishers, Ltd. 1989. 240p. $6.95 (paperback). ISBN 0-934601-70-4.

> This fascinating pocket guide offers hope and relief to travelers who find themselves in an airport, wondering what to do, either to avoid the excruciating numbness of waiting around, or to escape the organized chaos of other travelers rushing to be some-where else. This succinct guide is packed with useful facts on dining, shopping, ground transportation, and available traveler's services at 30 major U.S. airports. Also included are airport maps and listings of handicapped services, and local airline numbers and locations. An intriguing conclusion to each airport's information outline is a section called "Time To Kill," offering possibilities for sightseeing and entertainment by availability in one, two, three, or four hours from the airport. A final chapter offers helpful advice on possible airline problems and passenger rights.

Martin, Bob. *Fly There for Less.* Kissimmee, FL: TeakWood Press, 1990. 169p. $8.95 (paperback). ISBN 0-937281-02-6.

> This informative book supplies both novice and seasoned travelers with outstanding information on flying—and how to do it for less than standard fares. Coverage ranges from basic questions to ask to be sure one has gotten the lowest possible fare to what the author labels "creative techniques" for obtaining rock-bottom rates. Older adults with travel flexibility could avail themselves of many more of his suggestions than those with family or job obligations. *Fly There for Less* explains

little-known fare types, tells how to find low fares, reveals where to buy airline tickets for the biggest savings, and details circumstances offering air-travel bargains. A section on senior discounts amplifies even further the possibilities for flying for less.

Trains

Amtrak. *Amtrak's America.* 92p. Free (paperback).

Amtrak's America is an annual promotional directory of Amtrak's routes; tour, sightseeing, and hotel packages; train accommodations, including services for disabled passengers; and fare, reservations, and ticketing information. A valuable map delineates the national rail passenger system. Also included is information on rail/air/sail tours, escorted national park and circle tours, and other vacation packages. Available from travel agents or the Amtrak Distribution Center, P.O. Box 7717, Itasca, IL 60143; (800) 872-7245.

Scheller, William G. *Train Trips: Exploring America by Rail.* Charlotte, NC: The East Woods Press, 1984. $9.95 (paperback). ISBN 0-88742-000-1.

Train Trips offers a basic primer on routes and cities served by Amtrak and Canada's Via Rail. Scheller examines the history of America's passenger trains as well as present-day equipment. He covers dining on board or what to pack for do-it-yourself meals, as well as tips on baggage, ticketing, itineraries, and so forth. The remainder of the book serves as a guide to 52 major American and Canadian cities, including a detailed description of the railway stations, plus selected nearby attractions, accommodations, and restaurants. The latter information should be verified for up-to-date particulars.

Turpin, Kathryn S., and Marvin L. Saltzman. *Eurail Guide—How To Travel Europe and All the World by Train.* Malibu, CA: Eurail Guide Annual, 1991. 816p. $14.95 (paperback). ISBN 0-912442-21-2.

Having grown from 96 pages in its first edition to 816 in its twenty-first, this book—as the cover announces in bold letters— "describes every rail trip in the world a tourist might want to take." This fascinating, informative guide details departure and arrival times for thousands of trains worldwide. Train services such as eating, sleeping, and air-conditioning are covered, as well as what to see and do in nearly 2,000 cities and places in 112 countries. A travel tips section offers helpful advice about baggage, reservations, connections, and how to plan a rail itinerary, along with maps of Britain and 16 Eurailpass countries. Details for each country cover every particular from national holidays to a translation of train and railway-station signs. Train passes and discounts, including senior discounts, are specified. The book is published in a convenient size for carrying in a purse or hand luggage, and should be a high-priority item for every train traveler.

Group and Bus Touring

Gleasner, Diana C. *Touring by Bus at Home and Abroad.* An AARP Book. Glenview, IL: Scott, Foresman and Company, 1990. 158p. $10.95 (paperback). ISBN 0-673-24927-1.

Written in a breezy, friendly-as-a-tour-guide style, the author details every aspect of bus travel from intercity transportation to international luxury tours. Dispelled are the old myths of sleazy bus stations; hurried, regimented tours; or uncomfortable, smoke-filled, diesel-fumed buses. Introduced are modern motorcoaches with climate control, reclining seats, spacious aisles—even some with card tables, galleys, and portable bars. Gleasner offers important advice on all aspects of group travel from how to avoid a scam to the joys—as well as the possible disadvantages—of bus touring. Separate chapters consider mature, single, and disabled travelers, including helpful resources for each. The book is liberally sprinkled with Gleasner's reminiscences and personal experiences of bus tours, along with a large dose of inspiration to get up and go—and, more importantly, enjoy it.

Warren, Stuart. *Bus Touring: A Guide to Charter Vacations, U.S.A.* Santa Fe: John Muir Publications, 1989. 167p. $9.95 (paperback). ISBN 0-912528-95-8.

The travel trade publication *Travel Weekly* noted, "What many mature travelers want can best be found on a motorcoach tour." The definitive primer on motorcoach touring can be found in this useful handbook by Stuart Warren. The author, an experienced tour guide, offers valuable information on the styles and procedures of major tour operators, and advises how to select a tour. Also covered are tips on packing, health issues, and a myriad of other practical concerns such as carrying drinking water on board since bus water may not be potable, or keeping medications in a small ice chest, if necessary. The second section details eight popular touring corridors in North America, based on the routing practices of major tour companies. Not written as a guidebook, this segment instead highlights general trends about regional weather, comfort, shopping, cuisine, flora and fauna, and sites common to many itineraries in each region.

Recreational Vehicles

Alderman, Bill, and Eleanore Wilson. *Recreational Vehicles: Finding the Best Buy*. Chicago: Bonus Books, 1989. 123p. $6.95. ISBN 0-933893-78-7.

> This practical book answers key questions for those considering the purchase of an RV. Both authors have years of RV selling experience and have owned or worked with practically every type of RV mentioned in the text. They provide authoritative answers to the questions of whether to buy a new or used vehicle, as well as options available in each RV category. The book is well written, with good illustrations. There are checklists to help the buyer, trade-in hints, and even a chapter on how to get financing and insurance.

Boardman, John. *Living on Wheels: The Complete Guide to Motorhomes*. Blue Ridge Summit, PA: Tab Books, 1987. 296p. $19.95 (hardback). ISBN 0-8306-9218-5. $12.60 (paperback). ISBN 0-8306-9118-9.

> *Living on Wheels* is an excellent, clearly written, and easily understood technical book about RVs. Written in first person, the author describes his own experiences with RVs, backed up with expert information from RV manufacturers. The book covers RV design and construction as well as maintenance of everything from the drive train to roof air conditioners. Boardman also explains in detail how to differentiate a good warranty from

a bad one. Detailed illustrations and several good troubleshooting charts help give readers a sound basis to avoid as many potential problems as possible. An appendix lists defects by specific models for National Highway Traffic Safety Administration motorhome safety recalls from 1976–1986.

Dunlop, Richard. *On the Road in an RV.* Washington, DC: American Association of Retired Persons; Glenview, IL: Scott, Foresman, and Co., 1987. 194p. $8.95 (paperback). ISBN 0-673-24839-9.

> *On the Road in an RV* should be required reading for anyone considering RV travel. Valuable information ranges from a comparison of various kinds of trailers and rigs to suit individual needs, to driving tips on coping with such problems as wide turns, buffeting winds, backing up, and encountering other large vehicles on the road. Dunlop has included comprehensive information on financing and insurance, plus explicit details on taking an RV into Canada or Mexico, or traveling in an RV in Europe. Various appendixes outline RV rental sources; RV categories and descriptions, including price ranges; and campground and RV club listings.

Franz, Carl, and Steve Rogers. Lorena Havens, ed. *The People's Guide to RV Camping in Mexico.* Santa Fe: John Muir Publications, 1989. 308p. $13.95 (paperback). ISBN 0-912528-56-7.

> This useful guidebook covers every detail of camping in Mexico from repelling mosquitoes to exploding the "bandit myth." The authors describe driving conditions, how to find a campsite, how to stay healthy, and how to get a permit, license, and insurance. They also offer an extensive directory of formal and informal campgrounds throughout Mexico, including details (from personal experience) such as not parking in front of a soccer field's goalposts—to avoid waking up in the morning surrounded by an agitated team waiting to play. Appendixes include an extensive list of recommended reading, where and how to get maps (not in Mexico), and camping and travel clubs. A technical vocabulary list illustrates entire phrases for such needs as asking for an oil change or getting the wheel cylinders rebuilt.

Geraghty, John, and Bill Estes. *RX for RV Performance and Mileage.* Agoura, CA: TL Enterprises, 1983. 360p. $14.95 (paperback). ISBN 0-934798-06-0.

RV technical and diagnostic experts explain the tricks of getting maximum power from an RV engine, and help in determining the causes of engine problems. They also provide important facts about axle ratios, tire selection, and other factors affecting performance. Hundreds of diagrams and photographs provide tips on engine overhaul, troubleshooting batteries, and tuning various types of Ford, Chevrolet, and Dodge engines.

Groehne, Janet, and Gordon Groehne. *Living Aboard Your Recreational Vehicle: A Guide to the Fulltime Life on Wheels.* Merrillville, IN: ICS Books, 1986. 225p. $10.95 (paperback). ISBN 0-934802-31-9.

Living Aboard Your Recreational Vehicle is an interesting, easy-reading, no-nonsense book that explains in minute detail the pros and cons of living full-time aboard an RV. The authors, who've lived as full-timers for over 20 years, present important advice on everything from selling a houseful of possessions and making the break from home-base living to the real costs of living on the road. They cover the smallest details of everyday life: food preparation, housekeeping, traveling with pets, packing, keeping up with the mail, and even ways to maintain hobbies, volunteer, or earn money on the road. This book would be especially valuable for those contemplating living or traveling extensively in an RV.

Hanley Publishing Co. *Hanley's Buyer's Guide to Van Conversions.* Wheeling, IL: Hanley Publishing Co., 1989. 78p. $2.95 (paperback).

This handy guide lists over 50 van-conversion manufacturers and illustrations of their products. The reader service format provides access to additional data from manufacturers. The introduction provides tips on van selection, a discussion of each chassis manufacturer's product, and the contribution made by the converter.

Howells, John. *RV Travel in Mexico.* San Francisco: Gateway Books, 1989. 228p. $9.95 (paperback). ISBN 0-933469-08-X.

RV Travel in Mexico presents detailed advice on every aspect of RV travel and part-year living in Mexico. The author has interviewed hundreds of U.S. couples in RV parks all over Mexico and has blended their experiences and his own into up-to-the-minute advice on how to go, where to go, where to stay, and why RV travel is a safe, economical, and comfortable way to enjoy the country. Howells writes with a friendly, humorous approach to RV life and travel—and potential problems—in this foreign country. A particularly valuable vocabulary list shows English-to-Spanish translations of terms usually unavailable in the average pocket dictionary—words such as head gasket, lug wrench, Phillips screwdriver, and voltage regulator. An additional Spanish-to-English listing could be handed to a mechanic to point out words the American traveler might not be able to pronounce or would not understand when spoken. In short, the author leaves little to chance to stand in the way of successful RV living.

Intertec. *RV Owners Operation & Maintenance Manual.* Overland Park, KS: Intertec Publishing Corp., 1985. 160p. $5.95.

> Designed for the novice RVer, this manual provides explanations and illustrations concerning the electrical, LP-gas, and water systems. Useful information about winterization, storage, and other topics concerning the care, maintenance, loading, and operating of an RV is carefully explained. The book also includes tips on warranties and insurance, and suggests needed supplies for efficient operation.

Moeller, Bill and Jan Moeller. *Full-Time RVing: A Complete Guide to Life on the Open Road.* Agoura, CA: TL Enterprises, Inc., 1986. 340p. $14.95 (paperback). ISBN 0-934798-14-1.

> This solid and very readable reference text answers dozens of questions frequently asked by those who dream of traveling full-time in an RV. It covers what to expect in the full-timing RV lifestyle and its costs, RV selection, and driving procedures. It provides well-illustrated chapters on storage, maintenance for RV electrical and plumbing systems, LP gas, and climate control as well as electronic equipment. Campground selection, procedures, and manners, and traveling with children and pets are also covered.

National LP-Gas Association. *Directory of LP-Gas Refilling Stations.* Oak Brook, IL: National LP-Gas Association, 1986. 300p. $3.95 (paperback).

A handy resource guide for RV users to more than 10,000 LP-gas refilling locations in the United States and Canada. Some listings provide directions along with the address, phone number, and hours when service is available. The book also provides safety tips in the use of propane gas.

Peterson, Joe and Kay Peterson. *Encyclopedia for RVers*. Livingston, TX: RoVers Publications, 1989. 192p. $7.95 (paperback). ISBN 0-910449-06-1.

This book is an excellent compendium of facts and information for full-time RVers. Organized in an easy-to-read, easy-to-find style, the authors cover all facets of RV life from equipment and maintenance to money matters; getting mail on the road; handling medical, insurance, and legal needs; and RV housekeeping. Part II contains a useful directory of RV clubs and organizations, RV suppliers, special-interest clubs and organizations, and groups for single or handicapped RVers.

Thompson, John. *RV Repair and Maintenance Manual*. Agoura, CA: TL Enterprises, 1980. 288p. $12.98 (paperback). ISBN 0-934798-00-1.

A comprehensive technical guide to the do-it-yourself repair and maintenance of all systems found in all types of RVs—trailers, motorhomes, campers, and vans. Twenty-five chapters cover care of brakes, hitches, tires, electrical batteries, power converters, generators, and electrical, sanitation, and water systems. Also explained are the LP-gas system, air conditioners, furnaces, water heaters, insulation, toilets, and absorption refrigerators, plus exterior and interior care and storage. The book contains good, detailed explanations with hundreds of useful drawings.

TL Enterprises, Inc. *Trailer Life's Guide to Full-Time RVing*. Agoura, CA: TL Enterprises, 1982. 354p. $14.95 (paperback). ISBN 0-934798-05-2.

Subtitled "A Complete Guide to Life on the Open Road," this book is a comprehensive guide to all aspects of full-time life in an RV, including selecting the rig, making an RV more livable, and what to look for in a campground. Also covered in full detail are driving and handling practices, safety and protection, traveling with children and pets, and much more.

———. *Trailer Life's RV Buyer's Guide.* Agoura, CA: TL Enterprises, 1989. 280p. $4.95 (paperback).

> This annual Woodall guide lists recreational vehicles by type, by model and manufacturer's name, size specifications, standard and optional features, and materials used in manufacture. It also gives suggested retail prices, and offers a reader service to obtain specific manufacturer information.

Wolfe, Laura. *Living in a Motor Home.* New Hope, PA: Woodsong Graphics, 1984. 121p. $5.95 (paperback). ISBN 0-912661-02-X.

> *Living in a Motor Home* is an informal, personal account of a senior couple's full-time RV life, written for other seniors. The author includes some general tips on choosing an RV, making the transition to full-timing, and RV maintenance. She also covers cleaning and cooking, and offers personal accounts of trips she and her husband have enjoyed, such as a caravan adventure on piggyback rail to Mexico. Their travels in England in an RV are also described. The book may serve to pique one's interest in the full-time RV lifestyle, but lacks comprehensive practical details and resources.

Woodall Publishing Co. *Woodall's RV Buyer's Guide.* Lake Forest, IL: Woodall Publishing Co., 1989. 220p. $4.95 (paperback).

> This annual guide provides straightforward information on over 370 new recreational vehicles to help make informed choices. It provides size specifications, floor plans, photos, standard features, options, construction detail, and suggested retail prices. Chassis, tow vehicles, and RV and travel accessories are also covered.

Camping

CAMPGROUND GUIDES

These popular and informative campground guides are generally available in libraries, bookstores, newsstands, and camping or RV supply stores and dealers.

Armed Forces FAM Camp Guide
U.S. Army AG Publications Center
2800 Eastern Boulevard
Baltimore, MD 21220

> Free guide lists services at FAM camps, open to active and retired military and DOD civilians who travel in RVs.

Don Wright's Guide to Free Campgrounds
Cottage Publications
24396 Pleasant View Drive
Elkhart, IN 46517
$14.95.

> State-by-state listings of free parking places throughout the United States. Those with free water, electricity, or dump station are noted.

KOA Directory/Road Atlas/Camping Guide
Kampgrounds of America
P.O. Box 30558
Billings, MT 51994
$2 by mail, or free at any KOA campground.

> Complete listings of KOA campgrounds, including amenities and directions from nearest town or intersection, plus road atlas.

North America: Rand McNally's Campground and Trailer Park Guide
8255 N. Central Park Avenue
Skokie, IL 60076
$12.95 plus $2 postage.

> Comprehensive listings of campgrounds, plus related information. Updated annually.

Trailer Life's RV Campground and Services Directory
299091 Agoura Road
Agoura, CA 91301
(800) 234-3450
$13.95 plus $3 postage.

> Lists and rates campgrounds across the United States, Canada, and Mexico. Includes a road atlas and lists tourist attractions, as well as related RV services. Also lists Good Sam campgrounds and discounts. Updated annually.

Wheelers RV Resort and Campground Guide
1310 Jarvis Avenue
Elk Grove Village, IL 60007
(800) 323-8899
$10.95 plus $2.25 postage.

Comprehensive listings of campgrounds, plus related camping and RV information. Updated annually.

Woodall Tent Camping Guide
28167 N. Keith Drive, Box 5000
Lake Forest, IL 60045-5000
(800) 323-9076; (708) 362-6700 (in Illinois)

A guide to North American campgrounds, specifically catering to the special requirements of tenting.

Woodall's Campground Directory
28167 N. Keith Drive, Box 5000
Lake Forest, IL 60045-5000
(800) 323-9076; (708) 362-6700 (in Illinois)
Prices vary by edition.

Eleven different editions, ranging from a comprehensive North American edition to eastern and western editions, and eight regional camping guides targeting small groups of states. State-by-state maps, attractions, fishing license fees, etc., plus campground listings. Updated annually.

Cruising

Bannerman, Gary. *Bon Voyage: The Cruise Traveler's Handbook.* Lincolnwood, IL: Passport Books, 1984. $9.95 (paperback). ISBN 0-84429-547-7.

Although not a handbook of pertinent information for a novice cruise traveler, this chatty little book does offer some offbeat, amusing anecdotes about the happenings aboard a cruise ship. Readers will discover a number of "insider" tidbits ranging from who does what to whom—and how often—to what the ship's officers' lifestyles are like, or how much the ship's gift shop will gross in one week. It also includes some odds and ends of cruising information, from how long it may take to disembark to the fact that marriages are no longer performed aboard ship while at sea. There is a cursory overview of the major cruise lines and their ships. The book provides interesting reading for those who like to go beyond the ship's menu or tonnage statistics.

Black, Meme. *Tramp Steamers: A Budget Guide to Ocean Travel.* Reading, MA: Addison-Wesley, 1981. 165p. $6.95 (paperback). ISBN 0-201-03776-9.

> For those who already know they would enjoy the experience of budget cruising on freighters, this book provides important details for the "tramp steamer" traveler. Listed are specific lines, type of trip (i.e., one-way or multiple ports), departure port and destination(s), fares, duration of trip, frequency of trip, and number of passengers accepted. An interesting narrative describes each line's service, food, and accommodations. The author also offers incidental information on baggage limits and transporting cars or pets. Repeated frequently is the admonition: Book reservations for freighter cruises as much as a year in advance, as their popularity and devotees are increasing rapidly.

Deland, Antoinette. *Fielding's Worldwide Cruises.* New York: William Morrow and Company, 1989. 525p. $13.95 (paperback). ISBN 0-688-08047-2.

> This addition to Fielding's travel book series is an enjoyable, comprehensive guide to both ocean and freshwater cruises. It explains cruise details from immunizations and passports to the use of electrical appliances in one's cabin. A comprehensive glossary defines nautical terms. Numerous regional maps illustrate cruise waters and ports for the following areas: the Caribbean, Canada and the U.S. East Coast, the West Coast and Alaska, the Mississippi River, the Far East, the eastern and western Mediterranean, Egypt, the Hawaiian Islands, the South Pacific, South America, the British Isles, and Scandinavia. Descriptions of both fresh and ocean ports of call include attractions and geography, plus special tips on what to do and see. Various cruise lines are rated, including details on their owners, trip focus (singles, families, special-interest groups), type of entertainment on board, and more.

Herring, Charlanne Fields. *The Cruise Answer Book.* Bedford, MA: Mills & Sanderson, 1988. 316p. $9.95 (paperback). ISBN 0-938179-14-4.

This valuable cruise handbook well lives up to its subtitle: "A Comprehensive Guide to the Ships and Ports of the Americas." Herring begins with general information about choosing, booking, and planning for a cruise, including a few sample menus and types and costs of shore excursions. A section on amenities and activities for children will help those planning intergenerational travel. Descriptions of various ports of call include inland waterways of the United States as well as in the Caribbean, the Mexican Riviera, and Alaska and Canada. The author's descriptions of the various ships on each line constitute one of the most extensive and helpful lists available. In addition to the standard data on registry, tonnage, and accommodations, she also includes a full array of practical information such as: sales policy (deposit, final payment date, singles surcharge, etc.), services (from beauty shop and fitness director to room amenities such as telephones, television, and refrigerators), specific tipping policies for each ship, dress policies (number of formal nights, definition of "formal" and so forth), which credit cards are accepted on board, and finally, the type of entertainment offered. Appendixes include an explanation of nautical terms, ship's prefixes, and a guide to the crew and staff on board.

Kane, Robert B., and Barbara W. Kane. *Freighter Voyaging: A Guide to the Joys of Freighter Travel.* West Lafayette, IN: Voyaging Press, 1982. 119p. $7.70 (paperback). ISBN 0-910711-00-3.

The joys of freighter travel are readily apparent in this charming little book that explores the exciting possibilities of freighter travel as opposed to a passenger cruise ship. The Kanes offer good information on what to pack, activities available, the size and design of various ships' staterooms, and so forth. Their constant reminder is that a freighter passenger must be flexible: Cargo is king, and passengers must adapt to its particular schedule. They particularly recommend freighter travel for retirees who have the freedom from work schedules to adapt to variable freight scheduling. The book also describes various lines departing from several ports—the Gulf Coast, the Atlantic, and the Great Lakes, among others—and the ships' destinations. Names, addresses, and telephone numbers are provided for further information.

Murphy, Michael, and Laura Murphy. *Ferryliner Vacations in North America: Ocean Travel and Inland Cruising.* New York: E. P. Dutton, 1988. 277p. $10.95 (paperback). ISBN 0-525-48355-1.

Ferryliner Vacations presents intriguing possibilities for those who wish to explore the North American continent from a new perspective. Interesting, offbeat cruises on ferryliners range from those crossing lakes in a matter of a few hours to lengthy explorations of Alaskan waterways. Trips may be port to port, or involve round-trip cruising. Some ferries carry cars and RVs, while others are for passengers only. The book contains numerous maps of waterways and trips available on them. The authors provide valuable, detailed information on the type of ship, accommodations available (if any), prices, booking schedules and procedures, and descriptions of port towns. Various appendixes list information for each ship line, state tourist offices, and RV caravan organizers.

Springer, Marylyn, and Donald A. Schultz. *Frommer's Dollarwise Cruises*. New York: Simon and Schuster, 1989. 423p. $14.95 (paperback). ISBN 0-13-048596-9.

Typical of Frommer guides, this book is an outstanding resource for choosing the best cruise-travel values in all price ranges from deluxe to moderate or budget. It documents cruise costs, including cabin choices and prices, dining, and entertainment, plus the usual need-to-know facts about specific lines, their ships, and ports of call. Special chapters discuss children at sea, singles, and freighter travel. The authors offer explicit details—down to the paint job of a ship's swimming pool—in a breezy, wonderfully readable style. In sections from "Drinking, romancing and behaving yourself" to "Ahoy, buoy, get that hand off the fantail," both novice and experienced cruisers will find something they didn't know until reading this book. These authors even make some offbeat but interesting suggestions before taking a cruise: Read such books as Hemingway's *The Old Man and the Sea* or Robert Wilder's *Wind from the Carolinas* to get a special flavor of the ocean. Or pick up the videos for movies like *Shall We Dance,* with Fred Astaire and Ginger Rogers, or the Marx Brothers' *A Night at the Opera* to enjoy the enchantment and humor aboard ship.

Stern, Steven B. *Stern's Guide to the Cruise Vacation*. Gretna, LA: Pelican Publishing Co., 1988. 222p. $14.95 (paperback). ISBN 0-88289-693-8.

Stern's Guide to the Cruise Vacation explores and ranks each cruise line and its vessels, given all the possible factors in deciding which is the best cruise: ports of call, food, service, facilities, activities, accommodations, price, age of ship, fellow passengers, entertainment, size of ship, and the crew's nationality. Descriptions of various cruising areas, specific ports of call, and what to do with limited hours in each port are also given. In addition to general information on cruising, Stern also details individual specialties such as singles, children, tennis, and jogging. Descriptive information for every major ship is offered, including the history of the vessel, its vital statistics, physical details, an evaluation of the ship, and its price categories. Numerous photographs, sample menus, and activity programs round out this useful cruise book.

Ward, Douglas. *Complete Handbook to Cruising.* Lausanne, Switzerland: Berlitz Guides, Macmillan S.A., 1989. 287p. $13.95 (paperback). ISBN 2-8315-0369-8.

After 600 cruises and 80 transatlantic crossings, Douglas Ward has indeed put together a "complete handbook" of cruising. He presents straightforward capsules of cruising information— from the air conditioning (generally cooler than expected) to the engine room (off-limits, but technical information is available) to an explanation of wind force and many more topics, both practical and esoteric. A valuable section for disabled travelers offers good hints on cabins, where to be seated in the dining room, and pointers for embarkation. Included is a list of ports with elevators, escalators, and covered gangways, as well as difficult embarkation ports. Other sections briefly describe coastal and inland cruises in the United States, river cruising, and adventure cruising. Part II offers a complete evaluation and ratings of 134 major oceangoing cruise ships plus three adventure cruise vessels. Not included are specific prices, but a separate chart indicates ships by price range (low to high), tone/lifestyle (casual to formal), ambience (lively party cruises to mature or conservative, quality cruising), and educational (adventure or expedition cruises for life enhancement). Also helpful are rankings of cabin insulation/soundproofing and sports and health facilities, as well as a disabled-access rating.

Wright, Sarah Bird. *Ferries of America*. Atlanta: Peachtree Publishers, Ltd., 1987. 547p. $12.95 (paperback). ISBN 0-934601-13-5.

> Subtitled "A Guide to Adventurous Travel," this comprehensive directory lists complete information on 270 ferries in 39 states. The listings are arranged by region, including New England, the Mid-Atlantic states, the South, the Great Lakes and Midwest, the Rocky Mountain states and the Southwest, and the Northwest. The author covers local points of interest; ferry histories and anecdotes; fares, schedules, and restrictions; and tourist recommendations. Detailed for each trip are crossing time, ferry type, vessel capacity, operating season, and schedule. Several photos and maps round out this exhaustive ferry guide.

Health and Safety

Adler, Jack, and Thomas C. Tompkins. *Travel Safety: Security Safeguards at Home and Abroad*. New York: Hippocrene Books, 1988. 240p. $14.95. ISBN 0-87052-505-0.

> *Travel Safety* is an outstanding compendium of helpful tips. Beginning with securing one's home in preparation for being away, the authors detail for travelers every conceivable possibility for protecting themselves at airports, in hotels, on cruises or shore excursions, or in cars, trains, or motorcoaches. They explore various issues for solo women travelers, families, and special travelers (i.e., older adults and handicapped travelers), and offer helpful suggestions on everything from protecting one's pet to shopping pitfalls to problems encountered in casinos. Other chapters examine money and credit-card protection, health and insurance issues, coping with stolen or lost luggage, and dealing with terrorism or hijacking and hostage situations. A final chapter discusses the pros and cons of various travel-safety devices, and includes illustrations, prices, and distributors. This book is especially valuable to novice travelers, or those who may never have been abroad, but it also offers answers to problems even experienced travelers may not yet have anticipated.

Darwood, Richard, M.D. *How To Stay Healthy Abroad*. New York: Viking Penguin, 1989. 506p. $13.50 (paperback). ISBN 0-19261-8318.

Although the book is too heavy to carry in one's luggage, Dr. Darwood has produced an outstanding, highly technical volume covering all possible medical/dental problems travelers might encounter. The book covers information not generally available in other travel health books, such as descriptions and illustrations of venomous insects and fish, plus complete descriptions of various exotic diseases. The book might be especially appealing to those with scientific or medical backgrounds. For the not-so-scientifically-inclined, a helpful summary appears at the end of each chapter for quick scanning of salient points.

Lange, W. Robert, M.D. *The International Health Guide for Senior Citizen Travelers*. Babylon, NY: Pilot Books, 1988. 70p. $4.95 (paperback). ISBN 0-87576-139-9.

This helpful guide covers a gamut of health information from pretrip planning to a wide range of health concerns while away from home. The author begins with sound advice from what to do before departure, such as visits to the doctor and dentist, to basic medical travel kit supplies and what a good supplemental health-insurance policy should cover. There are also specific recommendations on traveling with such health concerns as heart disease, high blood pressure, diabetes or circulatory problems. Good advice abounds on such problems as jet lag, motion or high-altitude sickness, food and water precautions, and infections such as malaria, and even how to avoid car accidents in high-risk countries. Appendixes include resource organizations and a concise synopsis of special advice explained in detail in the body of the book.

Liebman, Robert L. *Traveling Right: The Quick Reference Guide to Efficient, Safe and Healthy Travel*. New York: Traveling Right, 1985. 152p. $12.95.

This handy pocket-sized book offers quick, concise tips on all facets of travel, with a special emphasis on scams. The author offers valuable insights on various modes of theft, drugging schemes, luggage theft, etc. He also discusses various cultural restrictions and customs. Currency restrictions and vaccination, passport, and visa requirements for each of 95 countries are listed, along with general information on holidays, climate, time zones, and more. Listed for hundreds of cities are police and other emergency telephone numbers, and information about local banks, car-rental agencies, hospitals, and translators. Although the author's overall perspective may seem overly suspicious, a traveler forewarned is certainly a traveler forearmed.

Scotti, Angelo T., M.D., and Thomas A. Moore. *The Traveler's Medical Manual*. New York: Berkley Books, 1985. 243p. $4.95 (paperback). ISBN 0-425-07758-6.

> *The Traveler's Medical Manual* offers a good overview of a wide range of travel risks and their prevention and treatment, including air, sea, and car accidents. Two maps illustrate areas at high risk for malaria and yellow fever. The book includes a list of International Association for Medical Assistance to Travelers (IAMAT) (see Chapter 7 under Health and Safety) and other English-speaking doctors worldwide. Also listed are required vaccines for various countries, and the highest medical risks in each country.

Silverman, Harold, M.D. *Travel Healthy*. New York: Avon Books, 1986. 184p. $3.50 (paperback). ISBN 0-380-89859-4.

> Subtitled "The Traveler's Complete Medical Kit," this useful little book provides valuable information on health-related problems travelers are likely to encounter, such as weather injuries, immunizations, jet lag, sunburn, insect bites, traveler's diarrhea, and more. A special section deals with information and advice for older travelers. Final chapters detail items that should be included in a traveler's medical kit, and a complete listing of foreign brand names for commonly used U.S. drug products is provided.

Weinhouse, Beth. *The Healthy Traveler: An Indispensable Guide to Staying Healthy Away from Home*. New York: Simon and Schuster, 1987. 223p. $6.95 (paperback). ISBN 0-671-61445-2.

> *The Healthy Traveler* focuses beyond which shots are needed for overseas travel to the broader questions of what health precautions should be considered for a trip. Examined are jet lag, motion sickness, traveler's diarrhea, altitude sickness, and car accidents. In addition to general health information, Weinhouse covers such topics as sports injuries and what to do if caught in an earthquake or hotel fire, plus descriptions of diseases that may not manifest until several days after the traveler has returned

home. Travel clinics across the United States that specialize in tropical illnesses and exotic diseases are listed as a resource for those with delayed onset of illness. The book also details immunizations required for all countries, and the malaria risk in each country.

Disabled Travel

Freedman, Jacqueline, and Susan Gersten. *Traveling Like Everybody Else.* New York: Adama Books, 1987. 175p. $11.95 (paperback). ISBN 0-915361-77-9.

> *Traveling Like Everybody Else,* written by an author who travels in a wheelchair, offers several insightful, practical travel tips for all types of disabled travelers—from those who may have only a slight handicap to those who are on dialysis. Particularly useful is a checklist/questionnaire for use in planning a trip to see if a traveling companion is needed. (For example: "Can I lift my own luggage? Can I reach the counter in a bank to exchange money? Is my balance good enough to open stuck dresser drawers so prevalent in Europe?") One useful section explains special services and questions to ask concerning train, plane, bus, and automobile travel, including renting a specially equipped car. There's advice on eating, shopping, and sightseeing, and on such problems as access, toileting, medications and supplies, and obtaining medical help when needed. Numerous appendixes outline helpful details on access information in the United States, hotel and motel chains with accessible units, tour operators who specialize in tours for the disabled, and more.

Hecker, Helen. *Travel for the Disabled: A Handbook of Travel Resources and 500 Worldwide Access Guides.* Portland, OR: Twin Peaks Press, 1986. 192p. $9.95 (paperback). ISBN 0-933261-00-4.

> This conveniently small and easy-to-hold handbook is, as noted in its introduction, "printed in large type on paper stock easy to turn with a pencil eraser." Hecker provides comprehensive lists of resources for the disabled traveler including helpful agencies, clubs, publications, books, and travel tips. Included are lists of access guides for the United States and foreign countries, plus hard-to-find travel resources. This book is a valuable aid to those

with heart or mobility problems, vision or hearing impairment, cancer, arthritis, asthma, and allergies, as well as to those with special dietary needs or any other disability.

Northern Cartographic. *Access America: An Atlas and Guide to the National Parks for Visitors with Disabilities*. Burlington, VT: Northern Cartographic, 1989. 464p. $89.95 (semihardcover). ISBN 0-944187-00-5.

> Participation from over 60 health/disability professionals and over 100 National Park Service personnel resulted in this outstanding reference book for the disabled traveler, offering detailed coverage on 37 major national parks. Information about paths of travel includes width, surface type, gradient, accessible parking, restroom evaluations, road elevations, medical services, lodging, dining, and campgrounds. Details of each park's programs for visitors with mobility, visual, hearing, or developmental disabilities highlight accessible vistas, tactile exhibits, captioned films, sign language, and special programming. The book contains nearly 300 detailed, full-color maps, drawings, and photographs, including regional maps showing selected support services within a 100-mile radius of each park. Also listed are hospitals, dialysis centers, prosthetic/orthotic services, wheelchair sales and service, and therapeutic oxygen suppliers. A series of poignant essays by disabled park visitors describe their personal travels. The book is printed in large type and incorporates a special binding format that allows easy use by people with motor impairments.

Reamy, Lois. *TravelAbility: A Guide for Physically Disabled Travelers in the United States*. New York: Macmillan Publishing Co., 1978. 298p. $9.95 (paperback). ISBN 0-02-601170-0.

> Although over a decade old, this book provides much good, basic, timeless information for disabled travelers. The author includes such topics as car-rental agencies that will rent cars with hand controls, how to deal with a travel agent who may be inexperienced with disabled travel needs, and how to travel with a respirator. Included is a sample letter to send to hotels inquiring about their facilities. Various medical concerns and insurance needs are also covered.

Walzer, Mary Meister. *A Travel Guide for the Disabled, Western Europe*. New York: Van Nostrand Reinhold Company, Inc., 1982. 284p. $18.95 (hardback). ISBN 0-442-23116-4.

> Beginning with wheelchair access to various U.S. airports, the author moves on to an extensive discussion of travel for the disabled in major European cities. Topics include: airports, ground transportation, restaurants, shopping and sightseeing, and where to call for assistance. Hotels and restaurants are rated by cost (luxury, expensive, or moderate), and whether they have been recommended by other disabled travelers. Descriptions include wheelchair lavatories, special bedrooms, and the number of steps involved to reach various parts of the building. General information about each country's average temperature and language are covered, along with specialized words in that language for items such as "lavatory," "wheelchair," "crutch," "battery," and so forth. The author also notes whether that country is well adapted to persons with handicaps.

Weiss, Louise. *Access to the World: A Travel Guide for the Handicapped*. Chicago: Chatham Square Press, 1983. 221p. $12.95 (paperback). ISBN 0-87196-786-3.

> *Access to the World* is a very readable, useful guide for any kind of disabled travel, from those who need kidney dialysis to heart patients, but is especially helpful for those who require a wheelchair. Weiss lists specific information on airlines worldwide, including their requirements or limitations on equipment, medical certification, guide dogs, special diets, etc. Similar information is included for travel on buses, trains, and cruise ships. Another chapter details modifications for cars and recreational vehicles. A cross section of major U.S. cities and a limited number abroad are listed with details on accessibility to historic areas, museums, theme parks, and other activities.

Travel Guides

> There are a number of useful travel guides available at libraries and bookstores. Some guidebooks are oriented toward sightseeing, special events, and attractions. Others offer specifics on hotels, restaurants, and entertainment. Some employ a rating

system to compare value; others publish specific prices for the budget-minded. A few delve deeply into the historical and cultural background; others are aimed at current attractions. It is advisable to compare several and carry along only one or two that best meet one's own personal travel style and needs.

A good starting place to compare travel guides is the following book:

Hayes, Greg, and Joan Wright. *Going Places—The Guide to Travel Guides*. Boston: Harvard Common Press, 1988. 670p. $14.95. ISBN 1-55832-003-2.

> This comprehensive directory offers brief, useful reviews of hundreds of travel guides, both series and individual titles. The guides are indexed by area and subject such as culture, special interests, and handicapped resources, including a section on guides for older adults. This book should be must reading for all travelers, even if they have a favorite travel guide series that has never let them down—so much more is available they might otherwise miss. Appendixes include: phrase books, travel bookstores and mail order travel book publishers, and travel newsletters and magazines.

TRAVEL-GUIDE SERIES

The following travel-guide series have proved popular with mature travelers and are recommended by them and by senior travel advisers. Each company publishes guides for a variety of cities, regions, and countries, and tends to follow a fairly similar format within the series. However, information and even format may vary depending on the local contributors and editors. Again, travelers are encouraged to compare several different guidebooks for a particular region and see which one best serves their travel style.

AAA Tour Books
American Automobile Association
1000 AAA Drive
Heathrow, FL 32746-5063

> Geared to automobile touring in the United States and abroad (AA series in Britain and Europe). Background information on history, climate, and culture. Listings, with prices, of AAA "approved" accommodations and restaurants.

American Express Guides
Simon & Schuster
1230 Avenue of the Americas
New York, NY 10020

> Pocket guides with plentiful information about sightseeing, excursions, hotels, restaurants, and nightlife, concentrating on cities or small regions. However, the type is small and many symbols are used.

Baedeker's Guides
Prentice-Hall Press
200 Old Tappan Road
Old Tappan, NJ 07675

> A classic guidebook series offering full-color photography; extensive descriptions of attractions, history, and culture; and practical information. Very readable, with in-depth information as thorough as if offered by a personal tour guide. Each book includes a foldout map of the area.

Berlitz Travel Guides
Macmillan Co.
366 Third Avenue
New York, NY 10022

> Very readable, beautiful books with full-color photography. Guides include historical and cultural essays along with practical tips and selected hotel and restaurant recommendations. Readers are offered a "short list" of things to see and do as well as "leisure routes" encompassing interesting but less important attractions.

Birnbaum Guides
Houghton Mifflin Company
2 Park Street
Boston, MA 02108

> Newly formatted guides are divided into the following practical sections: "Getting Ready To Go" (includes travel hints for older, single, and disabled travelers), "Perspectives" (understanding the culture and history), "The Cities," "Diversions," and "Directions" (itineraries and guide to attractions). Also lists

selected hotels and restaurants by price category (generally moderate and up). Very readable and extremely dependable information.

Fielding Travel Books
William Morrow and Company, Inc.
105 Madison Avenue
New York, NY 10016

Generally upscale and higher priced establishments are featured, with information on sightseeing, shopping, hotels, and restaurants (rated on a one-to-five scale).

Fodor's Travel Publications, Inc.
Random House, Inc.
201 E. 50th Street
New York, NY 10022

An old name in travel guides, some may be lacking in current attractions because of limited yearly updates. A new "Fun Guide" series has placed more emphasis on specific cities and small regions with more hotel and restaurant evaluations.

Frommer Books
Simon & Schuster, Inc.
One Gulf & Western Plaza
New York, NY 10023

Frommer guides are traditionally for the budget-minded traveler, with extensive, specific information on hotels and restaurants, including prices. Good background material on culture, sports, attractions, and so forth. Especially good for local transportation options.

Let's Go
(Harvard Student Agencies)
St. Martin's Press
175 Fifth Avenue
New York, NY 10010

An excellent series for low-budget travelers, with annually reevaluated information on both rural areas and big cities. Begun by Harvard students, the series appeals to many mature travelers as well for its good travel facts and solid information on excursions, attractions, and entertainment.

Lonely Planet Publications
112 Linden Street
San Francisco, CA 94607

> Offers over 70 "travel survival kit" guides to exotic, off-the-beaten-path destinations, none in the United States or western Europe. Information and format vary depending on the country and the focus of activity there, i.e., walking, trekking, sightseeing, etc. Useful guides for adventurous travelers of any age.

Michelin Green Guide Series
Michelin Guides and Maps
P.O. Box 3305
Spartanburg, SC 29304-3305

> Michelin Guides, nearly a century old, have been judged consistently good. The "Green Guides" (in English) present well-organized information for both driving and walking tours, plus extensive overviews of history, culture, economy, and ecology. The "Red Guides" (not in English but employ easily understood symbols) rate hotels and restaurants, with establishments living or dying on their Michelin rating.

Mobil Travel Guides
Prentice-Hall
15 Columbus Circle
New York, NY 10023

> The American equivalent of Michelin Red Guides, these rate an extensive number of U.S. hotels and restaurants, using space-saving symbols. Organized by various regions.

Periodicals

General Travel

Andrew Harper's Hideaway Report
Harper Associates, Inc.
P.O. Box 50
Sun Valley, ID 83353
(208) 622-3183
$90

A newsletter dedicated to the discovery of peaceful vacation retreats for the sophisticated traveler. Accepts no advertising or complimentary travel services. Includes various regular columns—answers to reader questions; critical reviews of travel services, accommodations, and destinations; and regional travel briefs.

Consumer Reports Travel Letter
Box 53629
Boulder, CO 80322-3629
$37

Published by Consumers Union of United States, Inc.
256 Washington Street
Mount Vernon, NY 10553

A no-nonsense, comprehensive travel newsletter with consumer information on a broad array of travel topics including discounts, scams, opportunities, advice, and so forth. Like its parent magazine, *Consumer Reports,* it accepts no advertising or travel compensation.

International Travel News
2120 28th Street
Sacramento, CA 95818
(916) 457-3643
$14

A consumer magazine for overseas travelers with candid, reader-written appraisals of airlines, tours, cruises, hotels, and more, plus travel tips and information. Includes a column and articles of specific interest to older travelers. Readers may solicit personal responses to travel questions at no charge. Free sample copy upon request.

The Mature Traveler
P.O. Box 50820
Reno, NV 89513
$27.50

The Mature Traveler is a no-nonsense travel newsletter aimed specifically at the "over-49" vacationer. It features current, verified information on discounts, tours, cruises, RVs, and travel companies, and other valuable data for older travelers. A specialty of the newsletter is regular exposés of both good and bad deals and "senior shucks" (i.e., when a so-called senior discount means a higher price than another available offer). Also includes reports on destinations for mature travelers and travel-partner want ads.

National Geographic Traveler
National Geographic Society
1145 17th Street, NW
Washington, DC 20036
(202) 776-6772
$17.95

A glossy, full-spectrum travel magazine with comprehensive destination travel features replete with outstanding National Geographic photography, plus a regular travelers' calendar of special events in the United States and Canada.

Passport
Enterprise Publications
MTH Corp.
20 N. Wacker Drive
Chicago, IL 60606
(312) 464-0300
$65

A general-interest travel newsletter for "the discriminating international traveler." Offers up-to-date news briefs of hotel/restaurant changes, critical reviews, and travel recommendations well ahead of published guidebooks. Accepts no advertising.

Travel 50 & Beyond
Vacation Publications, Inc.
2411 Fountain View
Houston, TX 77057
(713) 974-0445
$11.80

Aimed at mature travelers of all income levels, *Travel 50* offers practical, thoughtful tips and recommendations, all geared to finding the best travel value. Also included are reader profiles, destination travel articles and features, resources, advice, and more.

Travel Holiday
Reader's Digest Association, Inc.
Pleasantville, NY 10570
(914) 241-5700
$11

> Labeled as "the magazine that roams the globe," this glossy, full-spectrum travel magazine features travel destination articles accompanied by outstanding full-color photographs. Also features a regular "Travel Advisor" column with the latest travel tips and information.

Travel & Leisure
American Express Publishing Corp.
1120 Avenue of the Americas
New York, NY 10036
(212) 382-5600
$30

> An imposing, lavish travel magazine with regular departments covering travel health, money, photography, weather, and updates, plus destination travel articles and features.

Travel Smart
40 Beechdale Road
Dobbs Ferry, NY 10522-9989
(914) 693-8300
$37

> A newsletter offering a wide-ranging, frank look at the best values for travel dollars, including a section on discounts for seniors. Also included are new travel book/guide reviews, up-to-the-minute travel advisories, unusual travel opportunities, and much more. The newsletter accepts no advertising. Subscribers receive monthly issues; a yearly index; discounts on airfares, cruises, and tours; and copies of four travel reports: "Surviving an Aircrash," "Traveling Healthy," "Travel Ripoffs," and "Controlling Travel Costs."

Travel Tips
5281 Scotts Valley
Scotts Valley, CA 95066
(408) 438-6150
$9

Travel Tips is a newsletter for qualified travel and activity planners for senior groups, clubs, and organizations. It contains primarily paid advertising for travel opportunities, announcements, and special events on the West Coast, with an emphasis on group travel and discounts for seniors. It also serves as an outlet for information on one- to three-day trips, often not available in other media. The newsletter is free to senior travel planners and travel agents; mature travelers may subscribe for $9 per year.

Travelin'
P.O. Box 23005
Eugene, OR 97405
(800) 345-9828
Bimonthly, $18.95

This magazine accepts no advertising, offering little-known vacation spots and weekend hideaways "well wide of traditional tourist stops" in 11 western states, Alaska, Hawaii, and western Canada. The magazine is designed for the 45- to 65-year-old motorist vacationer.

Specialty Travel

American Hiker
American Hiking Society
1015 31st Street, NW
Washington, DC 20007
(703) 385-3252
Quarterly, $10

The magazine contains news and information on hiking, trail building and maintenance, volunteer vacation opportunities working on America's trails, and related features.

Backpacker
Rodale Press
33 E. Minor Street
Emmaus, PA 18049
(215) 967-5171
$16.97

A glossy, full-spectrum magazine of wilderness travel, including beautiful photography and features on equipment, techniques, and places, plus book reviews, maps, and useful travel hints and advertising.

Bicycling
Rodale Press
33 E. Minor Street
Emmaus, PA 18049
$17.97

> A glossy magazine for bicycle enthusiasts including news, features, helpful hints, reviews of new equipment, and advertising. Although aimed primarily at younger enthusiasts of sport bicycling, it also contains some useful tips and travel possibilities for senior bicyclists.

Golf Traveler
Golf Card International Corp.
1137 E. 2100 S
Salt Lake City, UT 84106
(800) 453-4260; (800) 321-8269 (Canada);
(801) 486-9391 (Utah)
$12

> News and features on golf courses worldwide, golf personalities, and related features and advertising.

Nude & Natural
The Naturists, Inc.
P.O. Box 132
Oshkosh, WI 54902
$25

> A family nudist magazine including discussions of the nudist lifestyle and worldwide nudist travel opportunities.

Romantic Traveling
Winterbourne Press
236 West Portal Avenue, Suite 237
San Francisco, CA 94127
(415) 731-8239
Quarterly, $15

> An eight-page newsletter focusing on travel to romantic spots throughout the world. A special column focuses on "Romance over Fifty."

Transitions Abroad
Transitions Publishing
P.O. Box 344-02
Amherst, MA 01004
(413) 256-0373
Five issues/year, $15

> Written for both young and mature travelers who want alternatives to packaged tourism, this magazine provides details on travel involving close interaction with the people of the host country through volunteering, employment, study programs, special-interest travel opportunities, and home and hospitality exchanges. Each issue focuses on a specific region: Latin and South America, Asia and the Pacific Rim, Europe and the Soviet Union, the Mediterranean Basin and the Near East, and the Americas, the Caribbean, and Africa south of the Sahara.

Accommodations

OAG Travel Planner Hotel & Motel Guide Redbook,
North American Edition
Official Airline Guides, Inc.
2000 Clearwater Drive
Oak Brook, IL 60521
(312) 574-6091
$88

> A technical reference guide including over 21,000 hotels, city data, ground transportation information, and more. OAG also publishes similar guides for Europe and the Pacific Asia area.

Trains

Go BritRail
BritRail
630 Third Avenue
New York, NY 10017
(212) 599-5400
Annual, free

> A promotional booklet of BritRail travel, passes, itineraries, day-trips, escorted tours, and various rail/air, rail/drive, and rail/sail

travel-package combinations. U.S. edition available from travel agents.

Official Railway Guide—Travel Edition
K-III Press, Inc.
424 W. 33rd Street
New York, NY 10001
(212) 714-3100
Five issues/year, $62

> Comprehensive reference guide; includes complete Amtrak, Via Rail Canada, and other passenger timetables for the United States and Canada. Also includes fares, equipment and on-board service information, bus and suburban rail connections, city-to-city sections, rail travel news digest, and a comprehensive station index.

RVs and Camping

> The following magazines offer a variety of camping and/or RV travel features, how-to columns, information and advice, and personal-experience articles. Annual subscription prices are listed; the periodicals vary from quarterly to monthly publication schedules. Most are available in libraries and bookstores; some may also be found in campground stores and at recreational vehicle dealers and service centers. Some focus on limited geographic areas, while others have a national or even international focus.

Camperways
P.O. Box 460
Spring House, PA 19477
(215) 643-2058
$12

> A tabloid-sized magazine of RV-related news, features, information, calendar of events, and travel tips for the Middle Atlantic region.

Camping Canada Magazine
2077 Dundas Street, East
Mississauga, Ontario L4X 1M2
Canada
(416) 624-8218
$22

A glossy, full-spectrum camping and RV magazine with travel information, test reports on new RV models, camping products and acessories, calendar of events, and destination travel features.

Camp-orama
6489 Parkland Drive
Sarasota, FL 34243
(800) 334-6808; (813) 756-6808
$12

A tabloid-format newsmagazine of RV lifestyle and travel information for the Florida area.

Disabled Outdoors
5223 S. Lorel Avenue
Chicago, IL 60638
(312) 284-2206
$8

Covers hunting, camping, fishing, and boating, with information on new products, services, special organizations, places to go, accessible resorts, and hunting and fishing regulations pertaining to the disabled. Also information on clubs and tournaments, how-to articles, and personal accomplishments.

Family Motorcoaching
8291 Clough Pike
Cincinnati, OH 45244
(800) 543-3622; (513) 474-3622
$24

The official publication of the Family Motor Coach Association (FMCA), this full-color magazine highlights RV news and features, technical and advice columns, destination travel features, and FMCA news and information.

Marine and Recreation News
27601 Little Mack Street
St. Clair Shores, MI 48081
(313) 777-8866
$10.50

A full-spectrum magazine for boat and water sports enthusiasts, with helpful advice and destination travel features.

MotorHome
29901 Agoura Road
Agoura, CA 91301
(800) 423-5061
$27.98

> A glossy magazine devoted to motorhomes, including travel features, service and repair articles, and regular advice and informational columns. Includes advertising and generally favorable reviews of motorhomes and related accessories.

New York RV
6489 Parkland Drive
Sarasota, FL 34243
(800) 334-6808; (813) 756-6808
Bimonthly, $6

> A tabloid-format newsmagazine for the RV lifestyle with camping information for the Empire State.

RV Life
P.O. Box 55998
Seattle, WA 91855
(206) 745-5665
$12

> A tabloid-format magazine with RV features, information, and advertising, plus destination travel articles focused on the western United States.

RV West
2033 Clement Avenue, Suite 226
Alameda, CA 94501-1317
(415) 769-8338
$12

> Newsprint magazine featuring RV mechanical and safety tips, destination travel features, and calendar of events in the western United States.

Southern RV
6489 Parkland Drive
Sarasota, FL 34243
(800) 334-6808; (813) 756-6808
$15

A tabloid-format newsmagazine for the RV lifestyle with camping information for the southeastern United States.

Trailer Life
29901 Agoura Road
Agoura, CA 91301
(800) 234-3450
$22

A glossy, full-spectrum magazine for travelers with motorhomes, trailers, truck campers, or folding trailers. Includes destination travel features, technical information and regular advice columns, product reviews, and calendar of events.

Trails-a-Way
6489 Parkland Drive
Sarasota, FL 34243
(800) 334-6808; (813) 756-6808
$12

A tabloid-format newsmagazine for the RV lifestyle, with camping and travel information and features, plus a calendar of events for the Midwest.

Cruising

Cruise Travel
World Publishing Co.
990 Grove Street
Evanston, IL 60201
(708) 491-6440
$18

A glossy travel magazine covering cruise ships, ports, schedules, and prices. Various travelogues of ports and itineraries, plus company and ship profiles; letters from readers round out the editorial format.

Freighter Travel News
Freighter Travel Club of America
3524 Harts Lake Road
Roy, WA 98580
$18

Magazine available as benefit of club membership. Features first-hand stories about freighter travel, tips on where to go, what to do while there, where to eat, stay, etc. Also included are news updates, book reviews, and comments/questions from club members.

OAG Worldwide Cruise & Shipline Guide
Official Airline Guides, Inc.
2000 Clearwater Drive
Oak Brook, IL 60521
(312) 574-6091
Bimonthly, $78

Comprehensive reference guide including individual cruise listings, organized by geographical area and departure date. Also ferry schedules.

Health and Safety

Traveling Healthy
108-48 70th Road
Forest Hills, NY 11375
Bimonthly, $24

Traveling Healthy is an eight-page newsletter containing information about traveling healthy and comfortably, edited by Karl Neumann, M.D.

Disabled Travel

Disabled Outdoors
5223 S. Lorel Avenue
Chicago, IL 60638
(312) 284-2206; (312) 366-8526
$8

Covers hunting, camping, fishing, and boating with information on new products, services, special organizations, places to go, accessible resorts, and hunting and fishing regulations pertaining to the disabled. Also information on clubs and tournaments, how-to articles, and stories featuring personal accomplishments.

The Itinerary
P.O. Box 2012
Bayonne, NJ 07002-2012
(201) 858-3400
$10

> A mix of valuable travel advice, along with advertisements of useful devices for travelers with physical disabilities. Topics include travelogues, accessible vacations, hotel/motel surveys, new products and services, books reviews, and more.

Pamphlets

General Travel

Grand Circle Travel. *Going Abroad: 101 Tips for Mature Travelers.* 24p. Free.

> A useful pocket guide divided into four information-filled sections. First, "Preparation" outlines travel documents, packing, home security, and last-minute suggestions. Next are details on plane travel, driving abroad, communicating, shopping, telephones, tipping, sightseeing, photography, and health care. "Return" explains clearing customs, what can and can't be brought in, and unused traveler's checks. A final segment explains useful travel terminology. Contact: Grand Circle Travel, 347 Congress Street, Boston, MA 02210; (800) 221-2610.

Henry, Harry H. *Senior Citizen Information and Referral Travel Directory.* 1988. 54p. Price unavailable.

> A self-published, typewritten listing of travel information, tourist services, and discounts in selected areas in the United States. Contact: Harry H. Henry, P.O. Box 1822, Oakland, CA 94612.

Institute of Certified Travel Agents. *Let's Talk Travel.* Free.

> A helpful flyer explaining frequently used travel terms, expressions, and abbreviations to help understand and evaluate travel brochures. Contact: Institute of Certified Travel Agents, 148 Linden Street, P.O. Box 56, Wellesley, MA 02181.

Partners-in-Travel. *Smart Traveler*. 12p. $5, plus self-addressed, stamped envelope.

> Explains money-saving tips on transportation, accommodations, dining, shopping, dealing with foreign currency, and protecting against loss. Free to members of Partners-in-Travel, a service club for single travelers. Contact: Partners-in-Travel, P.O. Box 491145, Los Angeles, CA 90049; (213) 476-4869.

U.S. Department of State, Bureau of Consular Affairs. *A Safe Trip Abroad*. Department of State Publication 9493. Rev. ed., 1987. 16p. $1.

> Offers advice and precautions for travelers on personal security, protecting valuables, vehicle security, where to get assistance abroad, and protecting oneself against terrorism or in hijacking/hostage situations. Contact: Superintendent of Documents, U.S. Government Printing Office, Washington, DC 20402; (202) 783-3238.

————. *Handbook and Directory of Consular Services*. 42p. Free.

> A valuable sourcebook for information on governmental citizens services overseas, passport services, visa services, and telephone listings for related government agencies. Contact: Public Affairs Staff, Bureau of Consular Affairs, Room 5807, U.S. Department of State, Washington, DC 20520-4818.

————. *Tips for Travelers*. $1 each; varying lengths.

> The "Tips for Travelers" series of pamphlets produced by the U.S. Department of State outline valuable, up-to-date information for travelers to various areas of the world, including some current "hot spots." They list passport and visa requirements; currency regulations; local dress and customs; important health, safety, and legal considerations; and where to turn for help. The booklet about Mexico, for example, details which highways to avoid using because of recent assaults on tourists. The pamphlets are available for the following areas: Sub-Saharan Africa, the Caribbean, Central and South America, the People's Republic of China, Cuba, eastern Europe and Yugoslavia, Mexico, the Middle East and North Africa, South Asia, and the USSR. Contact: Superintendent of Documents, U.S. Government Printing Office, Washington, DC 20402; (202) 783-3238.

————. *Travel Tips for Older Americans*. Department of State
Publication 9309. 16p. $1.

> A brief, informative overview of topics ranging from informa-
> tion on charter flights, trip insurance, and medical-assistance
> programs to practical shopping and safety tips for seniors travel-
> ing abroad. Contact: Superintendent of Documents, U.S. Govern-
> ment Printing Office, Washington, DC 20402; (202) 783-3238.

Specialty Travel

United States Master Swimming. *Places To Swim in the United States*.
38p. $2.

> Lists contact persons, swimming facilities, and, in some cases,
> lap and/or workout schedules at various pools around the coun-
> try. Contact: United States Masters Swimming, Inc., 2 Peter
> Avenue, Rutland, MA 01543; (508) 886-6631.

Group Tours

Brazelton, Louise. *Guide to Selecting a Group Tour*. Babylon, NY: Pilot
Books. 32p. $3.95. ISBN 0-87576-111-9.

> A basic, introductory guide for the novice traveler to assist in
> understanding and choosing group tours. Includes questions to
> ask when choosing a tour (food, attractions, seating, and so
> forth), plus tips on passports, packing, shopping, and sightseeing.

National Tour Association (NTA). *Travel Together!* 16p. Free.

> Details the benefits of escorted tours and how to choose the best
> tour. An additional 40-page booklet, *A Consumer's Guide to
> National Tour Association Operator Companies,* included with
> *Travel Together,* lists NTA members nationwide. Contact:
> National Tour Association, P.O. Box 3071, Lexington, KY
> 40596-3071; (800) 284-4NTA.

Palmer, Paige. *Guide to the Best Buys in Package Tours*. 1990 ed. 46p.
$3.95. ISBN 0-87576-124-0.

> This abbreviated guide to package tours lists and briefly
> describes more than 100 group tour operators and their travel

specialties. Palmer discusses how to choose a tour operator, health and insurance considerations, and travel tips for the disabled. Also covered are suggestions on creating package-tour variations and how to file travel complaints. Checklists inform novice travelers about precautions to take, trip preparations, and final details before departure. Contact: Pilot Books, 103 Cooper Street, Babylon, NY 11702; (516) 422-2225.

United States Tour Operators Association (USTOA). *Guide to USTOA Members, Their Programs, Services and Destinations.* Free.

Lists current USTOA members and the types of tour programs they offer. Contact: United States Tour Operators Association, 211 East 51st Street, Suite 12B, New York, NY 10022; (212) 944-5727.

————. *How To Select a Package Tour.* Free.

An informational flier listing guidelines for choosing a tour, how to read a tour brochure, and a glossary of tour travel terms.

Contact: United States Tour Operators Association, 211 East 51st Street, Suite 12B, New York, NY 10022; (212) 944-5727.

Accommodations

Gum, Cindy. *Your Place and Mine: A Guide to Vacation Home Exchanging.* 49p. Free.

This booklet is invaluable for anyone first considering this inexpensive way of actually "living" in a new area, as opposed to just visiting. Written in a spirited, exuberant manner, it should convince almost anyone that home exchanging is a viable option for vacation accommodations. It also reminds readers of the realities of opening one's home to strangers, as well as considerations of what exchangers may find in foreign countries. Several checklists, samples of advertising one's home, and points to cover— from an inquiry letter to an exchange agreement—leave no welcome mat unturned in handling the important details of home exchanging. Contact: Gum Publications, 18510 Hillview Drive, Los Gatos, CA 93030.

Airlines

U.S. Department of Transportation. *Fly-Rights: A Guide to Air Travel in the U.S.* 32p. $1.

> A valuable booklet explaining air travelers' rights and responsibilities. It offers outstanding consumer information on airfares, reservations, and tickets; delayed and canceled flights; overbooking; baggage; smoking regulations; contract terms; airline safety; and where and how to complain. Contact: Superintendent of Documents, Dept. 33, Washington, DC 20402, or U.S. Department of Transportation, 400 Seventh Street, SW, Washington, DC 20590.

RVs and Camping

National Forest Service. *Camping at Selected National Forests.* Free.

> Information and reservation application. Or call for reservations: MisTix, 800-283-CAMP. (National Forest Service, U.S. Department of Agriculture Office of Information, P.O. Box 2417, Washington, D.C. 20013.)

————. *Federal Recreation Passport Program.* Free.

> An informational brochure about the Golden Age Passport, a free lifetime entrance pass for persons age 62 and older to federal national parks, monuments, historic sites, recreation areas, and national wildlife refuges. The passport must be obtained in person from any National Park Service or Forest Service headquarters, or regional offices of other federally managed areas. Contact: National Forest Service, U.S. Department of Agriculture Office of Information, P.O. Box 2417, Washington, DC 20013.

————. *Forest Service Volunteer.* FS 342. Free.

> An informational brochure on volunteering in national forests. Contact: National Forest Service, U.S. Department of Agriculture Office of Information, P.O. Box 2417, Washington, DC 20013.

————. *A Guide to Your National Forests.* FS-418. Free.

> Full-color national map of national forest lands including regional listings and information. Contact: National Forest

Service, U.S. Department of Agriculture Office of Information, P.O. Box 2417, Washington, DC 20013.

————. *Rules for Visitors to the National Forests.* Free.

An informational brochure. Contact: National Forest Service, U.S. Department of Agriculture Office of Information, P.O. Box 2417, Washington, DC 20013.

————. *So You Want To Be a Forest Service Volunteer Campground Host.* Free.

Information and application for the campground host program. Contact: National Forest Service, U.S. Department of Agriculture Office of Information, P.O. Box 2417, Washington, DC 20013.

Recreation Vehicle Industry Association (RVIA). *Catalog of Publications about the RV Lifestyle.* Free.

A leaflet listing a number of helpful publications for RV travelers covering topics such as hints for buyers, the RV lifestyle, highway safety and driving tips, RV video camping aids, and RV maintenance. Contact: Recreation Vehicle Industry Association (RVIA), 1896 Preston White Drive, Reston, VA 22091, (703) 620-6003; or RVIA, 1748 W. Katella Avenue, Suite 108, Orange, CA 92667, (714) 532-1688.

————. *Recreation Vehicle Reference Lists.* Free.

A valuable packet of information sheets for RV owners. The lists include addresses, phone numbers, and prices, where applicable, for: RV public shows, RV rental sources, campground information, state campground associations, camping clubs, RV trade and related associations, publications for campers and RV owners, RV accessibility for the handicapped, and RV trade publications. Contact: Recreation Vehicle Industry Association (RVIA), 1896 Preston White Drive, Reston, VA 22091, (703) 620-6003; or RVIA, 1748 W. Katella Avenue, Suite 108, Orange, CA 92667, (714) 532-1688.

————. *RV Standards and RV Buyers.* Free.

A leaflet listing required standards for electrical, plumbing, heating, and fire safety systems as established by the American National Standards Institute. Contact: Recreation Vehicle Industry

Association (RVIA), 1896 Preston White Drive, Reston, VA 22091, (703) 620-6003; or RVIA, 1748 W. Katella Avenue, Suite 108, Orange, CA 92667, (714) 532-1688.

Recreation Vehicle Industry Association (RVIA) and American Association of Retired Persons (AARP). *Safety in RV's: A Moving Experience.* 40p. Free booklet; $1.25 postage.

> This valuable booklet is a basic primer on driving and safety tips for novice RVers. Chapters include an explanation of how various RV types differ; driving requirements, including maneuverability and driving in mountainous areas or on narrow roads; considerations on weight, tires, and weight distribution; towing procedures; dealing with emergencies; and proper understanding and use of equipment. Contact: Recreation Vehicle Industry Association (RVIA), 1896 Preston White Drive, Reston, VA 22091, (703) 620-6003; or RVIA, 1748 W. Katella Avenue, Suite 108, Orange, CA 92667 (714) 532-1688.

————. *Set Free in an RV.* 24p. Free.

> A beautifully illustrated booklet with basics for choosing an RV; rental tips; descriptions and illustrations of various RV types and interiors; information on driving, financing, and insuring an RV; camping; and a resource list for further RV information. Contact: Recreation Vehicle Industry Association (RVIA), 1896 Preston White Drive, Reston, VA 22091, (703) 620-6003; or RVIA, 1748 W. Katella Avenue, Suite 108, Orange, CA 92667, (714) 532-1688.

————. *Winterize Your RV.* 8p. Free.

> A helpful booklet with general tips for RV winter storage, inspection, and maintenance, as well as helpful hints for winter startup and camping. Contact: Recreation Vehicle Industry Association (RVIA), 1896 Preston White Drive, Reston, VA 22091, (703) 620-6003; or RVIA, 1748 W. Katella Avenue, Suite 108, Orange, CA 92667, (714) 532-1688.

Recreational Vehicle Rental Association. *Who's Who in RV Rentals.* 44p. Free. $5.

> A handy vacation-planning guide listing RV rental dealers in the United States and Canada. Rental dealers are listed by state and

city. Each listing includes the dealership's name, address, and phone number, plus the type(s) of RVs for rent, how many people the RV sleeps, the unit's length, approximate rental rates, minimum number of rental days, and the deposit required to reserve the unit. It also lists additional services such as one-way rentals, airport pickup, and livability packages (linens, utensils, etc). Contact: Recreational Vehicle Rental Association, P.O. Box 2999, 1896 Preston White Drive, Reston, VA 22091; (703) 620-6003.

U.S. Fish and Wildlife Service. *National Wildlife Refuges—A Visitor's Guide.* #024-010-00660-9. $1.50.

An informational brochure. Contact: U.S. Fish and Wildlife Service, Public Affairs Office, Washington, DC 20240.

U.S. Government Printing Office. *Camping in the National Park System.* #024-005-01028-9. $3.50.

An informational leaflet. Contact: U.S. Government Printing Office, Superintendent of Documents, Washington, DC 20402.

————. *Lesser Known Areas of the National Park System.* $1.50.

An informational leaflet with maps. Contact: U.S. Government Printing Office, Superintendent of Documents, Washington, DC 20402.

Cruising

Cruise Lines International Association. *Cruising—Answers to Your Most Asked Questions.* Free.

An interesting informational leaflet about cruising. Contact: Cruise Lines International Association, 500 Fifth Avenue, Suite 1407, New York, NY 10110, (212) 921-0066; or from travel agents.

————. *101 Reasons To Take a Cruise.* Free.

An informational leaflet promoting cruising. Contact: Cruise Lines International Association, 500 Fifth Avenue, Suite 1407, New York, NY 10110, (212) 921-0066; or from travel agents.

TravLtips Cruise & Freighter Travel Association. *Twenty Most Commonly Asked Questions about Freighter Travel.* Free.

An informational leaflet on freighter cruising, including currently available lines and shipboard accommodations, rates, itineraries, and schedules. Contact: TravLtips Cruise & Freighter Travel Association, P.O. Box 218-Q, Flushing, NY 11358; (800) 872-8584 (nationwide) or (718) 939-2400 (New York or Canada).

Health and Safety

The Hartford Insurance Company. *Get Out Alive: Surviving a Hotel Fire*. Free.

An informative, detailed leaflet on fire safety. The life-saving suggestions it contains should be valuable not only to travelers staying in hotels, but to any resident or visitor of a high-rise building. Enclosed with the flier are a convenient wallet card and two adhesive-backed labels containing a synopsis of pertinent details for surviving a fire. Contact: The Hartford Insurance Company, Hartford Plaza, Hartford, CT 06115.

Partners in Travel. *To Your Good Health*. 20p. Free.

A typewritten booklet of practical tips and guidelines to ensure a safe, healthy, problem-free trip. Contact: Partners-in-Travel, P.O. Box 491145, Los Angeles, CA 90049; (213) 476-4869.

Travel Assistance International. *Consumer's Guide to Travel Assistance*. Free.

A leaflet listing questions consumers should ask when considering purchasing medical and travel assistance insurance. Contact: Travel Assistance International, 1133 15th Street, NW, Washington, DC 20005; (800) 821-2828.

U.S. Department of State, Bureau of Consular Affairs. *The Citizens Emergency Center*. Free.

A brief flier describing how the Citizens Emergency Center can help travelers abroad regarding arrest, death, missing persons, financial and medical assistance, and travel advisories. Contact: Superintendent of Documents, U.S. Government Printing Office, Washington, DC 20402; (202) 783-3238.

————. *A Safe Trip Abroad*. Department of State Publication 9493.
16p. $1.

> Alerts travelers abroad of potential problems and offers solid tips
> in such areas as pretrip planning, personal and vehicle security,
> protecting oneself against terrorism, how to deal with a hijacking
> or hostage situation, and finally how to get assistance abroad.
> Contact: Superintendent of Documents, U.S. Government Print-
> ing Office, Washington, DC 20402; (202) 783-3238.

Disabled Travel

Amtrak. *Access Amtrak*. Free.

> An excellent flier detailing handicapped services by type of train
> and the accessibility of various rail cars. Contact: Office of
> Customer Relations, Amtrak, P.O. Box 2709, Washington, DC
> 20013.

Eastern Paralyzed Veterans Association. *Ten Questions and Answers
about Air Travel for Wheelchair Users*. 24p. Free.

> A valuable informational booklet answering common questions
> about airline travel for those using wheelchairs. Includes a useful
> chart showing various airlines' accessibility features. Contact:
> Eastern Paralyzed Veterans Association, 75-20 Astoria Boule-
> vard, Jackson Heights, NY 11370-1178; (718) 803-EPVA.

Organization for the Promotion of Access and Travel for the
Handicapped. *Cruise Ships for Wheelchair Users*. Free (enclose
stamped, self-addresed envelope).

> An informational flier listing specific vessels and the number of
> cabins accessible to wheelchairs. Contact: Organization for the
> Promotion of Access and Travel for the Handicapped, Box
> 15777, Tampa, FL 33684.

Society for the Advancement of Travel for the Handicapped. *The Guide
to Riding Wheelchair-Accessible Buses in NYC*. Free.

> An informational leaflet describing bus travel for those in wheel-
> chairs in New York City. Includes explanations of wheelchair
> lifts, private bus companies, and subways. Contact: Society for
> the Advancement of Travel for the Handicapped (SATH), 26
> Court Street, Suite 1110, Brooklyn, NY 11242; (718) 803-EPVA.

————. *The United States Welcomes Handicapped Visitors*. Free.

Lists hotels with accessible rooms, tips for renting cars with hand controls, and bus lines that allow a companion to travel with a handicapped passenger at no extra charge. Although written for foreign tourists, it is equally valuable for Americans traveling in the United States. Contact: Society for the Advancement of Travel for the Handicapped (SATH), 26 Court Street, Suite 1110, Brooklyn, NY 11242; (718) 803-EPVA.

U.S. Customs Regulations

Department of the Treasury, U.S. Customs Service. *GSP and the Traveler*. Publication No. 515. Free.

A flier explaining the Generalized System of Preferences devised to help developing nations improve their financial or economic condition through export trade. Travelers can ascertain which of a wide range of products from certain countries can be brought home duty-free. Contact: Department of the Treasury, U.S. Customs Service, Washington, DC 20229.

————. *International Mail Imports*. Publication No. 514. 16p. Free.

Provides information about parcels mailed from abroad to the United States. Contact: Department of the Treasury, U.S. Customs Service, Washington, DC 20229.

————. *Know Before You Go*. Publication No. 512. 32p. Free.

A complete listing of U.S. customs regulations for returning residents. Contact: Department of the Treasury, U.S. Customs Service, Washington, DC 20229.

————. *Pets, Wildlife*. Publication No. 509. Free.

A leaflet explaining U.S. customs regulations for those who travel with pets outside the United States or who wish to bring animals back into the country. Contact: Department of the Treasury, U.S. Customs Service, Washington, DC 20229.

————. *Pocket Hints*. Publication No. 506. Free.

A pocket-sized leaflet of capsule information for returning U.S. residents about customs exemptions. Available at various customs entry points or from the Department of the Treasury, U.S. Customs Service, Washington, DC 20229.

Video and Audio Tapes

Video Tapes

The electronic era has spawned a proliferation of video and audio tapes of interest to travelers, far too many to list here. From the National Geographic series of documentaries on various regions of the world to cruise lines and resort areas' promotional videos, there is little that the questing tourist can't see on a TV screen before leaving home. Series such as the National Geographic travel documentaries are available in most public libraries and retail video-rental stores. Travel agents carry a full supply of promotional videos for travel products they handle. Sporting goods outlets often have promotional tapes on golfing vacations or outstanding fishing spots, for example. Recreational vehicle outlets often carry RV and camping-related videos or information on where to get them.

Most of the early travel videos were designed to market particular travel products or destinations. They were generally produced by companies offering travel services (i.e., cruise lines, hotels and resorts, restaurants, and local attractions). Travelers should check with any of the travel organizations listed in Chapter 8 for video presentations on products they offer.

Recently, less commercially oriented travel videos have been produced, highlighting and describing a particular travel destination much as a travel guidebook might. The following organizations distribute some of the best travel videos currently available. Free catalogs are available upon request from these distributors.

International Video Network
2242 Camino Ramon
San Ramon, CA 94583
(800) 767-4-IVN; (415) 866-1121

The Video Travel Library collection of travel adventures and documentaries includes 70 "Video Visits" and special collection sets from *Fodor's* and *Reader's Digest*.

The Maier Group
235 East 95th Street
New York, NY 10128
(212) 534-4100

The "Travelview" series offers 24 videos covering 45 popular vacation spots worldwide. Each video is endorsed by the American Society of Travel Agents and includes Berlitz Travel Tips.

Questar Video, Inc.
680 North Lake Shore Drive
Chicago, IL 60611
(312) 266-9400

> Produces and distributes informative and educational travel, history, and wildlife/adventure video programming.

TRAVEL VIDEO DIRECTORIES

The following directories offer extensive listings for travel videos currently available.

ABC-CLIO, Inc. *Video Rating Guide for Libraries*. Santa Barbara, CA: ABC-CLIO, Inc. Published quarterly. $89.50/year. ISSN 1045-3393.

> Reviews and rates hundreds of current videos, including information on intended audience, price, and availability for home or public performance use. Arranged alphabetically by category. Additional indexes include: Best of the Issue, Title, Subject, Audience (by age level), and Producers and Distributors.

R. R. Bowker. *Variety's Complete Home Video Directory*. New York: R. R. Bowker, 1989. 1,319p. $100. ISBN 0-8352-2588-7.

> Arranged by titles with brief annotations. Additional indexes include: Cast/Director, Genre, Series, Spanish Language, Laser Video, 8mm, Closed Caption, Awards, International Standards, Manufacturers and Distributors, Subject/Specialty, Service and Suppliers, Toll-free and Fax Numbers, and Latest Releases.

Weiner, David J., ed. *The Video Source Book*. Detroit: Gale Research, 1991, 12th ed. 2,371p. $220. ISBN 0-8103-4299-5.

> Evaluations of current videos in the areas of entertainment, education, culture, medicine, and business. Arranged alphabetically by title. Additional indexes include: Subject, Videodisc, 8mm, Captioned, and Credits (by actor/actress, narrator, and director).

SOURCES FOR TRAVEL VIDEOS

The following outlets market travel videos.

Chronicle Videocassettes
P.O. Box 708
Northbrook, IL 60065
(800) 445-3800

International Adventure Video
680 Waverly Street
Palo Alto, CA 94301
(415) 321-9943

Preview Media
1160 Battery Street, Suite 100
San Francisco, CA 94111
(800) 992-8439

Vacations on Video
1309 E. Northern
Phoenix, AZ 85020
(602) 840-2732

Audio Tapes

Audio tapes have also become a valuable traveler's aid and, like video tapes, are too numerous to specify. Tapes available range from language lessons to audio tour guides for a museum, a city walking tour, a national park driving tour, or even complete travel books on tape. Public libraries and private companies lend or rent various books on tape. Both general-interest and travel bookstores carry a wide array of audio tapes. Guided tours on tape are available at visitor centers at a number of tourist attractions, museums, city hospitality centers, and other tourist locations.

A good reference book to consult for available audio tapes is:

R. R. Bowker. *On Cassette: A Comprehensive Bibliography of Spoken Word Audio Cassettes.* New York: R. R. Bowker, 1989. $95. ISBN 0-8352-2465-1.

The "Travel and Geography" and "Foreign Language" sections are especially helpful.

Online Computer Databases

Electronic travel databases, once available only to professional travel agents, are now available through a number of computer networks that consumers can access by modem on their own personal computers. Some services allow reservations online; others merely provide the tools for searching out the best travel deals.

The following general- and special-interest networks offer one or more online travel services such as the Official Airlines Guide (OAG), Eaasy Sabre, Travel+Plus, and more. Signup fees, hourly charges, and accessibility vary from company to company. Per-hour or per-minute charges depend on use during "prime" or "nonprime time" hours, which also vary according to each company's definition. The telephone numbers listed are for further information and are not access numbers.

The Electronic Edition of OAG (Official Airlines Guide) is the most commonly subscribed-to computer travel service. Both travel professionals and travel consumers can access OAG directly by computer (see listing below), or can access it through a number of both general and specialized computer networks.

OAG is an online booking reservation system with 25 databases covering a number of travel services, including sports specials, tours and discount travel, and cruise travel. Among the most widely used services are: information on airline fares and schedules; airline reservations; car rental and accommodations information; arrivals and departures at 13 major airports; worldwide, country, and traveler's information; World Travel Guide (information on holidays, customs, visa and immunization requirements, history, and weather); U.S. State Department travel advisories; weather forecasts and currency exchange rates for various countries; Vacation Florida (tourism information); ski resort information; Zapodel's Adventure Atlas (worldwide tour database, rates, etc.); Official Recreation Guide (festivals, B&Bs, hotels, things to see and do); and a tours and discount travel section—primarily to Las Vegas, Florida, Mexico, the Caribbean, and Hawaii—plus information on condos in California and Hawaii; the Bahamas; Mexico; Orlando, Florida, beaches; and St. John.

Eaasy Sabre (American Airlines) and TWA PARS (Trans World Airlines) allow consumers to check airline fares and schedules, make reservations for a number of airlines, and access information on hotel/motel accommodations and car rentals.

Travel+Plus database offers extensive information on tours and package travel.

General- and Special-Interest Networks

America Online (for Apple users)
(800) 227-6364
Eaasy Sabre

American People/Link
(800) 524-0100
TWA PARS Travel Shopper

CompuServe
(800) 848-8199
Eaasy Sabre, OAG, Travel Shopper

> Also special-interest databases: "Discover Orlando," "Florida Forum" (Florida travel products), "Adventures in Travel" (travel articles for business and vacation destinations and special events), U.S. Department of State travel advisories, and an outdoors section detailing camping spots.

Delphi
(800) 544-4005
Eaasy Sabre, OAG, TWA PARS Travel Shopper

> Other databases: MetroLine City Search (provides profiles of hundreds of cities worldwide), WorldLine Country Search (information on various countries worldwide), ABC Hotel Services (listings), Bargain Finder International (searches for low-cost international airfares), CruiSearch (cruise information), and Adventure Atlas (adventure tours and trips), plus a bulletin board to request information from travel experts. No signup charge for those interested primarily in travel services; some services require membership in Delphi's Travel+Plus Club for $25/year.

Dialcom
(800) 435-7342
OAG

Dialog
(800) 3-DIALOG
OAG

Dow Jones News Retrieval
(609) 452-1511
OAG

EasyLink
(800) 779-1111
OAG

Genie
(800) 638-9636
Eaasy Sabre, OAG

> Also provides Travel Roundtable, a bulletin board, software library, and conference area.

I-NET America
(800) 322-4638
OAG, Travel+Plus

Minitel
(914) 694-6266
Eaasy Sabre

> Also provides Club Voyage, a travel information service for discounts for tours, cruises, and other travel services.

NewsNet
(800) 345-1301
OAG

> Also full text online of two travel publications: *Business Traveler's Letter* and *Frequent*.

OAG
(800) 323-4000

> Can be accessed directly without using other computer networks. No charge to make or cancel reservations.

Omnet/SCIENCEnet
(617) 265-9230
Eaasy Sabre

ORG (Official Recreation Guide)
(800) 826-2135; (406) 862-4484

Can be accessed directly without using other computer networks. A comprehensive vacation and leisure travel database and reservation system for over 65,000 travel services and opportunities, from sports and fitness to adventure travel, plus weather information, maps, travel agents, transportation, regional calendars, and more.

PC-Link (for IBM compatibles)
(800) 458-8532
Eaasy Sabre

Prodigy
(800) 822-6922
Eaasy Sabre

Also provides Accu-Weather (worldwide weather forecasts), Accessworld (24-hour travel agency for airfare, hotels, and car rentals), NCL (cruise information and bookings), Discount Travel International (discounted tourist flights and cruises), TWA Travel Services (senior citizen discounts available), Amtrak (New York and Washington train schedules, tour packages, and reservations), Premier Dining Club (directory of 500 restaurants across the United States), Quest International (hotel discounts), Hilton International (rate information), and *Consumer Reports* travel newsletter text online.

QLink (for Commodore users)
(800) 392-8200
Eaasy Sabre

Reuters
(800) 387-1588

Carries text of three travel publications: *Travel News, Travel Trade Gazette Europa,* and *Travel Trade Gazette UK and Ireland.*

Telenet
(800) 835-3638
Eaasy Sabre, OAG

Also provides Ultran, an adventure travel network.

Unison
(800) 334-6122
Travel+Plus

Glossary

cancellation insurance   Cancellation insurance reimburses fees paid in advance for travel by air and sea, and often bus and rail, as well as ground arrangements such as hotels, meals, car rentals, escorted tours, or any other travel service, if the services must be canceled. The reason for collecting is usually restricted to illness or death of the covered traveler, or death or alarming illness of an immediate family member or close relative, whether on the trip or prior to leaving.

drop charge   A drop charge is the additional fee charged by many car rental agencies for returning a car to a location other than the one where the car was originally rented.

escorted tour   On an escorted tour a professional escort or manager accompanies the participants from one destination to another and oversees the technical details of the tour operation.

full-timer   Full-timer is the term applied to those who have chosen to forgo a home base for living year-round in a recreational vehicle.

guaranteed share rate   Used on cruise ships, a guaranteed share rate means the cruise company will either find a roommate to share a cabin or will guarantee the regular double-occupancy rate if no one can be found.

guaranteed single rate   Used on cruise ships, a guaranteed single rate guarantees space at the standard rate but does not specify a particular cabin. At sailing time the single traveler is placed in any cabin still available, which cannot be valued at less than the amount paid, and, in fact, is often a much higher priced cabin.

guaranteed tour departure   If a tour operator announces a guaranteed tour departure, the tour will go whether or not enough people have signed up to fill the tour quota.

hosted tour   On a hosted tour, hosts, or representatives of the tour operator, provide information and optional sightseeing and entertainment arrangements in particular locations in lieu of a full-time tour guide.

local guide   A local guide is a travel professional engaged to point out places of interest and qualified to conduct tours of specific locations and attractions.

RV   Acronym for recreational vehicle. An RV is a vehicle that combines transportation and living quarters for travel, recreation, and camping. RVs are either motorized (motorhomes and van conversions) or towable units (folding camping trailers, truck campers, travel trailers, and park trailers.)

RV caravan   An RV caravan is a group tour in which participants move from destination to destination in their camping rigs and meet each evening at a planned rendezvous point. They drive at an individual pace and pick the sightseeing stops of their own choice along each day's route. Caravans are often combined with a guided tour of a local area, ferry travel, or fly/drive combinations.

RV rally   At an RV rally, owners of recreational vehicles gather at a designated rendezvous point for planned activities and socializing. Participants may be transported by motorcoach for tours or activities in the local area.

single supplement   A single supplement is an extra charge levied by most cruise lines and hotel accommodations that may mean paying up to 200 percent of the normal double-occupancy rate. For example, if the regular rate for a room is $80, each person is being charged $40. The rate for a single to occupy that same room might be $65 or even the full $80.

tour package   A tour package is not necessarily a guided tour, but rather a certain combination of transportation, accommodation, meals, and frills, usually cheaper than if each item is purchased or arranged separately.

vouchers   A voucher is a document or discount coupon that is exchanged for or applied to the purchase of certain travel services. It must specify exactly what it may be used for. For a hotel room, for example, it would specify the name of the establishment, period of time the voucher may be used, description of the room ("ocean view," "run of the house"), and the price that will be charged.

Index